EMERGENCY POLITICS

EMERGENCY POLITICS

PARADOX, LAW, DEMOCRACY

Bonnie Honig

PRINCETON UNIVERSITY PRESS   PRINCETON AND OXFORD

Copyright © 2009 by Princeton University Press
Published by Princeton University Press, 41 William Street,
Princeton, New Jersey 08540
In the United Kingdom: Princeton University Press, 6 Oxford
Street, Woodstock, Oxfordshire OX20 1TW

Library of Congress Cataloging-in-Publication Data

Honig, Bonnie.
Emergency politics : paradox, law, democracy / Bonnie Honig.
p.   cm.
Includes bibliographical references.
ISBN 978-0-691-14298-2 (hardcover)
1. Executive power—Developing countries.   2. Democracy—Developing countries.
3. Sovereignty.   I. Title.
JF251.H66 2009
352.23′5—dc22   2009004663

This book has been composed in Sabon

Printed on acid-free paper. ∞
press.princeton.edu

Printed in the United States of America

10   9   8   7   6   5   4   3   2   1

To
James Moore
William Connolly
George Kateb
teachers and friends

If yearning were to forget what it already possesses, that would be a lie, but if possession forgot to yearn, that would be death.
   —*Franz Rosenzweig*

Contents

Acknowledgments

THE ESSAYS COLLECTED here began as occasional pieces for presentation at conferences or for specific edited collections. In the years they were written, democratic theorists had good reason to want to think deeply about emergency and sovereignty. The essays reflect that but they define *emergency* broadly to include food politics, animal welfare, and immigration issues, as well as the sovereignty-defining demands of war and terror.

In the context of the emergency politics of the last few years, it seemed important to identify not just tactics, strategies, and perspectives that might be useful to democratic theorists and activists, but also exemplars of democratic ideals and practices. Many years ago when a colleague asked if I had any heroes, I did not know how to answer what seemed to me at the time a strange question. I understand it better now and can say that some of the thinkers, actors, and movements I turn to in this book are heroes of mine if that means I admire them deeply albeit not uncritically. The subjects of chapters 3 and 4, Louis Post and Franz Rosenzweig, are in my view deeply admirable exemplars of democratic sensibilities from whom we have a lot to learn. Slow Food, a food politics organization discussed in chapter 2, models a humorous and serious global/local politics of taste and justice. I hope this book will inspire others to learn from these examples.

Imagining a book, just like imagining a political future, is both necessary and insufficient to its realization. Moreover, such imagining cannot be done alone in spite of the fact that writing, unlike politics, is a solitary endeavor. Each of the chapters in this book was delivered publicly several times, as large keynote addresses or at small colloquia, graduate seminars, and anonymous conference settings. I have benefited from questions, comments, and interventions at Johns Hopkins University, University of Virginia, Cornell University, Amherst College, University of California–Los Angeles, Yale, Princeton, Columbia, University of Missouri at St. Louis, University of Chicago, Essex University, University of California–Berkeley, University of Melbourne, Australia National University, University of Minnesota, and Northwestern University. I thank especially my hosts at these institutions: Jane Bennett, Bill Connolly, Richard Flathman, Stephen White, George Klosko, Jason Frank, Tracy McNulty, Austin Sarat, Lawrence Douglas, Martha Umphrey, Ali Behdad, Kirstie McClure, Seyla Benhabib, Steve Macedo, Philip Pettit, Bruce Robbins, Lyman Sargent, Patchen Markell, Aletta Norval, Ernesto

Laclau, Shannon Stimson, Hanna Pitkin, Marianne Constable, Wendy Brown, Judith Butler, Andrew Schaap, John Dryzek, Mary Dietz, Jim Farr, Jamie Druckman, Michael Loriaux, Sanne Taekema, and Roland Pierek. For commenting on some of the chapters, I am indebted to all these people and also to Leora Batnitzky, Patricia Daley, Juliet Williams, John Comaroff, Julie Cooper, Jill Frank, Larry Glickman, George Kateb, Jeff Lomonaco, Eric Santner, John McCormick, Marcie Frank, Hans Lindahl, Bert van Roermund, and the late and sorely missed Iris Young. At Tilburg University Law School, faculty and graduate students gathered to discuss the manuscript just as I was doing the final revisions. I am grateful to them for the attention they gave the work and to Hans Lindahl for organizing that event.

George Shulman and Mary Dietz read the book manuscript in its entirety, each offering those views of the whole that are so important in the late stages of writing. Ian Malcolm at Princeton University Press supported the project and two readers for the press helped give the book its final shape.

I was fortunate to be able to develop the ideas here presented in a series of graduate seminars taught at Northwestern University, where political theory is prized and supported. The political theory graduate students at Northwestern constitute the collective space of political imagination and critique that I am fortunate to share, along with Sara Monoson, Lars Toender, Mary Dietz, and Jim Farr. Theory's extended family at Northwestern includes many others as well, but I want to mention here those who read and commented on parts of this work—in particular, Sam Weber, Peter Fenves, and Beth Hurd. Lida Maxwell, Laura Ephraim, and Diego Rossello provided valuable research assistance. Douglas Thompson prepared the final manuscript for publication. The American Bar Foundation provided support, funding not only my research assistants but also my appointment there. I am most grateful for the interdisciplinary intellectual environment supported by the leadership of Bob Nelson. The ABF has introduced me to approaches, literatures, and colleagues I would not otherwise have had the opportunity to know. For their help with parts of this book, I especially want to thank Bill Novak, Terry Halliday, Laura Beth Nielsen, and John Comaroff.

The American Philosophical Society provided a Sabbatical Fellowship that helped me finish this manuscript and start the next one. I profited as well from the APS Sabbatical Fellows conference where I met Richard Dunn and Mary Maples Dunn, then stewards of the APS sabbatical program, and was inspired by their commitment to the program and its ideals.

This book could be called a work of Jewish political theory, drawing as it does throughout on the inspiration of Franz Rosenzweig but also on midrashic tales and biblical interpretation. Bringing these essays together here for the first time, I myself was struck by how prominent a theme this was over the course of the book. For this I may have to thank my children, whose education has provided one of the occasions of my re-immersion in these materials. More generally, my family—Michael Whinston, Noah Whinston, and Naomi Honig—provide me with a challenging, joyous, and deeply satisfying experiment in living that I hope has found some expression in this book.

Finally, this book is dedicated to Jim Moore, Bill Connolly, and George Kateb in acknowledgment of my deep debt to them as teachers and friends. That it is this book I dedicate to them, and not the last and not the next, is appropriate because this one more than any other, I think, bears the marks of my past and continuing conversations with these men, mostly influential and intersecting, and once in a while at parallel play. Jim Moore introduced me to the work of Hannah Arendt and taught me the importance of historical approaches to political theory. He is the reason I pursued an academic career; he made it imaginable and he made it look fun and fulfilling. It is. Bill Connolly draws on Spinoza, Nietzsche, Deleuze, and Bergson to theorize politics for a world of becoming, while I draw here on Rosenzweig, Wittgenstein, Mendelssohn, Derrida, and Arendt on behalf of similar aims. It was Connolly's work on new rights that first made me realize the promise, importance, and fecundity of a central theme of this book: the paradox of politics. George Kateb never loses sight of the absolute importance of constitutionalism for democracy. He always says to write for posterity, and he leads, in this as in other things, by fine example.

The volume's Introduction and Aftermath appear here for the first time. The other chapters, as mentioned, appeared first in earlier versions as articles in journals and edited volumes. I appreciate being granted permission to collect them here, though I note that all have been substantially revised for this volume. Chapter 1 appeared originally as "Between Decision and Deliberation: Political Paradox in Democratic Theory" in *American Political Science Review* (101, no. 1, March 2007). It was reprinted in abbreviated form with four commentaries and a reply in *Rechtsfilosofie en Rechtstheorie* 2 (2008). Chapter 2 appeared as "The Time of Rights: Emergent Thoughts in an Emergency Setting" in *The Politics of Pluralism: Essays for William Connolly* (edited by Michael Shapiro and David Campbell, Duke University Press, 2007). Chapter 3 appeared as "Bound by Law? Alien Rights, Administrative Discretion, and the Politics of Technicality: Lessons from Louis Post and the First Red Scare," in *The Limits of Law* (edited by Lawrence Douglas, Austin Sarat, and Martha Umphrey, Stanford University Press, 2005). Chapter 4 appeared as "The Miracle of Metaphor: Rethinking the State of Exception with Rosenzweig and Schmitt" in the special issue of *Diacritics*, *Taking Exception to the State of Exception* (with guest editors Tracy McNulty and Jason Frank, 2008). Chapter 5 appeared as "Another Cosmopolitanism? Law and Politics in the New Europe," a response to Seyla Benhabib, in *Another Cosmopolitanism, The Tanner Lectures* (edited by Robert Post, Oxford University Press, 2006).

*   *   *

Four people particularly important to democratic theory died in the period during which I was writing the essays here published: Bernard Williams, Michael Rogin, Jacques Derrida, and Iris Young. All were models of what academics should be—politically engaged, intellectually curious, open: committed to their projects but not dogmatic in their opinions. All were also warm and funny people who never took the ups and downs of academic politics more seriously than real life. All of them are deeply missed.

Preface _____

FOR CARL SCHMITT, theorist of the state of exception or emergency powers, the decision to declare the exception is the mark of sovereignty, the moment at which sovereignty as a unitary power is revealed or performatively comes into being.[1] Schmitt's accounts of emergency and sovereignty have captured the imagination of political theory for the moment. In the essays collected here, I explore alternative conceptualizations of emergency and sovereignty that may better fit the needs of democratic theory and practice.

Giorgio Agamben is one of those for whom emergency closes out the possibility of any worthwhile democratic politics. His figure of the camps as the central scene of biopolitics supports what often seems to be an apocalyptic perspective. His aim, no doubt, is to enable opposition to biopolitics. But the idea he promotes, that emergency brings an end to any real politics, itself cements, it does not penetrate, emergency's closures. This book, by contrast, seeks to make clear actually existing opportunities, invitations, and solicitations to democratic orientation, action, and renewal even in the context of emergency. The basic resources of democratic citizenship—from the language of rights to the rule of law to a faith in progress—leave citizens ill prepared to work themselves out of the forms of submission into which they are interpellated by emergency situations. This book recrafts those concepts, highlighting their aptness for an emergency *politics*, finding in retheorized concepts of paradox, rights, law, hope, and politics hidden resources and alternative angles of vision that might motivate action in concert in emergency settings, finding even in narrowed times opportunities for democratic renewal.

It is the wager of this book that such opportunities open up when we de-exceptionalize the exception. If we normally think of emergency politics as identified with a "decision" that puts a stop to ordinary life under the rule of law, then it might be useful to note that ordinary democratic practices and institutions under the rule of law also feature "decision," those forms of human discretion presupposed by the rule of law but with which the rule of law is also ill at ease. In addition, if we think that sovereignty is sharpened and unified by emergency, we might also note that even the neo-Hobbesian, emergency-reproduced notion of sovereignty as unified and top-down itself has democratic qualities: It postulates popular subscription to sovereign power.

These are among the moves made here in a series of linked essays on democracy and emergency. First, I seek to move attention away from the exceptional decision to legally suspend law—the state of exception—and toward the operations of plural elements of that state of exception in ordinary democratic politics. Thus, instead of decision, rupture, or new beginning, I look here at discretion, maintenance, and orientation in ordinary and crisis politics. And second, seeking to highlight opportunities for democratic engagement even in the exceptional situation of emergency politics, I note the dependence even of Schmittian decisionism upon popular receptivity and orientation. I look at how political theorists evade invitations to rethink democracy and emergency and I ask what alternatives might open up to us were we to focus not on the paradoxical state of emergency as Schmitt and Agamben give it to us—the legal suspension of law—but on a different paradox: the paradox of politics.

The paradox of politics names a fundamental problem of democracy in which power must rest with the people but the people are never so fully who they need to be (unified, democratic) that they can be counted upon to exercise their power democratically. As Rousseau put it, you need good men to make good law, but you need good law to make good men. How to break the vicious circle? Deliberative democrats call this *the paradox of democratic legitimation*. Chapter 1 argues it is better viewed as the *paradox of politics*, if we recast that paradox from a problem thought to pertain only to origins (which mirrors emergency's threat of destruction) into a feature of daily democratic life in which subjects are perpetually (re)interpellated into citizenship. Every day, democracies face the problem, theorized by Rousseau, posed by the mutual inhabitation of the people/multitude and the effects of their undecidability on democratic politics. The paradox of politics and its implication—that the people are always also undecidably a multitude—reappears in different guises in all the chapters that follow.

Chapter 2 explores, by way of readings of Wittgenstein, Connolly, Arendt, and Agamben, the potentially productive connections between emergency and emergence by way of the *paradox of new rights*, which political theory has historically evaded by positing a natural or transcendental ground for rights. Cases looked at here include the right to suicide, animal rights, and the politicization of the infrastructure of consumption by food politics groups. Chapter 3 looks at a different case of emergency politics, focusing on the actions of U.S. Assistant Secretary of Labor Louis Post during the United States' First Red Scare. Here new rights (providing aliens with due process protections) begin to come into being by way of frictional contact between dissident collective action and the discretionary power of a government agent. I focus here on the role of decision in democratic action and governance, and not in its exceptionality—as "the decision" or "decisionism"—but in its ordinariness, as discretion. Decision as discretion calls attention not to the suspension of the rule of law but to its daily operations. The central paradox here is the *paradoxical dependence of the rule of law on the rule of man* in which law and discretion are mutually implicated.

Chapter 4 looks directly at the paradox of the state of exception's legal suspension of law. Here I turn to Franz Rosenzweig for an alternative to the decisionistic view of sovereignty promoted by the Schmittian state of exception. I argue for a more fragile and fraught understanding of sovereignty for democratic politics, in which the people who are part of sovereignty's constellation are not a unity but are rather undecidably both people and multitude and this is not just a danger for democratic politics but also a resource. In this chapter, I highlight the importance of preparedness, receptivity, and orientation even to the sort of exceptional politics seen as impositional, relentless, and irresistible by theorists of the Schmittian state of exception.

The undecidability of the people is also an issue in chapter 5. Here it surfaces around the question of how to treat the contingent boundaries that once defined peoples: Are those boundaries morally relevant? The question names what deliberative democrats call the *paradox of bounded communities*. But emergency remains an issue here as well. Chapter 5 looks at how the invocation of emergency licenses not just law's suspension but also law's expansion. Such expansion or innovation may be necessary and even welcome but when emergency is invoked the democratic energies on which institutional innovation also depends are undercut. The case in question is Seyla Benhabib's focus on the establishment of the International Criminal Court as an instance of cosmopolitanism. At issue in particular is her effort to motivate subscription to and faith in the new International Criminal Court by invoking the emergency of Nazi genocide by way of the Eichmann trial.

Linking these essays, my hope is to decenter the paradox of the state of exception and see it in connection with other paradoxes addressed here, most of which are proxies for the most fundamental and fecund paradox of all: democracy's *paradox of politics*. The irresolvable paradox of politics commits us to a view of the people, democratic actors and subjects, as also always a multitude. The paradox of politics posits democracy as always embedded in the problem of origins and survival: how to (re)shape a multitude into a people, daily. From the perspective of this paradox, we see democracy as a form of politics that is always in emergence in response to everyday emergencies of maintenance. The assumed antagonism between democracy and emergency is to some extent undone from this angle of vision and new sightlines are opened up. The work of democratic politics can better be seen to entail not just rupture but maintenance, not just new beginnings but preparation, receptivity, and orientation.

One implication of the work begun here is to lay the groundwork for questioning contemporary political theory's identifications of action with event, and politics with singularity. In chapter 4, where I analyze the idea of "miracle," Schmitt's metaphor for the state of exception, I ask whether these identifications are themselves remnants of earlier debates in political theology about the status of the extraordinary—god and miracle or divine agency—in the ordinary human world. Indeed, it may be worth noting that the theorists most important to me in these essays are for the most part theorists of the ordinary. This is certainly true of Wittgenstein and Rosenzweig. On my readings of them here, it is true of Rousseau and Arendt as well. In a way, my call to de-exceptionalize the emergency is mirrored by my readings of the last two of these thinkers. Here, in this volume, I see their work for the first time as not about the exceptional beginning but rather about the everydayness of politics and its paradoxes. Rousseau is often cast, especially in his treatment of the lawgiver, as a theorist of the problem of origins and yet I read him here as concerned in those very same passages with the problem of maintenance. What seems to be a paradox of founding in his work is actually a paradox of politics. And Arendt, with her account of action as ruptural or inaugural, is usually seen as a theorist of the extraordinary. In this book, however, I argue that we can find in her work another, different dimension, something that cuts across the binary of extraordinary versus ordinary, rupture versus procedure: In Arendt we find a commitment to a politics of the ordinary that is quite distinct from the proceduralism or deliberation with which her deliberativist interpreters affiliate her in opposition to action as rupture. We find rather a commitment to the inaugural, even ruptural or revolutionary political powers of daily political practice out of which procedures and other elements of political self-governance may come but by which such daily practice is not always already guided.

Practice is guided by vision and imagination as well as by need. And so the theoretical arguments parsed here are developed in the pages that follow along with stories of those who found ways to move beyond the life-narrowing survival orientation of emergency. That such stories surprise us is a measure of the powers of emergency to limit and narrow democratic aspirations. But survival, as I argue in the Introduction, "Surviving Emergency," carries promisingly plural meanings, connoting not just the mere life to which emergency seeks to reduce us, but also the more life—sur-vivre—of emergence. Together, in their agonistic partnership, these two aspects of survival—mere life and more life—set the parameters of democratic life and emergency politics and invite us to deliver on their promise.

EMERGENCY POLITICS

Surviving

MERE LIFE AND MORE LIFE

> Everyone should philosophize at some time in his life, and look
> around from his own vantage point. But such a survey is not an
> end in itself. The book is no goal, even a provisional one. Rather
> than sustaining itself, or being sustained by others of its kind, it
> must itself be "verified." This verification takes place in the
> course of everyday life.
> —*Franz Rosenzweig*

IN RESPONSE TO emergency, some political and legal theorists have focused on moral-political questions of justification: What may we do in
response to emergency? The question, now again a mainstay of democratic and legal theorizing, seems to point toward justification: What
justifies the suspension of civil liberties? Under what conditions can sovereign power declare emergency, legally suspend law, or, less radically,
implement and normalize extraordinary measures to protect or defend
democracy from destruction by its enemies? When is it permissible to
torture, detain without habeas corpus rights, deport, use rendition, or in-
vade another country? Such questions are not unimportant, not at all,
but in addition to proposing answers to them, we do well to wonder
what we are doing, as democratic theorists, when we focus on them. One
worry is that we contribute to the very account of sovereignty we mean
to oppose: If we ask what rules, procedures, norms, or considerations
ought to guide or constrain the decision to invoke emergency, we may
think we constrain or limit sovereignty—and we may indeed do so, when
our arguments find favor with judges or administrators—but we also
adopt a certain kind of sovereign perspective and enter into the decision.
When we treat sovereignty as if it is top down and yet governable by
norms we affirm, we help marginalize rather than empower important
alternatives, such as forms of popular sovereignty in which action in
concert rather than institutional governance is the mark of democratic
power and legitimacy. The focus on institutional governance as the central question of democratic theory is not only a product of the centrality
of emergency—there are other reasons for it as well—but the experience
of emergency has enhanced that focus and it is a problem.

The considerations we generate at the level of ideal theory when we imagine ticking time bombs and ask what may legitimately be done when we are faced with them, those considerations of right and wrong with their appeals to universalizability or consequentialism and other standards or principles, are not likely to inform the deliberations of actually existing executive branch members of the government who make these decisions. We might say that such work generates norms and considerations that may filter in to the consciousnesses of those in power or into the courts that may pass judgment on them, and this is not untrue. Or we may argue that we arm the public and its media with the arguments and perspectives they need to engage in the most powerful sort of critiques while doing the naming and shaming that the international human rights community calls for. These are among the contributions democratic theorizing focused on legitimation and normative considerations might make to emergency politics.

But we must at the same time call attention to how these very engagements—the work of democratic theory in generating norms and the exercise of justifying or criticizing emergency measures—do not just enact public accountability. When democratic theorists imagine the considerations that may legitimate such measures, they also possibly inadvertently contribute to (even while trying to undercut) the emergency-think that legitimates the sovereign decisionism that for Schmitt was per se extramoral and extraprocedural. By asking "when may we invoke emergency and suspend the normal order of law?" we concede there may be times when this may be done and that sovereign power may legitimately do this. We may add to the calculation considerations of right that Schmitt saw as extraneous to the sovereign decision, and this is no small improvement over his account. But we also move the terrain for debate away from the critical questions of how emergency (re)produces sovereignty (a question as old as Hobbes's state of nature) and how democratic actors can respond otherwise. We move to focus instead on questions of when do the facts justify the (newly constrained or proceduralized) decision and what sort of decisions are justifiable at all: Was there an immediate threat? Were there no other alternatives available? Did they get a warrant for the torture? And so on.

Facts do not offer a safe harbor. Hannah Arendt hoped facts could offer a kind of extrapolitical security to political life, but she knew that facts are as subject to political manipulation as anything else. Michel Foucault also alerted us to the problem when he called attention to the constructed nature of crises. For both, the fate of facts depends on other things. A certain kind of sovereignty, for example—unitary and decisive, committed to its own invulnerability—is most vulnerable to experiencing the political, with its contingencies and uncertainties, as a crisis. That sort of sovereignty is most likely to perceive crisis where there may be only conflict and to respond to perceived crisis with antipolitical measures of emergency rather than with more pliant, engaged measures appropriate to the needs and uncertainties of democratic politics and conflict.

Arendt and Foucault, along with Wittgenstein, Rosenzweig, Connolly, and others prepare the way for thinking of democratic sovereignty as plural and contingent, a constellation, as Connolly puts it, of contending forces. Such an "accidental sovereignty" stands in contrast with the deliberate democracy at the center of much of today's political theory. By contrast with deliberative democratic theorists' emphasis on justification, I attend to the remainders of political or legal settlement: Where they seek consensus (overlapping or better), I seek out agonistic contention as a generative resource for politics; where they focus on a series of paradoxes (democratic legitimation, constitutional democracy, bounded community, and so on, all of which I discuss in the chapters that follow), I focus on the paradox of politics as the key, central one.

The insoluble paradox of politics, which thematizes the concern that good citizens presuppose good law (to shape them) but good law presupposes good citizens (to make good law), teaches an important truth of democratic theory and practice: The people, the so-called center of democratic theory and practice, are always inhabited by the multitude, their unruly ungovernable double. And the law, to which liberal and democratic theorists look as a resource in their efforts to privilege the people over the multitude, is itself undecidable as well, just like Rousseau's own lawgiver, who Rousseau acknowledges may be a charlatan. In the end, it is not the lawgiver but the people/multitude's decision to accept him that is decisive for their political future. I present the argument for this view in detail in chapter 1 by way of a reading of Rousseau and conclude from it that the task of reinterpellating people into the demands of democratic practice is never over or complete. The paradox of politics is not a paradox of founding, a problem only at a regime's beginning, but rather a problem of everyday political practice in which citizens and subjects try to distinguish general will from will of all without knowing for sure whether they have got it right (or whether it has got them right).

Unlike the paradoxes to which Habermas and his followers are drawn, the paradox of politics does not elicit from us justification or confront us with the need for legitimation. The paradox of politics is not soluble by law or legal institutions, nor can it be tamed by universal or cosmopolitan norms. The paradox of politics highlights the chicken and egg circle in which we are law's authors and law's subjects, always both creatures and authors of law. Thus, the paradox teaches us the limits of law and calls us to responsibility for it. And it teaches that the stories of politics have no ending, they are never-ending.

They have no unitary beginning either. While deliberative democrats too seek out the promise of open-ended political practice, they anchor that practice in a unitary beginning that promises to deliver on the promise of legitimation. As we shall see in chapter 1, when Habermas himself refers to democracy's eventful beginnings, he uses the synecdoches of "Paris" and "Philadelphia," thereby marginalizing the aconstitutional politics that goes by other names—instanced by various political actors and thinkers from the antifederalists to John Brown and James Baldwin—and on which democracy also depends. When Habermas immediately shifts from those idealized city names to refer rather to their "rational trace," he marginalizes in turn those elements of Parisian and Philadelphian political practice that may violate the ideal norms of discourse ethics, notwithstanding the fact that these unruly practices may not only trouble current democratic activisms but also inspire them. Habermas's rational trace sifts through the historical record for elements that can anchor a democratic tradition whose original, plural radicalisms committed it to the rejection of such anchors. Retelling democratic history in terms of its rational trace rather than its many contingencies evinces the faith in progress that guides deliberative democratic theory and rules out the plural timelines by which agonistic democratic theory and practice are otherwise riven, engaged, and animated.

In the essays that follow, I explore an alternative to deliberate democracy. From an agonistic perspective, I thematize the promise and limits of accidental sovereignty, forms of action in concert that postulate and produce new public goods, rights and popular orientations upon which diverse democratic forms of life are deeply dependent.

First, though, I want to stay for a bit with the normative question as posed in order in a different way to generate an alternative critical orientation to it. When might it be permissible or even necessary to torture, detain, or otherwise violate the rule of law's most expansive expectations? Here I turn to Bernard Williams's moral theory on behalf of a politics of emergency. I do so mindful of my own past criticisms of the colonization of political theory by moral philosophy. I turn to Williams's theory for inspiration and seek to translate it into more political terms, not to adopt it as such. And I find in Williams's moral theory a welcome departure from the more systematic and justificatory kinds of moral philosophy whose example has, in my view, influenced political theory in less than salutary ways.

What interests me in Williams's work is his treatment of tragic situations, situations in which, as he puts it, there is no right thing to do but something must be done. Here, even inaction is action. For Williams, the question posed to the moral agent by the tragic situation is not simply what should we do in a tragic situation but what does the tragic situation do to us and how can we best survive it with our moral integrity intact? That is, the goal of moral theory in response to tragic situations is not to guide choice but to enable the moral actor to survive the situation, to do the right enough thing or the thing that is right enough for him or her, and then to survive the action's potentially crippling effects on his or her moral agency in the future. The goal is to salvage from the wreckage of the situation enough narrative unity for the self to go on.

Williams thinks of that narrative unity as "integrity." Integrity on Williams's account is both the product and condition of moral action. Most of the time, our actions are moral when they are consonant with the goals and values that define us and mark our character. In tragic situations, however, that consonance is sacrificed. We already know, by the nature of the choice we confront, that we will have to sacrifice something fundamental to our sense of integrity, and we want to come through that choice in a way that does not totally destroy us. While I have elsewhere criticized Williams's overly unitary view of moral agency, in particular the seemingly essentialist idea of a core self that he calls integrity, here I find that assumption of unitariness useful. For here we are looking into the conditions of a democracy's survival; we are, in short, committed not to national unity but to the preservation of a regime's identity as democratic—its democratic integrity.

The entirely problematic premise of the emergency measures question is that we have no choice. The bomb is ticking and we can either risk destruction or torture someone to find out its location and defuse it. Both options are unacceptable and yet we must act. In practice, democratic citizens do well to contest such claims. Governments often claim to have no choice when the facts do not support the claim or when the sense of choicelessness seems to be a product of a lack of imagination rather than a lack in the situation. Indeed, as others have pointed out, such situations, by way of which arguments are made to justify warrants for torture, are unreal. Real life never provides such stark and incontestable alternatives. But moral philosophy does. What might it teach us?

When Bernard Williams thinks about tragic situations, he does not have the state of exception in mind. But his thought may usefully inform ours insofar as he is imagining a kind of moral emergency, a situation in which something must be done and the only options available seem unacceptable. Are they equally unacceptable and how should we assess our options?

In *Utilitarianism: For and Against* Williams provides two examples by way of which to think through the problem.[1] His examples are that of George, an unemployed pacifist chemist who is offered a much-needed job but in a laboratory that does chemical weapons research, and Jim, a hapless botanist who stumbles on a horrific scene of mass violence in an unnamed South American country and is offered by the state militia the opportunity to save nineteen of twenty native people randomly rounded up to punish a village, which is charged with harboring guerillas. If Jim shoots one Indian, the commander says, he will let the rest of those rounded up go free.

Both situations pose a problem for the agent's integrity. But the challenges in question are importantly different: Were George to accept the job, it might wear away at him, compromising in small almost unseen ways his fundamental moral commitment to pacifism and, more important, his sense of self. Through the daily grind of work in this laboratory he will be implicated in violence. George will never actually see a weapon or fire one at any victims but he will be implicated in something he rejects, nonetheless. On the other hand, he may use his position for good and seek to alter the organization's aims from the inside. That is why he has a dilemma. He may decide that it is not only morally permissible but perhaps even incumbent upon him as a pacifist to take on this work and try to redirect, hinder, or even sabotage the organization. Williams does not think so, however. For Williams, this tragic situation has a right answer. George should not take the job. Contra utilitarianism, George is under no obligation to insert himself into the political situation even if he thinks he might thereby do some good. The damage to George's integrity that would be the likely result of such an insertion is for Williams the overriding consideration here.

As I have argued elsewhere, when Williams locates this example in England, he telegraphs its manageability but does not analyze the conditions of that manageability.[2] Staying home—literally and metaphorically— is an option for George in England in a way that it simply is not for Jim in South America. On the other hand, it is surely precisely because our home institutions distance us from the violence in which they and we are implicated that George's dilemma is difficult: It lacks clarity. The violence in which he may be implicated is real but it is distant and alien. For Jim, by contrast, the scene of his dilemma is distant and alien (South America) but the violence in which he is about to be implicated is undeniably real and clear.[3] This may suggest implicitly that we, as moral agents, have some responsibility to do what we can to avoid encountering tragic dilemmas, to stay home rather than risk home leaving. If so, Williams ought to have done more to analyze the not unproblematic forms of institutional and political work that render home a safe moral space. He ought also to have thought not just about moral but political integrity. We do not need to be Sartrean existentialists to see that political integrity may, more than moral integrity, demand of us that we put ourselves at risk, rather than insulate ourselves from it.

Jim is less lucky than George.[4] For Jim, there is no way out. He stumbles on his tragic situation when he is abroad, away from home and its guarantees, insulations, or attenuations. He finds himself in a situation in which he will, no matter what he does, be directly implicated in a violence that is undeniable. He will witness the shooting of twenty Indians who are begging him to intervene in order to save nineteen or he will intervene and shoot one. Either way, he will suffer; so will they. Thus Jim's situation points to a different consideration than George's. George can decide to stay out of trouble (even if he will regret not doing the good he might have done). But Jim does not have that option. Thus, for Jim the question shifts. It is not just "what is the right thing to do?" but also "how will I survive this situation?" For Williams, since the moral integrity of the agent is what is at stake here, the two questions meld in Jim's case: What Jim should do is whatever course of action he, being who he is, is more likely to be able to survive. Thus, Williams says, Jim should "probably" shoot one Indian, but not definitely so.[5]

With this second example Williams moves us away from one subject-centering question: What should I do? and toward another: How can I survive what I did? Survival points us beyond moral choice to its aftermath. Survival more than choice has intersubjective implications: How can I express remorse for what I did or did not do? How can I exhibit fidelity to those I may have wronged even though I did what I thought was best? Decision isolates. But acting can force us into connection with others. On Williams's account, acting for the best in a tragic situation includes remaining around for the cleanup. Where other moral theories give guidance ad hoc, they are nowhere to be found post hoc. Take the question of torture. Kantians will say it is never permissible. Utilitarianism will tell us to do the felicific calculus. As long as we act in ways called for by these moral theories, both will treat any post hoc regret on the agent's part as irrational or irrelevant to the moral situation. Williams, however, argues that regret is a *moral* emotion and that it is an appropriate response to a tragic situation.[6] Because of his focus on the agent's integrity, he has a broader understanding of the moral situation—it lasts longer—and he includes in it a concern for the self's future moral agency. His focus on the integrity of the core self may, as I have argued elsewhere, diminish the pull of politics in ways that undermine democratic energies that require plurality, shifting coalitions, and a willingness to put oneself at risk.[7] But if we think here of the integrity of democracy rather than the self, the effect may be different. By broadening what counts as part of the moral situation and focusing on surviving it rather than on doing the right thing, per se, Williams may provide a useful template for democratic theorists confronting the problem of democratic survival of the state of emergency.

Most of us in daily life do what Williams counsels George not to do. In little ways everyday we put or find ourselves in situations that compromise our principles and put pressure on our commitments. This daily and all too familiar compromise is opposed by Williams in no uncertain terms insofar as it threatens an erosion of self. Here we can say no—I cannot do this and still remain who I am or become who I want to be. And so it may be that we should say no to the opportunity to do good by changing corrupt institutions from the inside. But what about Jim's situation? With that second example, Williams moves us from our little seemingly costless yeses onto a different register of moral challenge. Shoot one person to save nineteen or stand by while twenty are shot and do nothing to save them? Now schooled by Williams's example of George, we may be inclined to say no—sorry, can't help you. I cannot get my hands dirty like that. But Williams says no, it is not that easy. Jim's case is importantly different from George's. In the end, in a case like Jim's, only you can decide what you can live with. Whatever you do, you will have cause for remorse. And the act of doing it will put into question your integrity as a moral agent. Thus, what course of action you choose should express what best will secure your continuation as a moral agent in the aftermath of tragic moral choice. Not only that, your actions after the fact should also express a commitment to your survival as a moral agent. In other words, whatever you do, you ought to feel remorse and you ought to find ways to express it in action afterward. Here remorse is a mark of moral character not a symptom of irrationality. And integrity is both the condition and the product of moral action in extended time.

Williams's two examples share a concern for the moral agent as a continuing entity in time, a commitment to his or her ability to continue acting as an agent of moral integrity in the future. In both examples, and this is what makes them consistent with each other, the aim is survival. Here is the key point of contact for democratic theorists dealing with the problem of emergency. Rather than focus on what is allowable or defensible on behalf of integrity, Williams invites us to switch the question's emphasis, away from surviving *emergency* and toward *surviving* emergency. What do we need to do to ensure our continuity as selves and/or our survival as a democracy with integrity? Our survival depends very much on how we handle ourselves in the aftermath of a wrong. We will not recover from some kinds of tragic conflict. But when faced with such situations, we must act and we must inhabit the aftermath of the situation in ways that promote our survival as a democracy.

So to return to the question of torture: Kantians will rule it out and utilitarians will calculate its costs and benefits. But Williams seems to refuse to say decisively what to do in any particular situation, and counsels that we think about it in the context of considering the problem of how we will live with what we did, *how* we will live with what we did, so that we can survive what we did or didn't do. He calls attention to the postulates of moral agency—in particular, integrity. He chides Kantianism for its refusal to let us consider dirtying our hands in such a situation and he chides utilitarianism for treating our hesitations to do so as mere self-indulgence rather than granting that such hesitations may themselves be expressions of a sort of moral care for the self.

Politically, surviving the emergency situation with integrity as a democracy might mean engaging in a kind of political care for the self. It may mean refusing to legitimate the use of violence that your democracy does engage in.[8] An example of this might be Justice Robert Jackson's dissent in Korematsu, which focused on the dangers of a Court-approved internment that to Jackson were distinct and importantly different from internment without Court approval.[9] Political care for the self may mean being clear that there is no justification, no proceduralization, no clever legal argument that can cleanse or insulate the regime that tortures from implication in a wrong. It may mean, as I think it does, simply refusing to engage in torture. For those democracies that do torture, their survival as a democracy (not intact, but survival nonetheless) would require they hold themselves responsible and answerable to those they harm. This may mean offering restitution for harms done, empowering those harmed to make claims against them (as we provide public defenders for those accused of criminal wrongdoing), recognizing their claims on behalf of the democracy's own survival as a democracy, supporting the international criminal court that may bring charges against one's own citizens. It may mean offering safe harbor to those facing torture elsewhere. And, in a different vein, it might also mean being responsive to the fact that, as Clinton Rossiter claims, expansions of executive branch and administrative powers will not simply or automatically recede after emergency's end.[10] Surviving as a democracy therefore commits us to revisiting regularly such expansions from the perspective of democracy's needs rather than those of emergency.

In sum, the current focus on the question of what we are legitimately allowed to do in response to emergency, while important, tends to privilege the moment of decision and obscure its also important aftermath. It tends to focus attention on the moment of emergency and not on the afterlife of survival. It tends to make us feel like everything is justifiable and there can be no cause for regret when our survival is at stake. But a democracy's survival requires quite the opposite attitude. Regret is a morally and politically productive emotion and survival requires it. Thus, if there is a moral theory by way of which democratic theory and practice might be well instructed, that moral theory is Bernard Williams's.

There is a risk of analogizing emergency and the tragic situation, however. Williams's most tragic situation, that of Jim in South America, is one in which our hero stumbles haplessly into a conflict in which he is unimplicated. That supposition provides Williams with analytic clarity but it also is a point of dis-analogy with emergency. Political emergencies rarely occur as a result of mere innocent wanderings. Instead, emergencies are usually the contingent crystallizations of prior events and relationships in which many are deeply implicated. This combination of responsibility and chance is missing in Williams's analytic examples but it is at the core of the ancient Greek tragedies in which the tragic heroes are not hapless; they are, in modern terms, both guilty and innocent of wrongdoing. Oedipus unknowingly killed his father and married his mother but he did so trying to escape his fate, about which he did know. Similarly, emergencies in the real world have a history, and one of the requirements of political integrity, as with personal integrity, is surely the need to own up to our implication in the histories by which we, at any particular moment, may feel unfairly assaulted.

Here it is useful to recall Jacques Derrida's explication of the French term for survival: *survivance* as *sur-vivance*—more life, surplus life.[11] In Classics, the term overliving applies to those who ought to have died but go on to more life.[12] Survivance, survival, here means something like that overliving: it is a dividend—that surprise extra, the gift that exceeds rightful expectations, the surplus that exceeds causality. Often survival's needs reduce us, they make us focus on specifics, immediacies, the needs of mere life. For that reason, Arendt saw the focus on survival as a problem for politics. For her, not need but rather overlife was the condition and goal of political life. But Derrida rejects the starkness of a choice between mere life and more life. He offers a concept of survival that signals in its doubleness both the needs of life and the call to overlife. As Derrida puts it, we have in sur-vivance both *plus de vie* and *plus que vie*: both more life and more than [mere] life.[13] This "survival" seeks to orient us toward overlife, toward the gifts of life, to the extra, the dividend, the unearned, and toward that which cannot be earned. The question here then is what resources, concepts, and practices might promise survival as life and overlife, mere life and more life, to contemporary democracies?

One important project of democratic theory in response to emergency is to diagnose the sense of stuckness that emergency produces in its subjects and to identify remaining promising opportunities for democratizing and generating new sites of power even in emergency settings. This is the overlife of democracy and it points beyond current apocalyptic diagnoses of our situation. The goal of the linked essays in this volume is to mobilize democratic theory on behalf of the doubled meaning of survival as mere life *and* more life. The propulsive generative powers of political action often seem at odds with its obligatory focus on the needs of mere life. But if democratic politics is about risk and heroism, it is also just as surely about generating, fairly distributing, demanding, or taking the resources of life—food, medicine, shelter, community, intimacy, and so on. The tensions of food politics are a matter of concern in chapters 2 and 4, where I look at battles over the infrastructure of consumption and its implications for human and animal life (chapter 2, in a discussion of the food politics group, Slow Food) and at the symbolic and material political implications of hunger (chapter 4, by way of a reading of an episode of food politics drawn from the Hebrew Bible's *Numbers*). These treatments of food and hunger highlight the ways in which radical founding and everyday maintenance, the people and the multitude, the lawgiver and the charlatan, mere life and more life are undecidably implicated in each other in ways we ignore at our peril.

Too many democratic theorists focus on either the heroic or the everyday, reinscribing rather than interrogating an opposition between the needs of mere life versus more life. But survival as mere and more life postulates both, acknowledging their agonistic tension and mutual indebtedness. The agonistic mutuality of mere and more life is discernible in all the chapters that follow. Sensitized to it, we start to see democracy's challenges in what Williams would call tragic perspective and we attend to the forces, temporalities, powers, agencies, and contingencies that thwart but also enliven human efforts to bring order, meaning, and justice to our universe. When Bernard Williams attends to the tragic situation, he generates insights regarding moral agency as such, highlighting the salience of regret as a moral emotion and the centrality of both choice and its aftermath to the moral situation. So too, I hope, democratic theory and practice are enhanced by a tragic perspective, one that alerts us to suffering, which is a way of saying we are alerted by it to our noncentrality in the universe. A sense of this noncentrality might induce in persons an attitude of defeatism. Kant issued a version of this criticism at Moses Mendelssohn, as we shall see in chapter 2. But a tragic perspective, no less than the ancient Greek tragedies themselves, can be seen rather to issue in a call to action, responsibility, and the creative communalities of festival and ritual—not an excuse to withdraw from them.

Chapter One —————————————————————————

Beginnings

THE PEOPLE, THE MULTITUDE, AND THE PARADOX
OF POLITICS

Everyone had opposed the Shah and wanted to remove him, but everyone had imagined the future differently. Some thought that the country would become the sort of democracy they knew from their stays in France and Switzerland. But these were exactly the people who lost first in the battle once the Shah was gone. They were intelligent people, even wise, but weak. They found themselves at once in a paradoxical situation: A democracy cannot be imposed by force, the majority must favor it, yet the majority wanted what Khomeini wanted—an Islamic republic. When the liberals were gone, the proponents of the republic remained, but they began fighting among themselves as well. In this struggle the conservative hardliners gradually gained the upper hand over the enlightened and open ones. I knew people from both camps, and whenever I thought about the people I sympathized with, pessimism swept over me.
  —*Ryszard Kapuściński*

Of course, it is appropriate to examine theories that insistently present themselves as exemplars of coherence to see whether they live up to the standard they impose on others and themselves. But what about those that seek to expose paradoxicality in daily life? These must be appraised, first of all, by the way they respond to the paradoxes they identify.
  —*William Connolly*

THE PARADOX THAT INDUCES pessimism in Ryszard Kapuściński is the paradox of founding. At a democratic regime's beginning, especially when that beginning emerges out of violent war or dictatorship, there may be agreement on what is opposed (a brutal dictator or the state of nature), but rarely is there agreement or clarity on what the new regime should look like. In postrevolutionary Iran, the liberals' vision of the future lost out first, then the republicans'. These losses were not foreordained. The revolution might have gone on another way. But it did not. Kapuściński says this is because "the majority wanted what Khomeini wanted—an Islamic republic." That may be; but there is no way to tell whether in wanting an Islamic republic, the majority all wanted the same thing or whether, in so wanting, they wanted the same thing Khomeini wanted. Still, that—or something like it—is what happened.

This chapter does not engage the particular events of the Iranian revolution. But it does take as its occasion the comment of Kapuściński in which the "paradoxical situation" of founding produces in the observer and in many participants as well a certain pessimism. Addressing the paradox of beginnings on a theoretical register, my aim is to explore what positive possibilities such a paradox might harbor, and what sort of orientations and perspective might open those possibilities to view. Under what sort of circumstances and from what angles of vision might such a paradox produce in those in its grip a sense of optimism and possibility? How might the paradox of beginnings be turned to democratic advantage?

The Paradox of Politics

For the democratic theorist, William Connolly, paradoxes are salient clues to political life's secrets; they are challenges to be negotiated, not puzzles to be solved or overcome. One paradox to which Connolly returns again and again is the paradox of politics.[1] Here is Connolly's parsing of the paradox, which he finds well expressed in Rousseau's *Social Contract*, bk. II, chap. 7: "For a general will to be brought into being, effect (social spirit) would have to become cause, and cause (good laws) would have to become effect. The problem is how to establish either condition without the previous attainment of the other upon which it depends." Rousseau raises the issue in the context of *founding* the ideal social contract, but Connolly insists that the problem attaches to politics more generally. If the paradox is real, then wherever good law is said to have come from the free and good willing of citizens, it will likely turn out that something else is (also) the case. Thus, where Rousseau posits "pure general will (which must be common and singular)," readers sensitive to the paradox of politics will, if they look hard enough, find "the concealment of impurities." For example:

> Rousseau's artful efforts to legitimize the subordination of women can be seen, first, to express the necessity of subordination (of either men or women) within the family so that the will of a unified family can contribute a single [undifferentiated] will to the public quest for a general will, and, second, to conceal the

violence lodged within the practices of male authority in the family by treating subordination as suitable for women as such.

Connolly concludes: "So Rousseau both exposes the paradox in the founding of the general will and conceals it in his presentations of that will once it has been founded."[2]

That concealment is achieved, in part, by way of the device of temporalization, Connolly argues: "Rousseau understood the founding of a general will to be paradoxical. He located the paradox in time (*perhaps to imagine another time when it could be resolved*)."[3] By confining the chicken-and-egg problem to the founding period, Rousseau seeks to prevent it and the unwilled violence that resolves it (personified by the lawgiver) from spilling over into politics more generally. In so doing, Rousseau leads his readers to infer that they must just somehow get through the founding, whether by way of a lawgiver's impositional guidance or if necessary by way of a more explicit violence that can produce by force that which will later come by way of education and culture. Hence his approval of the idea that people can be "forced to be free" (though, as Johnston points out, education and culture can be coercive as well).[4] If they can find that much-needed bridge over what Hannah Arendt calls the founding period's "gap" in time, the people might somehow limit to the founding period the violence that attends the paradox of politics. They might then avoid the violence that otherwise recurs daily in established regimes, in the name of law (which claims to be nonviolent by representing itself as purely self-grounding), or popular sovereignty (which claims to be nonviolent by representing itself as the true and total will of the people who are not yet formed).

As it turns out, however, the so-called paradox of founding—the vicious circle of chicken-and-egg—is not overcome by time nor is it just concealed, as Connolly argues, by way of unacknowledged, foundational violence in Rousseau. It is also replayed ad infinitum in Rousseau's own text, *as the paradox of politics*. As I argue here, close attention to bk. II, chap. 7 of the *Social Contract* indicates that each of Rousseau's several efforts to solve the paradox succeeds merely in moving it to another register where once again it defies resolution and inaugurates anew a contestatory politics. The repeated reappearance of the paradox of politics in Rousseau's text supports the idea that the problem of how to generate or recognize a general will recurs daily in democratic regimes.

Rousseau does at first present the paradox of politics as a paradox of founding in bk. II, chap. 7:

> In order for a nascent people to appreciate sound political maxims and follow
> the fundamental rules of statecraft, the effect would have to become the cause;

the social spirit, which should be the product of the way in which the country was founded would have to preside over the founding itself; and, before the creation of the laws, men would have to be what they should become by means of those same laws.

In order for there to be a people well formed enough for good lawmaking, there must be good law, for how else will the people be well formed? The problem is: Where would that good law come from absent an already well-formed, virtuous people?

But the seeming quandary of chicken-and-egg (which comes first, good people or good law?) takes off and attaches to democratic politics more generally once we see that established regimes are hardly rendered immune by their longevity to the paradoxical difficulty that Rousseau names. Every day, after all, new citizens are born, others immigrate into established regimes, still others mature into adulthood. Every day, established citizens mistake, depart from, or simply differ about their visions of democracy's future and the commitments of democratic citizenship. Every day the traces of the traumas of the founding generation are discernible in the actions of their heirs. Every day, democracies resocialize, recapture, or reinterpellate citizens into their political institutions and culture in ways those citizens do not freely will, nor could they. Every day, in sum, new citizens are received by established regimes, and every day established citizens are reinterpellated into the laws, norms, and expectations of their regimes such that the paradox of politics is replayed rather than overcome in time.

Indeed, the first thing to go, when we face the chicken-and-egg paradox of politics, is our confidence in linear time, its normativity and its form of causality. What is linear time's normativity? Belief in a linear time sequence is invariably attended by belief that that sequence is either regressive (a Fall narrative) or progressive. In both regressive and progressive time, the time sequence itself is seen to be structured by causal forces that establish meaningful, orderly connections between what comes before and what comes after (Decline or Rise), such that one thing *leads* to another rather than forming, as plural temporalities and tempos do, a random assemblage or jumble of events. *All* these elements—linearity, its normativity, causality—are thrown off balance by the paradox of politics in which what is presupposed as coming before (virtue, the people, the law) invariably comes after (if at all), and what comes after invariably replays the paradox of politics that time was supposed to surmount.

It might seem that acknowledging the vicious circularity of the paradox of politics must be costly to a democracy, or demoralizing: If the people do not exist as a prior—or even as a post hoc—unifying force, then what will authorize or legitimate their exercises of power? But there is, as we shall see, also promise in such an acknowledgment. Besides, denial is costly too, for we can deny or disguise the paradox of politics only by suppressing or naturalizing the exclusion of those (elements of the) people whose residual, remaindered, minoritized existence might call the pure general will into question. From the perspective of the paradox of politics, unchosen, unarticulated, or minoritized alternatives—different forms of life, identities, solidarities, sexes or genders, alternative categories of justice, unfamiliar tempos—re-present themselves to us daily, in one form or another, sometimes inchoate. The paradox of politics provides a lens through which to re-enliven those alternatives. It helps us see the lengths to which we go or are driven to insulate ourselves from the remainders of our settled paths. It keeps alive both the centripetal force whereby a people is formed or maintained as a unity and the centrifugal force whereby its other, the multitude, asserts itself.[5]

Connolly's insight about paradox and linear temporality comes up in relation to Rousseau, but the insight exceeds Rousseau and invites a new line of critical reflection on contemporary deliberative democrats who stage their reflections on democracy and rights by taking up a political paradox and rendering it manageable by embedding it in a linear time sequence. Unlike Rousseau (as Connolly reads him), Jürgen Habermas and Seyla Benhabib do not confine the paradox of politics to a distant past. They locate the paradox in the present and look to a future in which the paradox can be worked out by way of present political practices—which Habermas calls "tapping" and Benhabib calls "iterations"—and futural orientations. While Rousseau, on Connolly's account, thought to escape the paradox of politics by confining it to a distant past, and Habermas and Benhabib seek to escape it by reference to a hoped-for future, both would-be solutions depend upon their location in linear time. We may not know the future the way we know the past (although even the past exceeds our efforts to know it, given its availability in perpetuity for re-interpretation and appropriation), but that matters less than the fact that the linear temporality in which both past and future are lodged is itself what irons out the circularity of paradox and gives us hope that present conflicts can be surmounted in ways that will not generate new remainders. The paradox of politics, central to agonistic democratic theory, is replaced in the deliberative democratic literature by other paradoxes, two of which I focus on here: the paradox of democratic legitimation and the paradox of constitutional democracy. Deliberative democrats worry about these two paradoxes but, as I argue here, these two paradoxes are not a problem for them but a solution: They are soluble in and by time, something that is not true of the paradox of politics which recurs daily.

Reframing Rousseau's Paradox of Politics
as the Paradox of Democratic Legitimation

The problem of how to identify or generate the general will is reframed by deliberative democratic theorists as the paradox of democratic legitimation. Here is how the deliberative democratic theorist, Seyla Benhabib, understands the paradox:

> Rousseau's distinction between the "will of all" and "the general will," between what specific individuals under concrete circumstances believe to be in their best interest and what they would believe to be in their collective interest if they were properly enlightened, expresses the paradox of democratic legitimacy. Democratic rule, which views the will of the people as sovereign, is based upon the regulative fiction that the exercise of such sovereignty is legitimate, i.e., can be normatively justified, only insofar as such exercise of power also expresses a "general will," that is, a collective good that is said to be equally in the interests of all.

Democracy's regulative fiction affirms the sovereignty of the people but also limits or shapes its actual manifestations by requiring that it aim toward a collective good. The regulative fiction motivates the quest for a "moral standpoint" to guide or assess popular willing. Benhabib begins with Rousseau because she credits to him the worthwhile articulation of the paradox of democratic legitimation, but in the end she prefers Kant because Rousseau does not answer to the need for a moral standpoint.[6]

Rousseau himself makes no mention of regulative fiction, but he does seem to acknowledge the insufficiency of mere majoritarianism to democracy when he considers, in bk. II, chap. 3 of the *Social Contract*, the possibility that the general will can err. His response? The general will cannot err because if it erred it would not be the general will, it would be the mere will of all.[7] With this distinction between the will of all (what the people will) and the general will (the option that the people should will, whether or not they actually do so), the general will seems to move from being the purely procedural outcome of a political process to being, instead, an extraprocedural outcome by which to judge the products of supposedly pure, but now apparently imperfect, procedures.

The fact that the general will might go one way and the will of all another could have led Rousseau to reject the idea of a general will as such or to lose faith in the people whose willing legitimates the regime. But, Rousseau insists, "the general will is always right and always tends toward the public utility." The people may not see it. Their deliberations may lack "rectitude" not because they are corrupt; the people themselves are "never corrupted," rather they are "often tricked," Rousseau says.

The goodness of the people may be beyond dispute, but it becomes increasingly clear to Rousseau that not even their goodness can guarantee their rightness and, with the general will now operating as an external standard by which popular willing can be judged, the people may be found on the side of the will of all, not the general will, even if through no fault of their own. The problem is so serious that Rousseau refers only three chapters later in the *Social Contract* no longer to "the people" but to the "blind multitude."[8]

Benhabib rejects what she sees as Rousseau's two solutions to the paradox: the first because it fails and the second because, she says, it imports to the scene of deliberative rationality and its regulative fiction an idealized rationality that violates the legitimacy to which it ought to be committed. Rousseau's first solution Benhabib calls an "arithmetic solution," in which the will of all, which "is merely a sum of particular wills," can be used to calculate the general will as follows: "[T]ake away from these same [private] wills the pluses and minuses which cancel one another, and the general will remains as the sum of the differences."[9] Benhabib correctly argues that "Rousseau's 'arithmetic' solution does not satisfy, because it is not at all clear what the language of 'taking away the pluses and minuses of individual wills' could mean concretely or institutionally."[10] But caught up in the search for an independent normative standard to which Rousseau was not himself committed, and seeking a solution to the paradox rather than a diagnosis of it, Benhabib may dismiss too quickly the import of this first, flawed effort.

What other than a right solution might this arithmetic puzzle have to offer us? We might perhaps read Rousseau's odd arithmetic symptomatically: What if Rousseau's pseudoarithmetic solution illustrates for readers the deep inextricability that marks the will of all and the general will? On such a reading, Rousseau's casual directive—"take away some of this and some of that and count what's left over"—*is not meant to reassure but rather to illustrate for us the hopelessness of knowing for sure* when we have our hands on only one and not the other. Might this be the lesson of Rousseau's fuzzy math—that the general will is *inhabited* by the will of all and that we cannot know for certain when we have disentangled them and cannot hope, therefore, to guide our politics by such knowledge?

This possibility is borne out by Rousseau's full discussion of the lawgiver. Benhabib sees the lawgiver as Rousseau's second attempt to solve the paradox of democratic legitimation. In fact, Rousseau's turn to a lawgiver represents not a second solution but a second slightly different problem. The lawgiver arrives in response to a move away from the paradox of democratic legitimation and toward the paradox of politics, discussed above and construed by Rousseau initially (but only initially, as we shall see) in bk. II, chap. 7, as a paradox of founding. In the paradox of democratic legitimation, represented in bk. II, chap. 3, on whether the general will can err, the people loom as a problem for the general will that is supposed to be theirs. They may "err" by willing the wrong thing. They may be "tricked." Or their deliberations may lack "rectitude." In the paradox of politics, however, as in bk. II, chap. 7, the focus is on finding "the best rules" for an emerging nation on the brink of existence as such. Here the problem is not that the people might be misled or might miscalculate in their deliberations such that they mistake a particular will for a general will. Here the problem is that the people do not yet exist as a people and so neither does a general will. The solution cannot be the right procedure or standpoint, for the people are in the untenable position of seeking to generate, as an outcome of their actions, the very general will that is supposed to motivate them into action. They lack at this juncture all the necessary conditions of communal action. The problem is clearest in the moment of founding but, as I suggested earlier, it attaches to democratic politics as such partly because the people are never so fully what they need to be (virtuous, democratic, complete) that a democracy can deny credibly that it resorts to violence, imposition, or coercion to maintain itself. In some sense, that is, the "people" are always undecidably present and absent from the scene of democracy. That is why it is always part of the point of democratic political practice to call them into being rhetorically and materially while acknowledging that such calls never fully succeed and invariably also produce remnants.[11] Hannah Arendt alerted us to this dimension of democratic politics in *Origins of Totalitarianism* when she lamented Clemenceau's failure to try to call out the people from the Dreyfus-decrying mob of France. Clemenceau might have succeeded, Arendt thought, had he tried.[12]

Arendt's judgment is backward looking. With hindsight and from within the frame shaped by events that have already occurred, it may seem easier to distinguish people from mobs, real public goods from shiny golden idols. In the paradoxical moment of founding, however, no member of the community can yet be said to possess the needed perspective, which can only come post hoc, to form the rules or identify or advocate for a collective good by which the people need to have already been acculturated in order to be not a "blind multitude" but a "people" capable of the autonomous exercise of popular sovereignty.[13] Somehow the impasse is negotiated—Arendt in *On Revolution* speaks in this regard of the several good fortunes that allowed the American people and their founders to found rather than founder—but its trace remains. The general will can never be really equally in everyone's interest nor really equally willed by everyone. Even if it were so fully willed, its authors nonetheless experience it as alien when it becomes a source of rule and they are no longer only its authors but also law's subjects.[14] More to the point, given the vi-

cissitudes of legislative processes, there is always some divergence between what people will as authors and what emerges as law over them as
subjects.[15] Indeed, it may even be that this uncanny law, always somewhat alien and perpetually reproduced as such even by democratic institutions, is marked by the paradox of politics itself: In that recurring paradox, again and again, the subject postulated by politics is seen as never
quite the cause because also always the effect of political practice. As
Peter Fitzpatrick colorfully puts it, this is a moment in which "time runs
widdershins and the present precedes itself."[16]

On this reading the lawgiver, seen by some of Rousseau's readers as a
would-be solution to the problem (he is said to have the perspicacity to
get the law really right for the people who cannot yet do so for themselves), actually works to mark the problem rather than to solve it: The
lawgiver may get the law really right but he enables the people's self-
governance by compromising their autonomy. Just as the earlier arithmetic solution showed the general will was always inhabited by the will of
all, so here too the point seems to be that popular sovereignty is always
haunted by heteronomy, that the people are always undecidably also a
"multitude." In Rousseau (this is one of his great strengths as a democratic theorist), notwithstanding his aspiration for autonomous popular
sovereignty, there is a sense that the people are never just heroes of their
own story but always also protagonists in someone else's (represented
by the would-be lawgiver), the always undecidable bearers of forces
larger than themselves.[17] One way to ease the problems marked here
might be to focus less than deliberative democratic theory does on universality and the orientation toward consensus as conditions of politics
and more on their imperfect (re-)production as sociopolitical effects. This
would shift the main focus from proceduralism and constitutionalism toward a theorization of their remainders and of popular orientations to
those devices of (self-)rule.

However let's assume for a moment, with Benhabib, that the lawgiver
is a response to the same problem as the earlier failed arithmetic solution.
There is something attractive about this figure, a founder who addresses
the paradox of democratic legitimation by setting the material and procedural conditions for successful general willing. At a minimum, he facili-
tates or educates. At a maximum, he forcibly acculturates. To Benhabib, however, the lawgiver solution is no solution at all because the
lawgiver is an "instance of idealized rationality," not deliberative rationality. Rousseau, she argues, is willing to "trade off legitimacy (the will
of the people) for rationality (the legislator, 'an instance outside the united
will of the people . . . whose rationality transcends the legitimacy deriving
from the people')."[18] So Benhabib looks elsewhere for the missing "moral
standpoint" and moves on to Kant.

Benhabib is not alone in treating the lawgiver as a betrayal of Rousseau's democratic ideal. Whether we take the lawgiver to be a figure of idealized rationality who trades off legitimacy in the way Benhabib describes, or of some other force (whether rationality, foreignness, paternal authority, moral certitude, or just really good intuition about what a particular people needs to function as a unity), the lawgiver is taken by many of Rousseau's readers to represent the would-be sovereign people's dependence on an outside force to guide them to the general will that ought properly to be their own, free internal motivation and the expression of their political unity.[19] In short, it seems that whatever problems of founding or willing are solved by way of the lawgiver's agency amount to little by comparison with the problems caused thereby for a would-be democracy.

The failure of the solution is not what it seems, however. In fact, Rousseau's lawgiver is less of a solution, failed or successful, than most readers of the *Social Contract* assume. He simply does not provide the certainty or force that Benhabib and other commentators associate with him for good or ill. The lawgiver may offer to found a people, he may attempt to shape them, but in the end it is up to the people themselves to accept or reject his advances. They may be dependent upon his good offices, but he is no less dependent upon their good opinion. This idea would come as no shock to Moses, one of Rousseau's favorite lawgivers, who led a people repeatedly referred to in the Hebrew Bible as "stiff-necked." The ancient Israelites changed their minds more than once about whether to follow their would-be lawgiver or rededicate themselves to other leaders and gods. Contrary to those who see Rousseau's civic religion as, per se, a limit on popular autonomy, the Israelite example suggests that even absolute divine power can be resisted and engaged. Here, indeed, is the ineliminable moment of popular sovereignty in a nation (whose myths describe it as having been) formed by a lawgiver: The true lawgiver (prophet, god) is no more clearly identifiable by the "people" than is the general will. For democratic theory this is a good thing, for Rousseau's lawgiver, therefore, cannot help but inaugurate or represent a contestatory politics. The lawgiver forms a people into a unity that may or may not stay true to his leadership and he also generates remnants with plural and contending visions of the public good. The lawgiver does not transcend the political fray; he (or really law itself) is at the center of it.

In short, Rousseau is not using law or a lawgiver or even ideal rationality to solve a political problem from the outside. Instead, his treatment of the lawgiver considered in full suggests Rousseau has a political understanding of law, and perhaps even of rationality. The point is made clear when Rousseau ends his chapter on the lawgiver with a warning against cheap impersonators. "The great soul of the legislator is the true miracle that should prove his mission. Any man can engrave stone tablets, buy an oracle, or feign secret intercourse with some divinity, or train a bird to talk in his ear, or find other crude methods of imposing his beliefs on the people. He who knows no more than this may perchance assemble a group of lunatics [a "blind multitude?"], but he will never found an empire and his extravagant work will soon die with him. Pointless sleights-of-hand form a fleeting connection; only wisdom can make it lasting."[20] Just as the will of all can masquerade as the general will, so too can the charlatan impersonate a true lawgiver. As Geoffrey Bennington concludes, "Legislator and charlatan thus remain radically undecidable."[21] The people, still and always also a multitude, never so fully formed that they are uninhabited by anarchic waywardness, must nonetheless discern or decide the difference between the legitimate lawgiver and the pretender. The decision, as it were, rests with them; it reflects in true chicken-and-egg fashion who they are and/or it also forms them into the particular people they are and might be.

Thus, with the introduction of the lawgiver, the problem of how to know and/or generate the general will has not been solved; it has been shifted to a new register. Now in place of the earlier, supposedly arithmetic problem, we have a political problem: the would-be people's, the multitude's, performative choice to reject the overtures of one lawgiver who is or is said to have been a charlatan and to commit themselves to another, proclaimed authentic. In so doing, they choose and are chosen by their destiny. The decision may also divide them, however. They may split and become antagonists, as occurred after the prophet Muhammad's death in A.D. 632, when the people who later became Sun'ni or Shia decided differently how to answer the fateful question of who was to be Islam's next rightly guided caliph: Ali, a direct descendant of the prophet, or Mu'awiya Ummayad who, after beating Ali in battle, declared himself caliph? The Shia went one way, the Sun'ni the other.[22] Rousseau may have had this example in mind: He refers only a few lines later in his text to the children of Ishmael.

Even without such extreme division, the irreducibly political condition of the community is not ameliorated at this point in Rousseau's text; it is unrelieved. For, sure enough, the problem occurs again on a third register and then on a fourth and fifth. Perhaps to break out of the difficulty of distinguishing in the moment between lawgiver and charlatan, Rousseau moves to another indicator—durability of the laws given. "The Judaic Law, which still exists, and that of the child of Ishmael, which has ruled half the world for ten centuries, still proclaim today the great men who enunciated them."[23] Invoked by Rousseau as an authentic indicator of authentic lawgiving, durability does not function reliably, however. Not only can we not assess durability in advance and are thus not helped by this indicator if we are looking for guidance in the present moment, but even those who assess durability post hoc may not agree on the facts or on their significance. ("A durable state may always be a mere simulacrum of a good one.")[24] There is no way to distinguish deserved duration (based on wisdom) from contingent duration (based on chicanery or mere good fortune), so even judgments based on the fact of durability are contestable.

Indeed, as soon as Rousseau invokes durability as a true indicator of good lawgiving, he concedes the contrary. By arguing against those who disagree with his assessment of Judaic and Islamic law as the products of good lawgiving, he shows that he himself knows better than to think that mere longevity precludes people from passing plural and conflicting judgments: "[W]hile pride-ridden philosophy or the blind spirit of factionalism sees in [the laws of Moses and Ishmael] nothing but lucky imposters, the true political theoretician admires in their institutions that great and powerful genius which presides over institutions that endure."[25] If there is no sure way to distinguish the general will from the will of all, the people from the blind multitude, the true lawgiver from the charlatan, significantly durable institutions from those whose durability is a function of mere good fortune or successful violent imposition or, even further, the true political theoretician from the pride-ridden philosopher or blind factionalist, then the will or judgment of the people who are not yet (or no longer) a people remains crucial. There is no getting away from the need in a democracy for the people to decide—on which is the truly general will, whose perspective ought to count, who is a true prophet, what are the right conditions for their lives, which enduring institutions deserve to endure and which should be dismantled, which would-be leader to follow, whose judgments to take seriously, and so on. Appeals to god or divine power do not escape this predicament, they replay it; when the lawgiver resorts to signs and wonders, he seeks to end the cycle of contestation but now the people move from judging him to judging the authenticity of his signs. Disagreements may persist and are of lasting political import (as the historic split between Sun'ni and Shia Islam suggests). It is worth noting that this reading (by contrast with Bennington's) stresses the people's undecidability rather than the lawgiver's.[26] Thus, on this reading, Rousseau is not to be dismissed, contra Benhabib, for his too unified conception of the people, for the people though solicited as a unity by the lawgiver are never fully captured by his law.[27]

Benhabib could concede the cyclical undecidabilities tracked here in Rousseau and still insist that her fundamental argument survives intact. The paradox that interests her may occur on four or five registers in Rousseau and not just one or two; the terms of the paradox may even shift a bit as the argument unfolds, but fundamentally, she might say, we are still faced with the problem that defines democracy: When faced with distinguishing general from particular wills, true lawgivers from pretenders, or properly durable institutions from those that are falsely so, popular sovereignty must be exercised not in a decisionistic fashion that takes its bearings from mere, aggregate preferences or by orienting with Rosenzweig toward an alien divinity, but rather on the basis of a commitment to deliberative procedures that generate outcomes that pass the test of a moral standpoint of universalizability. The material conditions of successful general willing called for by Rousseau (defined and sheltered territory, small population, relative equality, civic religion) are, from Benhabib's perspective, simply not a substitute for such a standard, nor for that matter are they relevant to us in late modernity. Caught up in the search for an independent normative standard to which Rousseau was not himself committed, conceiving of the paradox as a binary conflict not a vicious circle, and seeking a solution to the paradox rather than a diagnosis of it, Benhabib concludes that the people need the missing moral standpoint that Rousseau never provided in order to mark out a procedural path and cut short the spiral of paradox into which Rousseau supposedly falls. In quest of this standard, Benhabib turns to Kant.

Why didn't Rousseau make this move? Perhaps Rousseau wanted to impart a different understanding of politics, one that takes its bearings from the real human world as we find it ("taking men as they are and laws as they might be," he says at the outset of his *Social Contract*), with its plural, conflicting aspirations, and vicious circles, and not from a regulative ideal, fictional or otherwise. Rousseau is a theorist of political culture, not of universality (pace Habermas).[28] But he is not therefore irrelevant to us now. Quite the contrary. Rousseau's material conditions of popular sovereignty may be impractical in our late modern world but they remain instructive. It is as true for us as it was in his day that under conditions of radical inequality, it is difficult to generate, identify, string together, and fight for public goods and against narrow factionalisms. Instead of addressing the problems of politics by way of a principle or a regulative ideal or fiction, Rousseau illustrates for us, time and again, the mutual inhabitation of general and particular will, people and blind multitude, lawgiver and charlatan, properly durable institutions and those stabilized by force. These are not binary paradoxes and they are not soluble by philosophical inquiry; indeed they are often generated by philosophical inquiries, which tend to harden tensions into hypostatized, polar alternatives. What is lost by way of such polarization? The fecundity of undecidability, a trait that suggests that our cherished ideals—law, the people, general will, deliberation—are implicated in that to which deliberative democratic theory opposes them: violence, multitude, the will of all, decision.

Rousseau does juxtapose the general will and the will of all analytically but he also repeatedly depicts them as inextricably intertwined. No law and no perspective, as such, could disentangle them. The best a democratic politics can do is set the material conditions of shared living in such a way as to relieve the propensity of these two to diverge and to harden into oppositional relation. Rousseau teaches that conflicts between general will and will of all will be more or less frequent and intense, and variously experienced, in different settings under different conditions. The frequency and intensity of their conflict are products of varying political circumstances and of the expectations we bring to those circumstances. Theories that lead us to expect such conflicts and speak of a quasi-logical paradox may themselves lead us into not out of the paradoxes they seek to avoid or resolve.

What problem might the paradox of democratic legitimation be solving for democratic theory? The paradox of democratic legitimation is a paradox much-beloved by democratic theorists who worry about mere majoritarianism (which is to say, it is beloved in some form by nearly all democratic theorists). Unlike the paradox of politics, the paradox of democratic legitimation seems soluble, and its supposed solution—a moral or juridical standpoint of universalizability, or the rule of law—underlines the waywardness of the people (their multitudinous character) and their need for legal or procedural institutions that are cast by contrast as merely stabilizing or enabling, not themselves wild or impositional. In short, if the paradox of democratic legitimation (bk. II, chap. 3) is preferred by many democratic theorists to the paradox of politics posed repeatedly in bk. II, chap. 7 (and only in its first iteration as a paradox of founding), that is because the paradox of democratic legitimation focuses our attention on law's regulative powers, specifically on the need to direct the energies of the people that are assumed to be independent of law rather than partly its products. The paradox of politics, by contrast, calls attention to law's formative powers, its never fully willed role in processes of subject-formation and the need, therefore, in a democracy, periodically or regularly to subject law to democratization by way of amendment, augmentation, or nullification.

Amendment, augmentation, or nullification are all forms of refounding that, as such, call the (not necessarily blind) multitude forth out of the people or manifest "the people themselves" acting in resistance to or in popular support of the institutions that form them.[29] These refoundings respond to the paradox of politics. But they may also cast us once again into that paradox, leaving us with no firm criteria or ground from which to distinguish with confidence the will of all and general will, multitude and people, because the perspective from which to do so and the identities at stake are themselves in question or in (re)formation. Thus, if the paradox of democratic legitimation takes the place of the paradox of politics in Benhabib's considerations, that is because the former paradox but not the latter allows us to take for granted the distinction by which it is supposedly troubled, the distinction between general will and will of all, while also rescuing law and proceduralism from implication in the phenomena they are entrusted to constitute and regulate. That is part of the point and attraction of the paradox of democratic legitimation.

When Benhabib mis-takes the paradox of politics for that of democratic legitimation (substituting, as it were, the problem posed in bk. II, chap. 3 for that posed in bk. II, chap. 7 of the *Social Contract*, or conflating the two), she sidesteps one of democratic theory's knottiest problems and renders the (revised) paradox soluble, by way of that "missing moral standpoint." She also paves the way to a kind of constitutionalism that serves as the moral standpoint's proxy in the human world of politics. And with that we arrive at a second paradox, also binary in structure, also set up to take the place of the paradox of politics: the paradox of constitutional democracy.

The Paradox of Constitutional Democracy

The problem of how to secure good general will in the absence of antecedent good law by way of which good willing is shaped is seen by some as soluble by way of constitutionalism. A constitution limits the damage that can be done by a poorly directed, confused, or wanton people by taking some things, like human rights, off the agenda. But constitutionalism, on this account, seems to take the place of Rousseau's awkward lawgiver (as he is traditionally understood) and to betray democratic ideals. Why should the people whose will legitimates the regime be bound by something they have not themselves willed? The paradox of constitutional democracy seems to restage the paradox of democratic legitimation. (Indeed, Judith Shklar identified constitutions with the general will.)[30] Have we simply traded in one paradox for another?

Yes and no. As we shall see, this new paradox does replay many of the issues at work in the paradox of democratic legitimation. Instead of will of all versus general will, we have popular sovereignty versus constitutionalism. However, there are important differences between the two paradoxes. In the translation of one into the other, something does change.

In the paradox of constitutional democracy literature, the problem that for Rousseau occurred synchronically at the founding and forever after—that which the law presupposes as its cause can only be produced by it as its effect—unfolds diachronically. In place of the present tense problem of (un)justifiable constraints on popular sovereignty that daily affect the people's relation to itself as both ruler and ruled (the paradox of politics), we get the rather different problem of constitutional democracy and its limits from the past on popular sovereignty in the present. Recasting the conflict in this way divides the ruled (the people) and ruler (law, the founders, or the constitution) and restages the paradox of politics as a generational divide, a problem articulated memorably by Thomas Jefferson when he asked whether the dead should have rights.[31] This new paradox of constitutional democracy is not a conflict that goes to the very heart of democratic politics, which impossibly promises both (self) sovereignty *and* freedom or, as Emilios Christodoulidis puts it, both self-rule and law-rule.[32] Instead, the tense elements of the paradox are split into two distinct objects: The constitution represents law-rule and the people represent self-rule, and these are seen as at odds[33] or somehow self-fulfilling.[34]

Thus, the paradox of constitutional democracy externalizes the conflict that the paradox of democratic legitimation, notwithstanding its flaws, subtly put at democracy's heart. The unwilled, constraining element of rule is now identified not with democracy, per se, but with the constitution, which may be right or necessary, and the paradox is now not internal to democracy (which seeks impossibly to combine will of all and general will, rule and freedom) but is rather a feature of one kind of democracy, *constitutional* democracy, which impossibly but necessarily combines written constraint with free popular sovereignty and then derives its legitimation from that impossible, tense combination. The result? We have come full circle, for we are left with the implication often, albeit erroneously, attributed to Rousseau: that a really, unmediated, unwritten, and unconstrained democratic regime could experience—simultaneously and without conflict or paradox—*both* freedom and rule, both general will and will of all, law-rule and self-rule. The implication here is that were it not for constitutionalism, we could have democracy. This attractive implication is surely one of the reasons the paradox of constitutional democracy commands more attention than the paradox of politics.

But since democracy is, or threatens always to be, in effect, a self-consuming artifact (those wayward, multitudinous people, again, on whom everything democratic depends but by whom everything democratic is threatened), democracy is said nonetheless to require the order and constraint of constitutionalism.[35] We cannot have democracy *with* constitutionalism, and we cannot have democracy with*out* constitutionalism either. Some democratic theorists see in this impossibility the plight and promise of democracy as such, a form of rule and freedom that forever seeks and rejects efforts to ground itself in something outside of itself.[36] But for most deliberative and liberal democrats, this dynamic represents a new paradox, one generated by constitutionalism's dissolution of the paradox of democratic legitimation. That new paradox, the paradox of constitutional democracy, immediately slouches toward its own solution by temporalizing the conflict, plotting the conflict between freedom and rule as one that occurs in time. In place of the synchronic paradox of politics (in which will of all and general will may be mutually inhabited), and in place of the paradox of democratic legitimation's difficulty of securing general will over will of all, we now have the still difficult but far less knotty problem of how to find freedom in relation to a past we are stuck with and did not author (a problem Nietzsche named the "will's antipathy towards time and time's 'It was'" and faced through the thought of eternal return).[37]

Taking this temporalized conflict between past and present as the problem to be solved, defenders of constitutionalism give many reasons for constitutional limits. Constitutions represent the general will or universal norms, or norms that represent the true political commitments of the people whether or not they would will them in a particular political moment (Peter sober rather than drunk, as Stephen Holmes puts it),[38] or they help shape the people into the stable agency of popular sovereignty that democracy presupposes and requires (Rubenfeld), or they supply a people with rules that are enabling not coercive,[39] or constitutions represent a multigenerational commitment that does not constrain freedom but rather actualizes it over time.[40]

Those who map the so-called paradox of constitutional democracy as a tension between past and present generations assume that governance across temporal distance is similar to governance across spatial distance in that both are alien to their subjects and impositional in nature. The analogy between time and space, temporal and geographic alienness, was deployed to good effect by Jefferson, who worried that an enduring constitution would (really, *should*) be experienced by subsequent generations as a foreign imposition.[41] Thomas Paine, too, spoke of rule from the grave as the "most ridiculous and insolent of all tyrannies."[42] Noah Webster shared the concern and memorably metaphorized the temporal imposition in the clearest, spatial terms: "'the very attempt,' he warned, 'to make perpetual constitutions, is the assumption of the right to control the opinions of future generations; and to legislate for those over whom we have as little authority as we have over a nation in Asia.'"[43] For these thinkers, "the past is a foreign country."[44]

The analogy, particularly Webster's version, subtly identifies certain of the Framers with the powers against which they had just rebelled: If seeking to govern over the future is no different from governing over those far away and is illegitimate for the same reasons, then, Webster implies, framers like Madison and Hamilton who found a constitution for the ages are not that different from the English king and Parliament. The point is underlined by Webster's reference to Asia, in which England had been involved since 1685.[45] But the analogy also has other effects. First, since the passage of time is held to be responsible for the alienness of the law, the analogy subtly implies that the people in the present might experience without conflict both freedom and rule. Indeed, it implies that the founders enjoyed that very experience, since the only expressed worry is about later generations, not the current one. Second, those who reject the space-time analogy deployed by Jefferson, Webster, and Paine do so by embedding temporal distance in national time. They point out that the founders may have lived a long time ago, but they are *our* founders. Any lingering sense of uncanniness of those who come before to those who come later is papered over by talk of beneficiaries and heirs, fathers and sons, or intergenerational community.[46] Habermas himself seems to do this when he notes the responsibility of each "generation" to fulfill the promise of constitutional democracy.

With his 2001 essay, "Constitutional Democracy: A Paradoxical Union of Contradictory Principles?" Habermas enters the constitutional democracy debates with the aim of showing that deliberative democratic theory is untroubled by their conundra. He counters the constitutional democracy literature's externalization and temporalization of democracy's conflict between freedom and rule. He rejects the idea that constitutional democracy represents a struggle between past and present. For him, constitutional democracy models the appropriate relationship of considerations of right (constitutionalism) to considerations of will (democracy). Deliberative democratic theory, he says, is committed to a view of these as mutually implicated. The problem of a possible conflict between them is unique to modern constitutional democracies because they have two distinct sources of legitimation, the rule of law and popular sovereignty: "This duality raises the question of how the democratic principle and constitutionalism are related," he explains. But that question is answerable. The two principles are "co-original," Habermas says, meaning that they are of equal conceptual import; neither is prior to the other. He differs from Chantal Mouffe, who argues that the two principles are antagonists in need of articulation. For Habermas, these principles are always already "co-implicated." Each depends on the other, and the rights that issue from each—public and private rights, taken together as basic rights— "are constitutive for the process of self-legislation," a kind of autonomy in which rule and freedom are experienced together.[47] The co-originality and self-legislation arguments are helped along by Habermas's procedural treatment of constitutionalism in accordance with his own discourse on theoretic requirements, and not as the reflection of a people's substantive norms and culture, in accordance with republican requirements.[48]

With the assumption of a procedural constitution (i.e., one cast as less impositional than the one Jefferson feared), we are some way out of the conflict Habermas is trying to solve (though see Ferrara on the unreality of this assumption in actually existing constitutions and Waldron on how even procedural constitutions impinge upon democratic autonomy).[49]

Although he attends to the paradox of constitutional democracy, the term "paradox" does not come up as frequently in Habermas's writings as in Benhabib's. He is less inclined than she is to engage with those who criticize deliberative democrats for being mired in paradoxes they cannot solve. Nonetheless, in *Between Facts and Norms*, Habermas theorizes what Patchen Markell refers to as "the constitutive tension of law and politics," one that needs "to be negotiated by citizens, not transcended by the theorist."[50] Similarly, in the essay examined here, Habermas turns to practice to aid theory in charting a way out of the paradox of constitutional democracy. Along the way, though, he runs right into the paradox of politics.

The problem arises when Habermas turns in his "Constitutional Democracy" essay to consider a question posed by Frank Michelman. Michelman appreciates the deliberative democratic view of constitutionalism as the nonconflictual partner to democracy but, Habermas notes, Michelman worries that the deliberative democratic solution is incomplete, and he raises a powerful objection: "'A truly democratic process is itself inescapably a legally conditioned and constituted process. . . . Thus, in order to confer legitimacy on a set of laws issuing from an actual set of discursive institutions and practices . . . those institutions and practices would themselves have to be legally constituted in the right way.'"[51] In Habermas's parsing: The "chain of presuppositions of legitimation reaches back even beyond the constitution-making practice. For example, the constitutional assembly cannot itself vouch for the legitimacy of the rules according to which it was constituted. The chain never terminates, and the democratic process is caught in a circular self-constitution that leads to an infinite regress."[52]

In *Between Facts and Norms*, Habermas's response to this concern was "that we understand the normative bases of constitutional democracy as the result of a deliberative decision-making process that the founders—motivated by whatever historical contingencies—undertook with the intention of creating a voluntary, self-determining association of free and equal citizens."[53] But in his essay on the paradox of constitutional democracy, under pressure from Michelman, Habermas sees his earlier solution as insufficient: "[T]he paradox seems to return [i.e., rather than disappear] when we trace matters back to the act of constitution-making and ask whether discourse theory allows us to conceive the opinion- and will-formation of the constitutional convention as an unconstrained democratic process."[54]

Habermas rejects the option of stopping the infinite regress with a "moral realism that would be hard to defend."[55] Nor does he try to resuscitate his model of the founders as deliberative decision-makers. Instead he embraces the regress he once sought to halt and he reorients its seemingly problematic openness: "I propose that we understand the regress itself as the understandable expression of the future-oriented character, or openness, of the democratic constitution." Reorientation shifts the burden of legitimation from the past to the present and future. It points to the responsibility of postfounding generations to "actualiz[e] the still-untapped normative substance of the system of rights laid down in the original document of the constitution." The present generation "tap[s] the system of rights ever more fully," expands the circle of rights to ever greater inclusion, and thereby brings constitutionalism and democracy into better balance.[56] The practice of tapping supports the co-originality thesis, by working further to harmonize the two elements of constitutional democracy, but also by directing us away from the problematic empirical past, which cannot by itself stop the infinite regress, and toward a not yet problematic future. Tapping also posits an origin for rights (in our tapping of the Constitution) that is less problematic than the not fully legitimate empirical founding that gave birth to the Constitution. Moreover, the "system of rights" itself works as a backstop to the threat of regress insofar as the system is said to bear within it "normative substance." True, for Habermas, that normative substance is formal, but its association with an empirical constitution clothes it.[57] Identified with a constitution but not completely captured by it, the normative substance becomes a potential object of affective attachment, via what Habermas calls "constitutional patriotism," while also retaining its universal character in accordance with discourse theory's requirement.[58]

Thus, Habermas's contribution to the constitutional democracy paradox literature is to endorse a thin constitutionalism situated between a conceptual co-originality (the ground) and a practice of tapping (the horizon) that together work to secure the sense of freedom that constitutional rule might otherwise threaten. He braids together the two sources of liberal democratic legitimation (rule of law and popular sovereignty), casts them as mutually constitutive, not antagonistic, and insists that each is dependent upon the other for eventual full realization: "The allegedly paradoxical relation between democracy and the rule of law resolves itself in the dimension of historical time, provided one conceives of the constitution as a project that makes a founding act into an ongoing process of constitution-making that continues across generations."[59] Launched into time, but anchored by a co-origin that is out of time, the paradox of constitutional democracy seems to Habermas to be resolved or dissolved.

Yet Habermas provides one more argument. He goes on to supplement the conceptual origin, co-originality, with an empirical event, the constitutional assemblies of Paris and Philadelphia. He provides the supplement in the context of a passing remark about Kant.

Recall that in Benhabib's treatment of the paradox of democratic legitimation, Kant was said to serve the deliberative project better than Rousseau. She had in mind the Kant of the 2nd Critique and so does Habermas, when he embraces (and modifies) Kant, who sought to render will and reason compatible by "subordinating law to morality." But Habermas is also critical of Kant because elsewhere, in "Conflict of the Faculties," Kant "went beyond the systematic boundaries of [his] philosophy and raised the French Revolution to the level of a 'historical sign' for the possibility of a moral progress of humanity."[60] Habermas seems genuinely puzzled by Kant here, but he misremembers Kant's position.

In "Conflict of the Faculties," Kant sought some sign that mankind might improve over time. "In human affairs, there must be some experience or other which, as an event which has actually occurred, might suggest that man has the quality or power of being the *cause* and . . . the *author* of his own improvement." What event might "serve to prove the existence of a *tendency* within the human race as a *whole*"? Not the French revolution. Its meaning, contra Habermas, was too volatile and uncertain to serve as a sign of anything. The revolution, Kant said, "may succeed or it may fail. It may be so filled with misery and atrocities that no right-thinking man would ever decide to make the same experiment again." Instead, Kant took hope from the spectatorial response to the revolution. The sign of possible human improvement was the universal sympathy for the revolution that "borders almost on enthusiasm," and the fact that spectators outside France, themselves still subject to monarchical rule, risked expressing their sympathy publicly: "[I]t proves," Kant says, "(because of its universality) . . . that man has a moral character, or at least the makings of one."[61] The details of Kant's account, the emphasis on the universality and the morality of spectatorship, admiration for non-self-interested action, and suggestion of a transnational public sphere, are all Habermas's own central commitments. Why then does Habermas miscast the account and distance himself from it?

It may be that Kant's uncharacteristic enthusiasm for enthusiasm, or something that "borders on" it, departs too much for Habermas from deliberative democratic commitments to dispassionate deliberate proceduralism.[62] But the problem is not just the affect, it is also the object. I think Habermas worries that Kant in his time, and we in our own, attach affectively to the wrong event, to revolution rather than constitution. For

Habermas, the vision of people rising up against unjust powers may be more passion-inducing than the daily toil of just self-governance. The storming of the Bastille fires up the political imagination more readily than a Supreme Court decision that in turn makes for much more fascinating reading than the minutes of most town hall meetings. But good drama and good politics are two different things, Habermas might say. He may worry that we, and even Kant, whom Habermas takes to be an otherwise reliable ally, tend to forget that. This worry may lead Habermas somehow to misidentify the event (mistakenly thinking it is the revolution itself rather than the public expression of sympathy for it) that, in Kant's view, grounds hope. Or perhaps the difference at issue here is minor. For Habermas, it may not actually matter whether we are talking about the revolution or public enthusiasm for it. Both endanger the context-transcendent constitutional project by orienting us toward rupture rather than continuity. Indeed, perhaps most dangerous of all, from his perspective, is precisely the very thing Kant did cling to (and that Habermas here erases from Kant's account)—the sight of people caught up, even at their own risk, in revolutionary fervor, but not in constitutional enchantment. For this contemporary theorist of constitutional patriotism and champion of a rights-centered democratic politics, the possibility that only the former inspires the heroism Kant admired is a dismal possibility indeed. So Habermas substitutes his own sign for Kant's, just as Benhabib substituted the paradox of democratic legitimation (bk. II, chap. 3) for Rousseau's more fundamental paradox of politics (bk. II, chap. 7): In place of the French Revolution, Habermas offers up for our (near) enthusiasm what Kant inexplicably left out: "the constitutional assemblies of Philadelphia and Paris" or at least the "*reasonable* trace of [that] great dual historical event that we can now see in retrospect as an entirely new beginning. With this event began a project that holds together a rational constitutional discourse across the centuries."[63]

Can rational discourse, the core element of Habermas's deliberative democratic theory, need the supplement of an event or, more aptly, its "reasonable trace"? Habermas here tries to take advantage of the exemplary power of the event without forsaking the transcontextual rationalism of discourse theory (not the event, but its "reasonable trace," not a constitution, but a "rational constitutional discourse"). His effort recalls that of Kant in the *Groundwork* to illustrate the moral law's power with phenomenal examples, while insisting that such manifestations of the law are always only partial. In both cases, the examples exceed and may even betray the reason or the law they are meant to serve. That is part of the attraction and risk of such examples, even to those who try to use them in a limited or constrained way. Habermas needs Philadelphia and

Paris to motivate his "constitutional patriotism." Without the events to conjure up a colorful human world of passion, loyalty, betrayal, idealism, and reason, the idea of affectively attaching to a constitution (which, after its characteristic nods to the people's virtue, is simply a list of offices, procedures, and rules) is about as attractive as kissing a typewriter.[64]

With the place names, however, a Pandora's box opens. Philadelphia and Paris represent not simply "constitutionalism" but two distinct revolutions and foundings, each characterized by its own unique, contingent drama, intrigue, public spiritedness, and remnants. In the U.S. case, "Philadelphia" conjures not just the assembly that produced the new national constitution, but also the many competing conceptions of the American experiment that were sidelined or minoritized by the assembly and its constitution. The revolution, the Articles of Confederation, the constitutional assembly in Philadelphia, the resulting Constitution itself, the antifederalists who fought it, the diverse crowds considered too unruly to be part of the deliberations, the various practices of popular constitutionalism delegitimated over the years, and the confederal practices of some native peoples are all the origins of contemporary American constitutional democracy. Not all of these are compatible, but all are part of American popular and democratic constitutionalisms, and all—including those defeated or marginalized—played a role in the historical shaping of American democracy. Some still do. If they are unrecollected in Habermas's invocation of "Philadelphia," that is because they are not, for him, part of its "reasonable trace." It is the trace, not the event, that he seeks to recollect. It is the trace not the event that he secures when he says that those who tap the system of rights must orient themselves toward a beginning from which they take their bearings and build a tradition. To do so, and by doing so, they must inhabit the perspective of the founders (they are "in the same boat") and take up the unfinished project of founding: "a constitution that is democratic . . . is a tradition-building project with a clearly marked beginning in time."[65]

But which is to be the beginning? Philadelphia or Paris? Habermas refers to that "great dual historical event" as if it does not or must not matter. But if it really does not matter, why utter the names Paris and Philadelphia at all? Clearly Habermas is aware that the names inspire; he wants to avail himself of their inspiration without the (for him) problematic particularities that make them inspirational but not universal, formative of a people but also productive of remnants.[66] Once we conjure up the event, however, there is no putting it back in the bottle. For democratic theorists more alert to the paradox of politics, such as Hannah Arendt, Sheldon Wolin, and Larry Kramer, "Philadelphia" is not the opening chapter in a bildungsroman, but a pivotal moment in a tragic story of almost irrecov-

erable loss (Arendt's "lost treasure" of the revolution) or theft (Wolin reflects on Jacob's theft or Esau's sale of his rightful inheritance).[67] To Arendt, Wolin, and Kramer, a democratic tradition built on practices now
lost would be very different from the one we have. This is not to endorse
their judgment over Habermas's but to highlight the latter's insistent
character, while calling attention to the genred nature of his reading of
the signs he favors. Rousseau's insight is apt here: Signs do not speak for
themselves. No criteria decide which event is a sign and which is its
(un)reasonable trace. We do, and the worth of our judgment depends on
its implications: What politics and public goods are generated thereby?
And, no less important, is the past rendered thereby entirely inalien, raw
material for our use and abuse? Or does it retain its otherness, that trait
which Franz Rosenzweig says might make the past a source of generativity for a future?

It may seem to Habermas that the paradox of politics calls us back repeatedly to the political moment of origins wherein it pulls the rug out
from under our feet, and it may seem to him that in such moments up-
heaval rather than settlement necessarily dominates, but this need not be
the case. The paradox of politics can be a generative force. Similarly, we
need not participate in any "democratic mysticism" to ask after the remnants of constitutionalism.[68] We can be clear-eyed about the undemocratic aims or implications of some popular and minority powers, but
without falling for any "constitutional mysticism." We can be clear-eyed
about the ways in which constitutions may operate not just to "canalize"
popular power, as Holmes says, but also to cannibalize it.[69] That is, it
makes little sense to talk of constitutionalism versus democracy, as such:
There are varieties of constitutionalism, including popular constitutionalism, many of which were casualties of Philadelphia and Paris.[70]

When Habermas's tappers choose "Philadelphia" as the beginning of
their tradition-building enterprise, the costs of alternatives foregone and
still sidelined daily are not viewed. Does Philadelphia win out over other
contenders now because it did so then, that is, because you go to politics
with the constitution you have not with the one you wish you had? If so,
then this seems to be one of those moments of decision that critics claim
are invariably discernible in deliberative democratic theory, notwithstanding its protestations to the contrary.[71] Habermas even seems to concede the point when he says: "we can now see in retrospect" that Philadelphia and Paris marked "an entirely new beginning." If our apprehension
of Philadelphia and Paris as new beginnings is, as Habermas says, retrospective, then that means we are making the judgment from inside the
frame we are supposed to be judging—and that means we are not out of
but rather firmly in the paradox of politics.

The Paradox of Politics, Revisited

Which came first, the chicken or the egg? Anaximander solved this, the oldest paradox, by postulating an infinite thing, an uncaused cause that functions not unlike Habermas's postulate of co-originality. Aristotle generated a different solution, the immortality of species, which, Roy Sorenson says, posits "an infinite relationship between finite things . . . an infinite sequence of parents and children, [in which] a parent could care for each child and there is no need to postulate an animal [or other] origin for human beings."[72] Aristotle's solution did not survive the theories of Darwin, Mendel, and Lamarck (evolution, inheritance, and acquired traits), which suggest that chicken or egg can be ranked first. Might Aristotle's solution be instructive nonetheless for politics?

Arendt may have had in mind something like Aristotle's infinite relationship between finite things when she remarked that the American revolutionaries succeeded because they practiced self-governance for decades before they rebelled. Although theirs was a revolutionary beginning, it was preceded by decades of acculturation in democratic habits, mindsets, practices, law, and institutions (an infinite sequence, as it were, of parents and children) made possible by their contingent distance from sovereign power.[73] That contingent distance was their "lucky break," the chance circumstance that helped secure their release from sovereign paternal power.[74] Recent scholarship underlines Arendt's central point with the suggestion that the enabling distance she noted was not simply a natural fact. According to Richard Ross, the American colonists, canny navigators of the seas of authority, sometimes pretended not to have received unwelcome directives from England, thus actively protecting the distance from monarchical power that was a condition of their successful self-governance.[75]

Arendt is often referred to as a theorist of beginnings. She repeatedly emphasizes the inaugural powers of action but her resort to something like Aristotle's infinite sequence to praise the American Revolution suggests a different notion of beginning than the ab initio variety with which she is usually associated (for good reason by many of her readers, including this one) and with which, as we saw earlier, Habermas also affiliates when he celebrates Philadelphia and Paris as an "entirely new beginning."[76] What are the two different ways of thinking about political origins? Michael Oakeshott is helpful when he distinguishes ab initio origin stories, which he disapprovingly associates with the opening line, "In the beginning," from those that that begin with "Once upon a time." The latter invite entry into another time and postulate many temporalities (that they imagine *a* time suggests there are others as well). They have "no unconditional conclusion; [their] end is the beginning of another

story. [They have] no over-all meaning; [they tell of] occurrences understood in terms of the meanings they acquire from their evidential contingent relationships." In the beginning stories, by contrast, posit one time,
one beginning and, as in Habermas's tradition-building project with its
clearly marked beginning in time, their energies are harnessed to an over-
all purpose. They are grand narratives, out "not to tell a story but to
construct a myth," Oakeshott says, though we need not accept his implication that the choice is between good stories and bad myths.[77] The paradox of politics resists that binary as well. Most narratives have elements
of myth and story, and partake of both sets of traits Oakeshott identifies
here. They can be turned to either purpose (story and/or myth) or, perhaps better, we can be turned by them to either purpose, or both.

When deliberative democratic theorists substitute binary paradoxes
for the vicious circle of Rousseau's paradox of politics, they evade the
conditionality tracked here in the work of Aristotle, Arendt, and Oakeshott.[78] Deliberativists do so in the hope that constitutional democracy
can be provided with a less contingent more legitimate ground, with what
Oakeshott refers to as a *justification* rather than a *vindication*. As I have
suggested, this lands them in the very paradoxes they then worry how
to resolve, manage, or transcend. If deliberativists prefer binary paradoxes, however worrying they find them, to the paradox of politics, it is
because the problems posed by the former (general will versus will of all,
constitutionalism versus democracy) are themselves the deliberative democrats' solution.[79] In their preferred paradoxes, the people are a problem
that rules might solve. In the paradox of politics by contrast, with its plural "once upon a time" and "in the beginning" temporalities, the problem is that the people are always also a multitude, the general will is inhabited by the will of all, the law(giver) is possibly a charlatan, and
political theorists' objectivity is also partisan. Here, we get neither deliberation nor decision as such; we get a politics, in which plural and contending parties make claims in the name of public goods and seek support from various constituencies and wherein the legitimacy of outcomes
is always contestable.

With their focus on conflicting principles (Habermas, Benhabib) or in-
commensurable "logics" (Agamben, Mouffe, Christodoulidis), binary
paradoxes shuttle us back and forth between decision and deliberation.
Even Chantal Mouffe's strategy of articulation, intended to respond to
the paradox of politics that she too theorizes and embraces, cannot help
but preserve the binary of law and democracy whose pragmatic settlements she seeks to rework.[80] Political events and dramas exceed such hypostatized categorizations, however. Politics occurs in the spaces between
them.[81] As Mary Dietz says of a different Habermasian binary, the two
tensions are never resolved. They are played out "along a continuum of

'more or less,'" not across a binary of either-or.[82] The categorizations, principles, logics are not entirely pernicious, however. The terms "general will" and "will of all," for example, capture certain elements of political experience and can provide a way to move people into supporting common agendas. But these advantages are lost when the terms in question are frozen into a binary paradoxical structure in which each term not only opposes the other but also props it up and between them the vast, complicated, and subtle terrain of politics is excluded. Recall here, for example, the elision of varieties of popular constitutionalism by Habermas's binary of constitution versus revolution.[83]

Rousseau's paradox of politics, like Aristotle's infinite sequence, explodes the reassuring binaries that structure many of contemporary political theory's debates.[84] The paradox of politics points to alternative domains of political work by depriving us of postulated points of origin (landing us right in the conundrum of which comes first, good law or the wisdom of self-governance?) and inviting us to see how (admittedly to different extents, in different ways, in different regimes) law and its authors/subjects fundamentally fail to intersect in the present in ways that satisfy independent standards of legitimation. This is not, contra Jefferson, Webster, and Paine, simply because others authored the law by which we are later, distantly governed. Nor is it, contra deliberative democratic theory, because we lack a moral standpoint from which rightly to distinguish the general will from will of all. Nor is it because we have failed our responsibility to tap the systems of right by which we are governed (though we may well have). Rather it is because this infinite sequence is the condition in which we find ourselves when we think and act politically, when we demand that the lawgiving/charlatan institutions by which we are always already governed and shaped be responsive to the plural, conflicting agents who together are said to authorize or benefit from them: the ever changing and infinitely sequential people, the multitude, and their remnants.

As we saw at the outset, Rousseau's aim is to launch the ideal regime of the social contract and secure its legitimation by insulating it from implication in violence, unfreedom, or partiality. The result, however, is rather different—a politics and a citizenry potentially ill equipped to respond to the daily, ongoing exercise of government powers unleashed by their social contract, yet unharnessed by real general willing and uninterrupted by agonistic democratic engagements. If the paradox of politics is real and enduring, then a democratic politics would do well to replace its faith in a pure general will with an acceptance of its impurity and an embrace of the perpetuity of political contestation made necessary by that impurity. In such a setting, democracy's necessary conditions (e.g., the reproduction of a supposed general will) may be found to offend some of its own commitments (to freedom and self-rule) in ways that call for (a certain model of) democracy's self-overcoming (i.e., in quest of a different democracy). This self-overcoming may take the form of civic commitments to practices of agonistic respect and to an ethos of pluralization that acknowledges the remainders of all forms of life by actively but not uncritically supporting the efforts of new identities to come into being without prior guarantees about the rightness or justice of their claims. It is to that problem that I now turn by way of an analysis of emergent rights claims.

Chapter Two.

Emergence

READING NEW RIGHTS IN THE PARADOX OF POLITICS

> For we say that there isn't any doubt that we understand the
> word, and on the other hand its meaning lies in its use.
> —*Ludwig Wittgenstein*

> How might paradox gain political richness when it is understood
> as affirming the impossibility of justice in the present and as
> articulating the conditions and contours of justice in the future?
> How might attention to paradox help formulate a political struggle
> for rights in which they are conceived neither as instruments nor as
> ends, but as articulating through their instantiation what equality
> and freedom might consist in that exceeds them? . . . And what
> forms of rights claims have the temerity to sacrifice an absolutist or
> naturalized status in order to carry this possibility?
> —*Wendy Brown*

WHEN IMMANUEL KANT DEVELOPED his late reflections on cosmopolitan right, he did so by way of a critique of a fellow Enlightenment thinker, Moses Mendelssohn. Mendelssohn formed half of the interreligious friendship with Lessing that the latter fictionalized and made famous in *Nathan, the Wise.* The issue for Kant was Mendelssohn's claim that "the human race . . . never took a few steps forward without soon afterwards, and with redoubled speed, sliding back to its previous position."[1] Individual persons might progress morally, Mendelssohn had explained, but the species as a whole does not.

Contra Mendelssohn, Kant claimed that the "hope for better times" is something "without which an earnest desire to do something useful for the common good would never have inspired the human heart." Hope grounds duty. Hope is therefore indispensable to Kantian morality, and so, to guarantee it, Kant paradoxically insists that we have a duty to hope, or at least a duty to act hopefully. The need is so dire that he ignores the vicious circle into which he is thrust by his solution—which comes first, the hope that grounds duty or the duty to hope?—and he even attributes to Mendelssohn the very trait Mendelssohn is said to be wanting: "the worthy Mendelssohn must himself have reckoned on [the hope for better times], since he zealously endeavored to promote the enlightenment and welfare of the nation to which he belonged"—a nation whose law Kant saw as fundamentally and merely regulative, but which Mendelssohn insisted was on the contrary deeply revelatory.[2]

"The worthy Mendelssohn," however, had been quite explicit in his rejection of something like the Kantian duty to hope and its premise (or what he took to be its premise), the progress of the species guided by nature. Criticizing Lessing's argument in *The Education of the Human Race*, Mendelssohn clearly opposed "the attempt," in Matt Erlin's words, "to force the entire species into a single framework of linear development."[3] Contra Lessing, Mendelssohn argued, man cannot be said *as such* to be in his infancy, childhood, or adulthood. For, at any point in human history, "man" is "child, adult and old man at the same time, though in different places and regions of the world."[4] This view is different from the eighteenth-century Scottish historiographers' for on Mendelssohn's account the ages of the different places themselves change too. What looks like adulthood in one historical moment may generate in that same place infancy for the next. Providence, Mendelssohn said, had a habit of wiping the slate clean (like the biblical flood). This was not mere futility or Sispheanism, as Kant feared.[5] Indeed, Mendelssohn himself in effect had already pitted that very same charge against Kant, via Lessing: Were a society to achieve the highest level of progress and achievement, Mendelssohn said, "what would our children do? Continue to march forward indefinitely?"[6] Providence did them and us a favor, Mendelssohn said, by occasionally making us start anew. That new start is secured, moreover, not just by Providence but also by the nature of individuation itself, which on Mendelssohn's account not only vehiculates progress, as Kant said, it also *thwarts* the progress of the species. In Mendelssohn's view, individuation involves resistance: What the father achieves, he says, the sons rebel against. A generation that loves liberty will be followed by one that embraces servitude.[7]

Thus on Mendelssohn's account, generational time is ruptural, discontinuous. This works to protect individuals from becoming mere cogs in the species machine, a charge that had been leveled against Kant—that his commitment to species progress violated his own principle of respect for persons insofar as it treated individuals not as ends in themselves but as means toward the end of species progress. And it addresses a second problem as well.

For those who saw human history in linear progressive terms, it was difficult to account for the stubborn persistence of Judaism in Enlightened modernity. Where Kant and even Lessing saw Judaism as a necessary stage en route to Christianity, Mendelssohn rejected any philosophy of history in which a fragment, *this* fragment, was necessary in/to a larger evolutionary plan whose progress it serves, under which it is subsumed, by way of which it ought to have disappeared or, put more positively, been redeemed. In short, Mendelssohn understood, as Matt Erlin puts it, that "It is not just the individual who suffers an implicit reduction in status in late 18th century theories of progress; entire cultures become vestigial once their historical function has been fulfilled."[8] Hence Lessing's argument, to Mendelssohn's disappointment and consternation, that the rites and rituals of ancient Judaism had been rendered nugatory by the arrival of Christ. In the Christian world, Judaism was a relic. It was the Jews' failure to see this that informed Kant's judgment that they were overly attached to literal law.

It was a view with which Mendelssohn was all too familiar, having himself been challenged on several occasions publicly to renounce ritual Judaism and embrace more fully the Enlightenment to which he was also devoted. In a way, that is to say, he was challenged to give up what appeared to his critics to be an assemblage-style subjectivity that was plural and perhaps conflicted for the sake of a unitary, sovereign, consistent model more like what Bernard Williams calls integrity, built around a single set of core beliefs. Of course, transforming the former into the latter was precisely Mendelssohn's project as an architect of the Jewish Enlightenment.

Still, Mendelssohn took a dimmer view of the species and its prospects than did Kant, and this is unsurprising. Mendelssohn, a Jew living in Berlin under Frederick the Great, had good reason to doubt the progress of the species. He had in his own lifetime been made painfully aware of the limits of Enlightenment for Jews.[9] As Sebastian Hensel, biographer of Moses Mendelssohn's famous grandson Felix, reports, it seems it was the case that

> under Frederick the Great every Jew had to purchase, on the occasion of his marriage, a certain amount of china from the newly established royal china factory in Berlin, and that not according to his own choice, but that of the manager of the factory, who made use of the opportunity to get rid of things otherwise unsalable. Thus Moses Mendelssohn, a man even then generally known and honoured, became possessed of twenty life-sized china apes, some of which are still preserved in his family.[10]

Knowing now about Mendelssohn's twenty porcelain apes, I reexperience with some discomfort my purchase of china when I myself got married years ago. Aware that I was participating in a ridiculous, bourgeois convention, I was not sufficiently disturbed by *that* to refrain from getting new dishes. I *was* getting married after all; how disturbed could I be by the trappings? But this story of the Jewish Mendelssohn's coerced acquisition of useless porcelain apes, life-sized no less, on the occasion of his marriage stands now for me as a trace in the current practice in which affianced couples "register" for china. Knowing it was once coerced, and specifically for Jews, something shifts in me and the idea of wedding china is less tolerable.

It may not, however, have been intolerable for Mendelssohn or at least so we are invited to conclude by the fact that the apes were kept in the family for years. The poet, Jean Nordhaus, imagines an explanation for this in a poem that personates a Mendelssohn who accepts and even wills a Nietzschean affirmation of the royal requirement:

> . . . With time, I've grown fond
> of my porcelain pets. They ask nothing more
> than a corner to stand in. And sometimes at night,
> one will gleam out from the shadows,
> bow, and give me a wink as I pass.
> For if you embrace your afflictions
> and call them your own, they will become
>
> your blessings. I've even
> given them names: This bent one
> is My Hump. And that one
> with his hands beside his open mouth
>
> I've dubbed The Stammerer.
> The one with the dagger
> is Lavater. And this one
> is known to the family
>
> as Frederick the Great.
>
> I could go on, but you understand . . .[11]

Mendelssohn did in fact refuse the affliction of circumstance: He wrote *Jerusalem* on behalf of tolerance and on several occasions and at their request pleaded the cases of his coreligionists to state authorities. He survived, surely not without suffering, several challenges to convert or recant. Mendelssohn may have been motivated by a kind of hope when he did all this but it was not Kantian hope. He did not share Kant's faith in "the morality of a wise creator and ruler of the world"—or at least the creator he was interested in was not the same as Kant's.[12] And he rejected what Kant thought were hope's necessary conditions: progress, evolution, and the duty to hope. These, Kant thought, would secure "man's most sacred rights." Mendelssohn, who lived in a more tragic universe, thought the opposite was true.

What are the necessary conditions of rights? Kantian hope or a more Mendelssohnian sensibility open to plural timelines and the eternal return of the same? We saw in chapter 1 some of the limitations of Kantian hope, which depends upon and licences a backward-looking gaze rather than a plural timeline and futural perspective. We also saw how Kantian hope works to elide rather than embrace the paradox of politics. In this chapter, I propose we look at rights not in terms of their past trajectories but rather in their fragile moments of emergence. This makes us alert to the ways in which new rights reactivate the paradox of politics: New rights presuppose the world they seek to bring into being.

I begin with two rights-claims to which William Connolly repeatedly returns in his work: gay rights and the right to doctor-assisted suicide. I focus not on the rights per se nor on the claimants but on the worlds potentially opened or closed by these rights. I worry about how a focus on rights is encouraged by a law-centered view of the world and risks distracting our attention from common goods, the generation of which is the glue and the goal of democratic life. Liberal and deliberative democratic theorists tend to approach rights with a juridical focus: Are they legitimate? Can they be subsumed under old, established ones? What if instead we ask: What new relations and new realities might a new right inaugurate, or is the new right desirable? Is it just?[13]

Beginning with Connolly's position on emergent rights, I highlight some of the larger issues surrounding doctor-assisted suicide, noting its possible implication in the biopolitics in which Giorgio Agamben says we are mired. And I find in Wittgenstein resources that may help us imagine rights differently, in a way that departs from what I call here the chrono-logic of rights. Finally, I turn to a relatively new movement, Slow Food, to illustrate the sort of political actions that might arise out of an alternative to established chrono-logical understandings of rights. Slow Food's success thus far has been due in no small measure to its embrace of the complex temporalities of the paradox of politics. First, it embraces plural tempos: It combines the slow seasonality of nature (by contrast with the fast tempo and repetitive productivity of industrial agriculture) with the fast pace of global communications and markets (by contrast with the slow-paced, face-to-face encounters preferred by some democratic theorists); and second, it uses a rights-claim to center its agenda and challenge the larger apparatus of the chrono-logic of rights. Slow Food claims the *right to taste*. In so doing, the movement acknowledges—by embracing while accenting—the apparent ridiculousness of new rights-claims from the perspective of the established schedule of rights; and Slow Food sutures rights to goods, convivial eating, healthy food, more human and humane food production processes, as well as the local autonomies, sustainability, and transnational connections that these require, while affirming pleasure as central to its politics and pointing to the capacity that Arendt, borrowing from Kant's aesthetics, thought was absolutely important to democratic politics: *taste*.

Slow Food, in short, points us toward the co-implication of the right and the good, rather than to the question of which is prior to the other. Since Rawls, debates within liberal theory have been largely framed by the neo-Kantian assumption of the priority of right. I do not here engage the Rawlsian literature in detail but I have it in mind when I close this chapter with Slow Food's declaration of the right to taste. The right to taste bridges liberal rights with the utilitarian focus on pleasure that Rawls sought to escape, though he never named that, in particular, as the problem with utility. Instead, he criticized the consequentialism of utilitarianism in the worry that it might violate individual rights and integrity. But for Rawls utilitarianism also posed another problem: Its focus on pleasure raised the spectre of subjectivism, which Rawls would see as potentially destructive to consensus or collective action notwithstanding utilitarian efforts to objectify subjective feeling by way of the quantification of utiles. With its call to a right to taste, Slow Food enters the paradox of politics—it enacts the pleasure it calls for, there is pleasure in laughter and the claimed right is funny—but it also offers a new hybrid political resource: A right to pleasure combines the powers of liberal and utilitarian theory and invites us to move beyond their well-established opposition.[14]

That well-established opposition is currently under pressure as well from proponents of animal rights and welfare, a cause to which Slow Food also draws our attention. This is where utilitarianism will yet experience a comeback. If the reason for its being discredited was the liberal critique of utility's inability to respect the distinction between persons, utilitarianism is now surely set to reemerge as a creditable moral theory because of its refusal by extension to take seriously the distinction among species. On this point, too, utilitarians take issue with Kant. Recall the charge leveled against Kant, that his commitment to species progress violated his own principle of respect for persons. Utilitarianism *embraces* that charge. Rather than seek to rescue individual integrity from Kantian species progress or vice versa, utilitarianism rejects both commitments and subjects the Kantian commitment to species progress to no less trenchant and difficult a critique than was leveled at his principle of respect for persons. The sum of pain and pleasure decenters even the species whose progress Kant hoped for. This utilitarian approach—with its quantifications and calculations—was easier to dismiss on humanist grounds when environmental politics was not yet formed and articulated. In recent years, however, things have changed. Animal welfare and rights have acquired more acceptance as serious political claims amid concerns about human safety and environmental health. Thus, it seems to me, the move to animal rights or welfare may well stage a reevaluation of utilitarianism in the coming years. Peter Singer has done a great deal to make this unavoidable by pressing the cause of animal welfare with consistency and rigor for decades.

Slow Food chooses a less consistent, more paradoxical path. It promotes human-centered pleasures by adding a new right, the right to taste, to the human rights arsenal while gently pressing upon us an awareness in particular of one of the remainders of the rights-centered human universe: animal life, whose existence under current food production conditions rises surely to the level of emergency and which cannot be best remedied merely by a further expansion of rights. The needed encounter with animality points beyond the chrono-logic of rights and calls for a different orientation, lodged in the paradox of politics and called for by Slow Food at its best. Perhaps by way of this encounter, we can rescript the story of Moses Mendelssohn and his twenty porcelain apes as an undecidable event that was certainly enabled by the evolutionary belief that the Christian world ought by then to have already left Judaism behind but also pointed beyond that belief, resisting evolutionary time by setting man and ape up in coexistence: The incident of the porcelain apes may unwittingly point toward a future it would not yet have comprehended.

The Politics of Becoming

As we saw in chapter 1, time is not plural for Habermas, who says that "The *allegedly* paradoxical relation between democracy and the rule of law resolves itself *in the dimension of historical time, provided one conceives of the constitution as a project that makes a founding act into an ongoing process of constitution-making that continues across generations*," provided, that is, that the present generation takes up the responsibility to "tap the system of rights ever more fully" and realize further its constitutional inheritance in time.[15] The past offers a system that needs only to be tapped, not overcome, transformed, or reinterpreted in light of new events, remnants, or ideas, and the future does not escape or transform the past— it merely fulfills the past or at worst forestalls its fulfillment. Habermas renders time itself inalien by casting it in familial terms. He portrays the relation between past and present as a generational passing; it occurs in generational time, and his familial metaphor somehow inoculates later generations against the trauma of norm-transmission, postulated by Mendelssohn and later analyzed at length by Freud.

In potentially originary moments, however, it is difficult to know what properly belongs to the future and what to the past, or to which future and which past. At such moments, William Connolly says, "Justice now trembles in its constitutive uncertainty, dependence and ambiguity."[16] There may well come what we later will call progress, and new identities may be allowed or ushered onto the threshold of justice, but progress does not come with its own guarantee, nor is it a meaningful criterion to guide us. In the moment we do not know in what progress might consist, and new claims may seem laughable. Looking backward, we can say with satisfaction that the chrono-logic of rights required and therefore delivered the eventual inclusion of women, Africans, and native peoples into the schedule of formal rights. But what actually did the work? The impulsion of rights, their chrono-logic, or the political actors who won the battles they were variously motivated to fight and whose contingent victories were later credited not to the actors but to the independent trajectory of rights as such?

Our moral clarity regarding identities or forms of life that were once but are no longer excluded is a product of political victories whereby some succeeded in their effort to migrate "from an abject abnormal subordinate or obscure Other *subsisting* in a nether world under the register of justice to a positive identity now *existing* on the register of justice/injustice."[17] Those victorious political actors *created* post hoc the clarity we now credit with having spurred them on to victory ex ante. They may have had clarity in their minds or been motivated by a commitment they shared with others. But that clarity and those commitments did not in the moment have the necessitarian quality that the past lends to them post hoc. On the contrary, in the moment emergent rights-claims are experienced as fragile, contingent, and paradoxical. They presuppose and claim already to inhabit a world not yet built. In short, they replay, they do not govern, the Rousseauvian paradox of politics, launching us into its nonlinear temporality, or can do so if we allow ourselves to be vulnerable to them.

Connolly's politics of becoming brings together critical responsiveness and an ethos of pluralization on behalf of those subjects, impulses, and forms of life remaindered by any current constellation of identity/difference. It is crucial to such a politics to shake off the perspective of the backward-looking gaze (the perspective of the dialectic) and the chronologic of rights from which developments in time appear necessary, chronologically if not logically; this is why the will rages against time's "it was," as Nietzsche and Arendt knew—because the will seeks freedom, not the necessity that the past seems to offer.[18] Instead a politics of becoming postulates the perspective of the present moment, that of the actor and not the spectator, situated between past(s) and future(s) and always infiltrated by their rumblings, in which practitioners of critical responsiveness, faced with new claims from emergent identities or discourses, lose their bearings, find they have no sense of direction, and are confounded.

Of course new worlds are built not just by way of rights-claims and new identities but also by way of new visions of political goods and goals. Seeing movements for political change in terms of rights-claims, or centering such movements on the politics of rights or identity politics threatens to limit our apprehension of new political events and narrow our political aspirations.[19] Connolly's focus on rights and identity as central goals of progressive political action in place of, say, goods, especially in *The Ethos of Pluralization* and *Identity/Difference*, points to a potential limit in his approach.[20] It may make him unmindful of the role of law in producing the unilinear temporality he seeks to decenter. As I argue in chapter 3, it is in the discourse of law that innovative actors are invariably depicted as having "anticipated" the law (rather than having made, countermanded, or hijacked it) when they work for new rights. Connolly tends, following Nietzsche, to see such future orientations as remnants of religious, redemptive thinking, whether in Kantian or Hegelian form, which they are too. Niklaus Luhmann, by contrast, notes (and *celebrates*) law's success in producing a future-oriented linear temporality that can resolve the paradox of politics.

According to Luhmann, the development of modern constitutionalism has effected (in Emilios Christodoulidis's parsing)

> a displacement of temporal perspectives. The overwhelming orientation to the past that characterized pre-modern society is displaced by *a new openness to the future made possible in the new constitutional order*. Openness to the future means that law foresees its own changeability and regulates it by positioning itself before political influx and placing all law under constitutional scrutiny. What is remarkable in these new developments is that the past is relieved of its function as a horizon of legitimation; the social imaginary, more generally, is re-oriented toward the future.[21]

But the past and future may not be so easily uncoupled. Some futures function a lot like the past that they supposedly replace; other futures remain haunted by pasts that they supposedly left behind or by other supposedly parallel (e.g., colonial) pasts that they claim not to know.

Those who see rights-claims as claims to membership in the universal will judge rights-claims in relation to a past (an already established universal as ground), or future (a universal whose promise is in place whose realization has yet to be brought about), or both. But as Connolly points out, although agitators for rights do often claim membership in a (but not *the*) universal (we are human too, or we are citizens too), they also claim membership in particulars. The success of homosexuals in rescripting themselves as gays and heterosexuals as straights (thus replacing a medicalized binary [homo- or heterosexual] with a more egalitarian difference [gay or straight]) was partly achieved by their insistence "we are everywhere," members of straight families, brothers, sisters, sons and daughters, mothers and fathers. The particularity of membership and exposure, coming out, played a big part in the move from one identity to the other because it claimed solidarity. Success was not preordained by or contained in or subsumed by previous victories, which took the protection of the universal for themselves and (re-)defined others—including homosexuals—as their constitutive outside, beneath the radar of the universal. Nor was success promised by already existing declarations of right, which may or may not have been found to "encompass" these new claims. Things could have gone another way. They may yet do so.

Connolly's politics of becoming rejects mere inclusion or subsumption; it is committed to the sort of mutual and unpredictable unsettlement that follows from real, risky engagement with otherness. Here we have another departure from the usual politics of rights and identity, an element of his more expansive approach. To stay with one of Connolly's favorite examples: Homosexuals could not reach real equality as homosexuals; they had to rescript themselves as gay. In so doing they also unsettled their former partner identity, heterosexuality. The demedicalization of homosexuality entailed the denaturalization and deprivileging of heterosexuality. That is why so many heterosexuals fought it and continue to fight it. And they were, they *are* right, right about the costs to their own form of life, that is. In the politics of becoming, gays and straights inhabit their desires and experience them with more of a sense of contingency and relation to the other than homosexuals and heterosexuals do.[22] By contrast, mere chrono-logical inclusion under the sign of the universal does not come at that high a price. It requires tolerance, but it itself tolerates and may even, on moral grounds, *demand* stasis in the identities it already harbors. Perhaps that is why mere inclusion almost always disappoints and sometime enrages the newly included. As any informed observer of the civil rights movement in the United States can see, so much changes and yet so little changes at the same time. This outcome is aided and abetted by the focus on civil rights and the concomitant reentrenchment of an absolutist conception of property rights that precludes any meaningful redistributive politics. A politics of becoming, by contrast, recognizes that each new inclusion comes with disturbance and possibly transformation for those people and rights that are already in, as well as for the antecedent rules that aspire to govern or subsume all new cases and events. That is why time never stands still in politics, a point noted not only by Connolly but also by a range of thinkers from J. G. A. Pocock to Luhmann. It is, however, a risk of real dedication to a democratic politics such as that envisioned by Connolly that one might feel as if one were living from one emergency to the next. Each new emergent claim can be experienced as an emergency by the existing order, by the identities challenged yet again to undergo redistribution or revision or to reexperience the contingency at their heart. Hence the need for arts of the self and the other ethicopolitical virtues of respect and generosity outlined by Connolly in a series of books written in the 1990s and since.

Hence too the need to recraft time itself. It is to this effort that Connolly turns his attention in detail in *Neuropolitics*. Perhaps having fun with his readers or possibly at their expense, he associates linear temporality with a past time (implying that linear temporality is therefore dead and gone)—or he notes that Nietzsche does so, anyway. Like Nietzsche, Connolly uses that pastness to open up a new space for a new time, not a cyclical one (the cyclical conception of time is also identified with a dead past, even older than its linear alternative) but rather a looping, unpredictable sort of time, multiple and various, that runs and ruptures all over the place. It forks. In response to democratic theorists like Sheldon Wolin who insist on democracy's need for a slower and less plural tempo than that characteristic of our cacophonous, late modern world, Connolly proceeds carefully. He is not merely resigned like Tocqueville sometimes is and Connolly does not promote one temporality in place of another. *He does not just embrace speed.* He commits himself and invites us as well to seek out the promise borne in our new conditions for democracy's possible futures.

"The challenge is how to support the positive connections among democracy, uneven zones of tempo, and the rift in time without legitimating a pace of life so fast that the promise of democracy becomes translated into fascist becoming machines."[23] Connolly does not finally reject linear time and its normative punctuality. He puts them in their place, demotes them from the sole regnant form of time and thrusts them into a plural and pluralizing play of temporalities. Linear, punctual time (and its normativity of progress or regress) is one temporal register on which we live but from which we are also sometimes driven by events (and must allow ourselves to be driven).

With heightened speed and plural tempos come new dangers but also new possibilities. We lose the guarantees of a single time sequence in which what comes later is unambiguously better or worse than what came before, but on the other hand we don't have to work so hard to maintain those guarantees either. And on the positive side, Connolly writes, fast pace and plural tempos unsettle hierarchy, one of democracy's oldest bêtes noires. He does not worry enough, perhaps, about how a fast pace also consolidates new hierarchies (notwithstanding his stated concern about democracy sliding into fascist becoming machines). Where speed, in Tocqueville's time, favored democratic upheavals, in our time speed seems to favor instead a force not obviously democratic: that of hardly visible capital over workers hopelessly rooted in increasingly rootless economies.

On the positive side, accelerated tempos called attention to by Connolly close down distances and permit new coalitions and partnerships to develop transnationally. These are opportunities, not guarantees: "[M]y wager is that it is more possible to negotiate a democratic ethos congruent with the accelerated tempo of modern life than it is either to slow the world down or insulate the majority of people from the effects of speed."[24] For the wager to work, we democratic theorists and actors have to attenuate our allegiances to the chrono-logic of rights. We have to open democratic theory and practice to the vicissitudes of plural timelines and emergent life forms. Without preparatory work, the pluralization of time will open huge distances between those who affirm the multiplicity and those who respond to it by uncritically embracing familiar certainties (capitalism, traditional gender roles, nationalism, racial hierarchies, natural rights, or conventional theologies) that may no longer "work" the way they once did.

Another example to which Connolly repeatedly returns is that of the still-emerging right to doctor-assisted suicide. As he puts it in *Pluralism*,

> Forty years ago that claim was not even simmering as a minority report among moralists who defined themselves to be defenders of the definitive list of human rights. The new demand is not *derived* from a thick set of principles containing it implicitly all along. [This, I would add, is how it is made to look from liberal and deliberative democratic perspectives.] If it eventually acquires a sedimented place in the order of things, it will be *pressed* and *negotiated* into being by an assemblage consisting of insurgents who demand it, respondents who combine attention to new medical technologies and sensitivity to human suffering, and the fatigue [and, I would add in more agonistic spirit, *as well as the active discrediting*] of erstwhile opponents.[25]

In relation to this emergent right, many feel that sense of emergency I noted above. Regarding this particular emergent right, that sense of emergency may be overdetermined by the question of the value of life that lurks beneath all this and that points to the issue much studied by Giorgio Agamben: that of biopolitics and what he calls the "biopolitical structure of modernity." Agamben notes that "the fundamental biopolitical structure of modernity—the decision on the value (or nonvalue) of life as such . . . finds its first juridical articulation in a well-intentioned pamphlet in favor of euthanasia" published in Germany in the 1920s. Agamben himself takes no position on euthanasia—"It is not our intention here to take a position on the difficult ethical problem of euthanasia."[26] But he has nothing good to say about it. He links it to the forms of sovereignty that he criticizes and to which he offers no particular alternative. Would he treat doctor-assisted suicide differently? It is admittedly somewhat different from euthanasia per se: Although we do speak of a right to doctor-assisted suicide, it would be odd to speak of a right to euthanasia. In any case, for Agamben, rights, whatever they lay claim to, do not stand outside nor do they provide much critical leverage on the machinery of biopolitics.

For me, the idea of a right to doctor-assisted suicide induces a sense of panic. The right is not settled. There is no reliable apparatus for its adjudication. And the country in which I live while contemplating it offers such haphazard medical care to so many that the idea of a right to suicide seems ridiculously inapt. In the United States, as the case of Terry Schiavo made clear in 2005, huge medical and political resources could be marshaled on behalf of sustaining the merest of mere life when the political will to do so exists. At the same time, innumerable lives are treated daily as unworthy of being lived, their bearers incapable of commanding the resources of medical care and compassion they require.[27] In this ambiguous context, the possibility of a right to doctor-assisted suicide is unsettling.[28] The possibility of this right's entrenchment is frightening. As with many emergent claims, a line is being crossed. Places supposedly committed to the preservation of life, hospitals, may become arbiters and administrators of death—more like hospices, or worse yet, death houses.

Of course that line is already thoroughly attenuated, as Agamben himself points out but, as things stand or have stood until now, we do not have to acknowledge its attenuation so forcefully and consciously. Until now we could feign ignorance of the myriad, complex negotiations and relocations of life-death boundaries that occur in hospitals daily. A right to physician-assisted suicide might change that. It might change our sense of the meaning and function of medical care, of aging, of disease, of time. It might even change our understandings of life and death themselves and how we relate to them. The possible change may turn out to be for the good, it may be progress, but confronted with the possibility of such an altered world, how can we tell? Is it biopolitics turned thanatopolitics, as Agamben claims—part of a new and destructive form of sovereignty, dispersed and dangerous? Or is it a restoration to, or taking by, individuals of a decision that ought never to have been usurped by the state in its guise as religious ethical watchdog? Or is it a sovereign nonsovereignty, a moment at which individuals give up sovereignty-serving practices that seek to control or prolong life and yield instead to their own sense that their time has come?

When I note the changes that might occur in the wake of this new right's entrenchment, I emphasize the word *might* because how things unfold depends very much on how a new right is received, defended, and practiced even after its entrenchment, politically engaged and contested after that. In short, the right opens some possible doors but all by itself (if we can say that) it means very little. The *practice* of the right, as Richard Flathman might say, means everything.[29]

To those who have been in a position where it was needed, beside a loved one suffering without hope of improvement, the right to physician-assisted suicide may seem especially appealing. Personal acquaintance with such suffering may move us past our hesitations. But it may not. It depends upon how attached we are to the boundaries by which we separate life and death, daily. It depends upon our sense of how our relation to life, as a species, as a culture, may be altered by endorsing this new right to death at one's chosen time. It depends upon whether we think of death as something that we might negotiate or as something otherworldly to which we must yield. It depends upon how we think about doctors and other professionals and what we make of the rather thin resources for accountability that now exist in modern American society. It depends on whether we think suffering is redemptive or meaningless, on an individual's own pain threshold (mine is low), and on how we assess the social situatedness of the pain: Could it be alleviated by access to better medical resources, community supports, ontologies of health and illness different from those that are current? It may also depend on whether we think, with Agamben, that our current commitments to preserving life are part of a sovereignty-enhancing biopolitics of bare life that is hegemonic and ultimately quite dangerous.[30] It depends on all these things and more, because, as Connolly points out, rights are not just new options to be exercised, like having more money in one's wallet. Each new right inaugurates a new world. It transforms the entire economy of rights and identities, and establishes new relations and new realities, new promises and potentially new cruelties. Cora Diamond knows this. It is the central point of her critique of animal rights theorists for their misguided assumption that once animals are included in the universe of rights-bearing creatures, human rights will go on as they were.[31]

Where liberals, deliberative democrats, and universalists invite us to assess new rights-claims as judges would—in terms of their analogical fit to previous ones, of the appositeness of the claim to legitimate subsumption under prior higher law (whether constitutional or universal) in a gradually unfolding linear time, in terms of whether the new rights were in nascent form always already somehow part of a rights machine—Connolly urges us to assess emergent claims as democratic theorists and activists should: by imagining and assessing a world, the world that might be opened by this new right, and the plural timelines, circles, and forks that might be ushered in with it. Here, once again, rights and goods meet.

These reflections on a possible new right to physician-assisted suicide reflect the deep sense of disturbance created in me by my contemplation of it. I am glad I am not in charge of this decision, though in my gut I tend to side with proponents of this new right because I believe that its *un*-availability represents greater and unwarranted (and perhaps even, contra Agamben, biopolitical) exercise of state and professional power than is implied by its availability to us. But something else also surfaces: a sense that the chrono-logic of rights may offer fewer resources than Connolly's politics of becoming for *resisting* the entrenchment of new rights like this one. For the chrono-logic of rights puts us into its temporality: "We are rationalizing and extending the system of rights," its proponents say. "This right is like the others that came before it. If you supported equal suffrage for women and blacks, how can you get off the bus here? This is the next stage of the same project." (The same argument can be used for *ex*clusion: "When we fought for civil rights, we did not have suicide in mind.")

In the chrono-logic of rights, the honest contemplation of the unsettling ramifications of a new right forces one into conservatism ("no, we had better not support that one; it is not like the others we fought for") or submission (to the march of progress or the chrono-logic force of rights: "I don't feel good about the likely ramifications of this new right, but I have to support it because not to do so is to cast in doubt the legitimacy of all the rights we supported until now"). In Connolly's politics of becoming, however, and this is one of the things about it that most appeals, neither conservatism nor submission is sought. Instead a certain reluctance and panic are expected, even hoped for. Reluctance and panic are markers of a disquieting awareness that we are in this moment partitioning a new time, creating a new world. New and unexpected things are occurring. Some may turn out to fulfill what we think of as the promise of rights; others may betray that promise in ways we will regret and want to resist. Still others may take us in unanticipated new directions that may yet win from us approval and support. In such contexts reluctance and panic in the face of emergent rights may bespeak a lack of moral bearings. But they may also signal our awareness that we have received an invitation to reenter the paradox of politics and open ourselves to the work on the self and community that a politics of becoming periodically demands.[32]

The Chrono-logic of Rights

The chrono-logic of rights treats constitutional or cosmopolitan rights like Wittgenstein's "machine-as-symbol" in which "the action of the machine seems to be there in it from the start." But the machine-as-symbol misleads us, Wittgenstein explains in *Philosophical Investigations*, insofar as it suggests that

[i]f we know the machine, everything else, that is its movement, seems to be already completely determined. We talk as if these parts could only move in this way, as if they could not do anything else. How is this—do we forget the possibility of their bending, breaking off, melting, and so on?[33] Yes; in many cases we don't think of that at all. . . . we are inclined to compare the future movements of the machine in their definiteness to objects which are already lying in a drawer and which we then take out [somewhat like "tapping" a system of rights?].—But we do not say this kind of thing when we are concerned with predicting the actual behavior of a machine [or of rights]. Then we do not forget the possibility of a distortion of the parts and so on. . . . But when we reflect that the machine could also have moved differently it may look as if the way it moves must be contained in the machine-as-symbol far more determinately than in the actual machine. As if it were not enough for the movements in question to be empirically determined in advance, but they had to be really— in a mysterious sense—already *present*. . . . *When does one have the thought: the possible movements of a machine are already there in some mysterious way?—Well, when one is doing philosophy.*[34]

Philosophy positions us in a relation of knowledge to the machine, and this misleads us. Recall that philosophy, on Wittgenstein's account, makes us like "savages, primitive people, who hear the expressions of civilized men, put a false interpretation on them, and then draw the queerest conclusions from it."[35] The machine-as-symbol bewitches us in ways that the actual machine with its plural actions does not. We look at the machine's actual operations when we move from *knowing* the machine to *predicting* its movements. Seeking to predict rather than know, we observe the machine's behavior. "'But,'" objects Wittgenstein's erstwhile interlocutor, uncannily channeling Habermas and Benhabib, "'I don't mean that what I do now (in grasping a sense [of the machine-as-symbol]) determines the future use *causally* and as a matter of experience, but that in a *queer* way, the use itself is in some sense present'" (i.e., we can tap it). Wittgenstein responds in his inimitable and commonsensical fashion: "But of course it is, 'in *some* sense!'"[36]

Following Wittgenstein, we might distinguish between the right-as-symbol and the actual behavior of a right. The right-as-symbol is the right as it is seen by those who privilege as its meaning its capacity to be extended and tapped in certain ways that fulfill what they see as its true function or promise, regardless of its operations. The right-as-symbol governs the imagination of David de Grazia when he says of animal rights, "This last frontier of bigotry will be hard to cross."[37] For de Grazia, the innovation or extension will not alter the fundamental functioning of the rights-machine. The behavior of a right, however, may go in many different ways and along many different temporalities. These differences

may be labeled malfunctions or perversions only from the perspective of
the right-as-symbol.[38] Indeed, this is where I part ways with Wittgenstein
because he here shows that he *himself* is drawn in by the machine as symbol's perspective when he depicts departures from the machine as symbol
as "*breaking*," "*bending*," "*distortion*." These are pejorative terms, like
the *infelicities* that J. L. Austin attributes to speech acts but that Jacques
Derrida insists are part of the productive working of performatives.[39]
Similarly here, the departure of actual rights from the blueprint of
the right as symbol need not mean that something is broken or distorted.
It may signal the *more life* of iteration, the birth of something new, and
is in any case not something to be cast into an "external ditch of perdi-
tion" because those iterations are in fact, as Derrida points out, positive
conditions of possibility.[40] More pointedly, from the plural perspectives
generated and testified to by the myriad operations of the actual right, we
can see how the more essentialist notion of the right-as-symbol harbors
residues of transcendentalist thinking, something its proponents would
deny.[41]

With Wittgenstein's help we see that a new right can generate events
unpredicted and unpredictable from within the normative framework
that supposedly acted as the guarantor for the right in the first instance
(the guarantor in terms of both securing the right's merits analogically
and guaranteeing that the effects of entrenching the right would not spin
out of control in ways that might upset old gains along with the guaranteeing system that harbored them). These new events can occur in all
their overliving novelty because the right-as-symbol is an ideological
commitment (or a philosophical one, as Wittgenstein points out), not an
accurate representation of a machine's (or a right's) behavior. Away from
the bewitchment of philosophy, the play of rights as undecidable contenders among other forces in plural time is more discernible, and for the
politics of becoming herein lies the promise of rights for the mere and
more life of democracy.

Plural timelines, circles, and forks make it difficult to identify any single event or norm as the *origin* of a practice. As I argued in the last chapter with regard to Habermas and Benhabib, those who stipulate such origins, calling something out of the melee of time to stand as a beginning,
often find themselves facing paradoxes that are generated by that very insistence. The paradox of politics puts pressure on those who want to assess new claims in terms of their fit in relation to that now unidentifiable
origin, the right-as-symbol: Does the emergent right fit under the um-
brella of existing understandings of rights, or is it amenable to being
understood analogically as an extension or fulfillment of earlier rights
declarations? Democratic theorists do best to follow the (il)logic of the
paradox of politics and seek out the promise that inheres in its impossible

circularity when responded to not with ressentiment but with something like Connolly's politics of becoming.

One Step Forward, Two Steps Back? Slow Food's Fork in Time

Hannah Arendt closes *Willing*, volume 2 of *Life of the Mind*, expressing the "frustrating" futility of turning to the will to seek freedom. She finds more promise in Augustine, who argued that time and man "were created together." For Arendt, this means that the purpose of man's creation was to make possible a beginning. Time and man are co-original, but not in Habermas's sense of co-originality. On Arendt's account, the two are agonistically related, they struggle, and man as natal interrupts the would-be time sequence (much as the miracle of life ruptured the miasma of causality, as she says in *The Promise of Politics*). But, she says, Augustine is "opaque" on the details. He "seems to tell us no more than that we are doomed to be free by virtue of being born, no matter whether we like freedom or abhor its arbitrariness, are 'pleased' with it or prefer to escape its awesome responsibility" (through fatalism, for example). So Arendt goes Augustine one better. Although her readers have rightly noted repeatedly that she ends *Willing* with a declaration of the need to turn to "another mental faculty" instead, that of judgment, *Willing* really ends with a more direct counter to Augustine. What Arendt says she hopes to find in judgment is the very thing that Augustine could not muster for freedom: "our pleasures and displeasures."[42] Pleasure and displeasure (not hope per se, nor judgment) are for Arendt the best counter to what she sees as Augustinian doom.[43]

I conclude with a brief discussion of an emergent movement, one of whose most attractive features is its unabashed pursuit of pleasure, a movement that illustrates some of the best aspects of a politics of becoming while also providing an opportunity to assess the stakes of interpreting new movements as expressions of the right-as-symbol or as permutations of actual rights that run along plural axes of time—or both. If Wittgenstein is interested in the errors we make in philosophy of language as a result of taking too seriously our notion of the machine-as-symbol, I am interested in the political errors that follow from taking too seriously the notion of right-as-symbol, especially as sole and regnant perspective. The rights discussed here are the focus because at this particular moment they put the most pressure on that perspective and its exclusivity.

Slow Food, whose icon is a snail, began as a protest against the first McDonald's in Italy in 1986. Slow Food called people to resist the bland homogeneity of fast food on behalf of diversity in taste—local flavors, crops, and species. Intending to defend the masses from the hegemony of fast food by making the diversity and nuance of haute cuisine accessible to them, the leaders of Slow Food soon realized that this one sybaritic and possibly elitist goal implied others that were less so. Having begun with a declaration of a right—the movement called for "the protection of the right to taste"—Slow Food soon understood correctly that the right to taste implied a form of life in which animals are raised slowly, locally rather than industrially, and meals are prepared and eaten slowly, perhaps even punctuated by conversation. "At the table," Alice Waters notes, "we learn moderation, conversation, tolerance, generosity, conviviality: these are civic virtues."[44] The tables at which I have eaten have been somewhat more agonistic, perhaps, often featuring immoderation, interruption, and the fraught unresolved tensions of everyday life, work, and family, but Waters is nonetheless right—the table, in particular the slow food table, is one site at which the virtues she names (but not only those) are learned and practiced. A commitment to slow food means living at least some of one's life at a pace slower than is presupposed by fast food chains, with other members of the food community (no solitary eating of anonymous mass food in the car), and in closer coordination with the slow, nonindustrialized tempo of regional and local food production. A commitment to slow food means intervening in the infrastructure and the ethics and politics of consumption.

An international movement, Slow Food is made up of convivia, grassroots offices responsible for putting on events and educational programs for people in their regions. They understand the paradox of politics—that the people for whom they work and to whom they want to appeal may not yet (or ever) exist. Their Taste Education Project offers events and classes to reeducate palates and sensitize people anew to diverse, complex, and subtle flavors to which they have been made indifferent by postwar mass food production. Slow Food's "Ark Project" parodies Darwin, seeking to intervene in and reverse rather than merely catalogue evolutionary trends, by supporting with prize money those who preserve vanishing fruits, vegetables, and animal species, most of which are too delicate, quirky, or unpredictable for commercial growers. Slow Food draws attention to fruits and vegetables at risk, like the Gravenstein apple, ramps, and the Southern field pea. (The Gravenstein, an early-ripening apple, is unpopular with commercial growers because it bruises easily and is difficult to ship.) And through its Ark of Taste, Slow Food "aims to rediscover, catalog, describe and publicize forgotten flavors . . . that are threatened by industrial standardization, hygiene laws, the regulations of large-scale distribution and environmental damage."[45] Slow Food's founder, Carlo Petrini, likes to note, "A hundred years ago, people ate between one hundred and a hundred and twenty different species of food. Now our diet is made up of at most ten or twelve species."[46]

> In Europe, half the breeds of domestic livestock became extinct during the course of the Twentieth Century. One species of plant disappears every six hours. In the seven years between editions of Slow Food's anthology of Italian cheeses—*Fromaggi d'Italia*—a hundred cheese varieties became unavailable on the market. Less than 30 varieties of plant feed 95% of the world's population.[47]

Although preservation, authenticity, and tradition are valued highly by Slow Food, this is not a nostalgic movement. On the contrary, the movement represents nothing other than a fork in time: It refuses to move forward on the temporality of supposedly inexorable agribusiness, but it also refuses to move backward:

> [T]he secret to Slow Food's appeal is not that it offers a nostalgic backward glance at a world of vanishing pleasures. Globalization, in Slow Food's view, has the potential to help as well as harm the small food producer. On the one hand, globalization has the homogenizing effect of allowing multinational corporations to extend their reach to virtually every corner of the world. But at the same time, by making it easier for members of small minorities (beekeepers or Gaelic speakers) to communicate at a distance, it creates openings for niche cultures to thrive."[48]

That is to say, "commercial viability," to which Slow Food is very much attuned, is expanded along with the communications reach of the local producer. This international network, which Slow Food is helping to build, is named by Petrini "virtuous globalization." Slow Food's straddle of slow and fast temporalities becomes more evident when compared to another, also attractive new movement, the "localvores," whose chapters challenge members to eat for a month at a time only food grown within one hundred miles' distance. To mark their difference from a merely nostalgic position, localvores adopt the slogan "Eat Locally, Spice Globally."[49] Nonetheless, with their emphasis on localism, they are some distance from Slow Food's virtuous globalization.

Gastronomic pleasure entails education, biodiversification, localism, and transnationalism. It also entails political action. Beyond funding and supporting farmers, environmentalists, scientists, and others who advance the goals of the movement, and beyond creating local networks across the world (though still mostly in Europe), Slow Food has also lobbied the EU to prevent such measures as the imposition of standardized food safety requirements (developed by NASA and Kraft Foods) that would put small food producers out of business. Recently Slow Food has also turned its attention to another effect of postwar food production—obesity, which it calls *globesity*—to call attention to the connection between the expansion and export of fast food and growing rates of obesity worldwide.

The Second World War is the emergency that lurks in the background of all that Slow Food opposes. That war provided the opportunity for new, mass-oriented industrialization, and its devastation also created the hunger, especially in Europe, that made possible and even welcome the postwar degradation of taste by cheap, industrial food. When starvation or hunger seem the only alternatives, the focus will be (to recur to the distinction made in this book's Introduction) on mere life not more life. In the context of survival as mere life, the right to taste does not stand out as a pressing concern; it seems like a luxury. The genius of Slow Food has been its capacity (admittedly against a background of plenty in Europe by contrast with that continent's immediate postwar condition) to rescript that supposed luxury as a necessity for human health and well-being, and to orient our gaze toward a different emergency: the contemporary infrastructure of consumption. In so doing, Slow Food remobilizes the doubleness of survivance—as both mere and more life. And Slow Food highlights a new emergency, one caused rather than solved by the mere life aims of standardization and mass production. This is the setting for the emergence of a new right—the right to taste—and although it is a human right, it implies, unlike many other human rights, which tend to remainder rather than imply, a set of animal rights as well: the right to be preserved from careless extinction, to be treated well and in accordance with natural health requirements.[50]

To some, Slow Food seems elitist, a pseudopolitics designed to make elites feel good about their self-indulgence. In fact, one critic suggested, poor people need fast food, both as a source of employment and as a source of cheap food. Many democratic theorists are also uncomfortable with the notion of taste and pleasure as resources of progressive politics. Here is Alice Waters's response:

> We get hammered with the message that everything in our lives should be fast, cheap and easy—especially food. So conditioned are we to believe that food should be almost free that even the rich, who pay a tinier fraction of their income for food than has ever been paid before in human history, grumble at the price of an organic peach—a peach grown for flavour and picked, perfectly ripe, by a local farmer who is taking care of the land and paying his workers a fair wage! [Maybe: Another article in the food issue of *The Nation*, "Hard Labor," questions the identification of organic farming with job fairness, though that article does look at large corporations, not at the small farmers whom Waters has in mind here.] And yet, as the writer and farmer David Mas

Masumoto recently pointed out, pound for pound, peaches that good still cost less than Twinkies. When we claim that eating well is an elitist preoccupation, we create a smokescreen that obscures the fundamental role our food decisions have in shaping the world. Organic foods seem elitist only because industrial food is artificially cheap, with its real costs being charged through the public purse [through subsidies], the public health, and the environment [i.e., shipping, and its environmental impact]."[51]

Slow Food also understands well the ruses of procedure and standardization. For example, it exposes how neutrally imposed new health standards in food production have asymmetrical effects, exacting unaffordable costs from small local food purveyors and giving market advantages to large industrial food manufacturers.[52] It notes that local food purveyors have not been found responsible for outbreaks of illness, and that one of the largest food health scares in recent years, over mad cow disease, came not from the unmonitored local food producer but rather as a direct offshoot of industrialized agriculture, which specifically spearheaded the feeding of processed meat to cattle. That practice, in turn, was the result of a combination of pressures and incentives, ranging from the introduction to Europe of supermarkets over the last fifty years (replacing European capitalism's own "commercial ethic that still sought trust in the longevity of contacts and the solidarity of face to face contacts") to the relentless pressure for cheap food and the quest for ever greater economies of scale.[53] In response, Slow Food champions what Petrini calls "the good, the clean and the just." The good "means paying attention to the taste and smell of food, because pleasure and happiness in food are a universal right." The clean means making food "sustainably, so that it does not consume more resources than it produces." And the just means making food so that it "creates no inequities and respects every person involved in its production."[54] Thus when Slow Food supports coffee growers in Guatemala, training them to heighten and control the quality of their product while helping to bring the product to the global market (the "good and the clean"), the organization writes into the contract that children may not pick coffee during school hours, and that women must go to the doctor at least once a year (part of the "just"). Unschooled children and poor health care violate the quality control, broadly understood, of the local coffee-growing community.[55]

How shall we interpret the Slow Food movement? We might embed it into some nonparadoxical precedent as the American founders, on Hannah Arendt's account, sought to do when they set about researching prior constitutions rather than embracing the radical novelty of their own event.[56] Would Slow Food acquire greater legitimation if it were cast as the heir of prior declarations of human rights and as an anticipatory fulfillment of later ones? Or might it be better for democratic actors to note the boundary-breaking qualities of a new movement? It is not easy to position this new movement under existing liberal or cosmopolitan rights because those rights presuppose the very standardizations to which Slow Foods is as a matter of principle and practice opposed. Nor is it easy to subsume Slow Food's activities under a schedule of formal constitutional or universal human rights because it would be difficult to say, as with Wittgenstein's machine-as symbol, that the action—the right to taste—was "there in it from the start." From a human rights perspective, a right to taste seems laughable. It makes a mockery of serious rights won heretofore and now entrenched as universal human rights. But is a pleasure-based radical critique of the infrastructure of consumption really so far-fetched? *The new is always laughable*, a point worth recalling when called to the "serious" work of real politics.[57] This is one effect of the operation in practice of the right-as-symbol: its marginalization of anything that does not analogically fit its expectations or rubric, its sense that anything not already in the drawer violates the spirit of the machine.

In an article on precommitment and the paradox of democracy, Stephen Holmes illustrates my point about the connection between innovation and laughter:

> Present decisions set in motion irreversible processes which, in turn, necessarily box in future generations. This is true whether we embody our decisions in "irrevocable" charters or not. We must adjust to this fact about historical continuity even if it violates Paine's and Jefferson's curious belief that each generation has an inviolable right to start from scratch, ex nihilo, with no inheritances from the past.

Then, playing Burke to their Paine, Holmes says, "In retrospect, nothing could appear more laughable than the French Revolutionary attempt to restart the calendar at year I."[58] Laughable, yes, but this is what new claims and new orders do: elicit laughter, especially at the moment of their still contested emergence or, as with the revolutionary calendar, after they have failed (hence Holmes's honest "in retrospect"). What Holmes does not note is that this incident is an apt metaphor for revolutionary politics generally, since what revolutionary politics aims to do is restart time. Without defending this particular effort to restart time, I note that the distinction between the serious and the nonserious and the connection between the new and the laughable do a lot of unacknowledged theoretical work here. It is worth noting that other restartings of time—such as that by way of which the eras of B.C. and A.D. were distinguished—do not provoke Holmes. They are, presumably less laughable. Is their seriousness secured, boxed in, by their success?

The kind of critique carried out by the Slow Food movement does not depend on the resources of universal human rights. Those rights do *enable* those who want to make such efforts by providing juridical guarantees of free speech that can make a difference to free thought and critique; and for that and much else human rights are to be valued, defended, and expanded. But they are neither a substitute for, nor do they in and of themselves guarantee, the sort of scorching insights into the effects of industrialization and globalization that Slow Food names (along with many other critics and organizations). Nor do universal human rights secure movement along the trajectory that Slow Food maps and names "virtuous globalization."

And human rights do have remainders. In our rights-centered world, the capacity to make a claim has become an overly prized signifier of value and has helped to secure the very distinction between human and animal that Slow Food tries to attenuate by decentering Kant's species progress and stressing lines of dependence and connection across species. Others have written about the costs of universal human rights to local cultural and symbolic (rather than bio-) diversity. Another remainder of human rights is surely animal rights or welfare. Pressing the cause of animal rights seems out of step with the times, especially when human misery is so abundant. But in the spirit of Connolly's plural tempos (which make it harder to be "out of step with the times"), and in the spirit of Slow Food's commitment to its own fork in time, and in the spirit of Arendt's intuition that the intimate if agonistic connection noted by Augustine between man and time requires the suturing powers of pleasure, it may be time to step out of one time and broach another, in which we attend to the pleasures forgone in the name of mass food production, and ruminate on the massive cruelties daily committed by humans upon animal species' in the name of human well-being.[59] Such a move would be supported by a wager: The human cannot but fare better in a world in which animals are seen as having a claim upon humans who therewith treat them with dignity and respect. It would also be supported by an image—of Moses Mendelssohn surrounded by his twenty porcelain apes, sent hurtling backward in evolutionary time by a bigoted enlightened ruler and an opportunistic factory manager. Mendelssohn somehow rescripted his interpellation into the nonhuman world and accepted the invitation unwittingly issued to him, as it is to all of us—to ape full citizenship: to claim its rights and take its goods from outside the permitted boundaries of its exercise.

When we so act, we partition new worlds and something in the current chrono-logic rights machine may break or bend or malfunction. Or the machine may simply operate in a new, unanticipated way. It has happened before. But how do we tell the story, once it has occurred? Do we fold it into a narrative of law's progress and tell it as a tale of legal triumphalism? Or do we tell it as the outcome of a politics of pleasure that somehow, in the process of becoming, reoriented the rights machine in unanticipated ways and, laughingly, inaugurated a new time?[60] As we shall see in the next two chapters, both focused centrally on the politics of emergency, the law capaciously folds such innovations into its narratives and turns them to law's advantage. Analyzing how this happens is of central importance to thinking democratically about the politics of the exception and the state of emergency. As is so often the case in democratic politics, how we tell the story matters a great deal. It also matters what stories we tell.

Chapter Three

Decision

THE PARADOXICAL DEPENDENCE OF THE RULE OF LAW

> This was our paradox: no course of action could be determined
> by a rule, because every course of action can be made out to
> accord with the rule. The answer was: if *any* action can be made
> out to accord with the rule, then it can also be made out to
> conflict with it. And so there would be neither accord nor conflict
> here. . . . What this shews is that there is a way of grasping a rule
> which is *not* an *interpretation*, but which is exhibited in what we
> call "obeying the rule" and "going against it" in actual cases. . . .
> [W]e ought to restrict the term "interpretation" to the substitu-
> tion of one expression of the rule for another.
> —*Ludwig Wittgenstein*

THE SUBJECT OF THIS CHAPTER, U.S. Assistant Secretary of Labor Louis
Post, was trying to inaugurate a new time when he was caught up short
by the emergency politics of the First Red Scare. In this chapter, I look at
what Post did and at how his story has been recounted by legal historians. Post, in my view, had the ambitious aim of recasting the role and
function of executive power itself. He lost. Part of this loss is apparent in
the one thing he is most famous for: He is now said to have anticipated
the law when he exercised his administrative discretion to grant to aliens
rights they did not have under the law in 1919. That "anticipation" of
the law is what, for most legal historians, marks him as a hero. He was,
as we say, ahead of his time. When we say that, however, we position "the
past [so that it dons] the traits of the present. Only in this way," explains
Franz Rosenzweig, "does it become quite inoffensive to the present."[1]
In my view, this is what the legal historians' figure, "anticipation," does:
it renders Post himself "inoffensive." "Anticipation" captures potentially
inaugural and radical innovations that might have opened up a new time
and sets them to work on behalf of dominant forms of law and politics.
One way of summarizing the aim of this chapter then is to say that it
seeks to recapture the dangerous Post, the one whom J. Edgar Hoover
and others thought was worth hounding out of American politics.

The figure, "anticipation," is at work in the 2000 film *Civil Wrongs
and Rights*, which depicts the decades'-long legal battle to vindicate Fred

Korematsu after he lost his World War II Court challenge to the U.S internment of Japanese-Americans. One scene in the film is particularly
striking. Hearing of the court's finding in their favor, Korematsu's lawyers, who had been shown working many hours with no financial reward
and at great personal cost, joyously declared the law had won. Had the
law won? Or had it been pressed into service by creative, devoted individuals joined to a common cause? What impact might the belief in law's
independent, progressive trajectory have on democratic political action?
If the victory was the law's, the implication is Korematsu would have
been vindicated anyway. Democratic actors are often inspired by claims
of an independent trajectory of progress and the idea of service to a higher
cause ("I have been to the mountaintop!"); but a faith in law's independent progress might be costly as well. One of the costs, explored in this
chapter and the next, might be an overly limited repertoire with which
to respond to sovereign re-forming invocations of emergency. The law-
centered or rights-centered resistance to emergency politics, now dominant in the United States and elsewhere, is important. But it is also insufficient because, as I argue here and in the next chapter, it is in deep ways
partnered with its antagonist, the mechanisms of state sovereignty, and
together these limit opportunities for the more democratic energies that
survival—as mere and more life—requires.

The question Arendt posed facetiously with reference to women's rights
and femininst politics—"What will we lose if we win?"—may be apt
here.[2] Human rights lawyers win victories too valuable to dismiss on behalf of clients caught in the security net of the American war on terror.
But these very victories, won against executive power, reaffirm the central
identification of the executive branch with sovereign political power even
while they also attenuate some of its strength. That view of sovereignty
tends to immobilize popular political action, accents a sense of dependency by ordinary people on the prowess of professionals, and hides from
view the many capillaries of sovereign power that run through the regime
and on which executive branch power is deeply dependent. Also hidden:
the paradoxical dependence of the rule of law on the rule of man, the
law's dependence on administrative and judicial discretion as well as on
forms of popular political action that engage in agonistic struggle with
legal structures and institutions.

Against the Exceptionalism of the State of Exception

The tendency to treat emergency politics as exceptional or as sui generis
is encouraged by Carl Schmitt's term for the phenomenon: the state of
exception. This is a condition in which ordinary law is legally suspended

and sovereign power operates unfettered, by way of decision. Schmitt's apparent defense and even celebration of decisionism combined with his own Nazi party involvement have led many to criticize him for promoting a dangerously immoral and warlike conception of politics.[3]

But to say that the state of exception privileges decision need not mean that all powers redound to a single unaccountable sovereign dictator, though that is the term Carl Schmitt himself used, and that was his apparent meaning. Nor, contra Schmitt, need it necessarily mean that sovereignty is unified in and by way of the singular decision. In the context of American liberal democracy, decisionism has a place but it is somewhat differently described: In the United States, emergency politics occasions the creation of new administrative powers and the redistribution of existing powers of governance from proceduralized processes to discretionary decision, from the more proceduralized domains of courts and legislatures to the more discretionary domains of administrative agency.[4]

Such agencies are decisionistic by design: Highly discretionary, relatively unaccountable, for the most part ungoverned by the requirements of due process, and even possessed of law-making power of their own, they are referred to by their proponents (like the Progressives) as efficient, flexible agents of good political judgment and by their critics as dictatorial and unaccountable. Where proponents of administrative discretion see administrators as responsible agents entrusted to humanize and particularize the law that might otherwise be a blunt, harsh instrument, its critics see the arbitrary, capricious rule of man taking the place of the rule of law. Simply put, then, within the rule-of-law settings that Schmitt *contrasts* with decisionism, something like the decisionism that Schmitt approvingly identifies with a dictator goes by the name of discretion and is identified (approvingly or disapprovingly) with administrators and with administrative governance.

This way of thinking about decisionism takes emergency politics out of its exceptionalist context and sets it in the context of larger struggles over governance that have marked American liberal democracy for over a century.[5] This account invites us to consider emergency-occasioned "trade-offs" between, for example, security and rights not as sui generis. Debates about them belong to larger debates about the risks and benefits to democracies in emergency as well as nonemergency settings of administrative versus judicial power, rule of man versus rule of law, efficiency versus fairness, speedy versus fully deliberative decision-making, outcome versus process orientations and secrecy versus transparency or publicity.[6] The focus on security versus rights, to which we are driven by the government's use of its powers to imprison, detain, deport, and denaturalize in times of emergency, does not capture all the dimensions of emergency politics. Beneath the security versus rights issue is a more fundamental problem: the (re-)distribution of governing powers and the mechanisms by which such powers are held accountable or not. The liberty versus security debate is, from the perspective of administrative jurisdictional jockeying, a second- or third-order issue: Important, to be sure, but it is the tail, not the dog.

The to and fro between administrative and judicial governance is most visible in exceptional settings that are least domesticated (emergency, national security, immigration politics, border policing, colonial governance).[7] But the to and fro is not itself exceptional. It is part of a larger pattern of daily, ongoing vying for power, a quotidian jurisidictional jockeying among bureaucrats, administrative political appointees, judges, lawyers, civil libertarians, as well as citizens and activists from across the political spectrum.[8]

As part of that pattern, critics of administrative discretion and civil libertarians tend to respond to executive expansions of discretionary power not with counterpolitics, per se, but with claims of rights. They try to re-judicialize the terrain in question in two ways: They turn to courts and contest the relocation of decision-making power from judicial settings to administrative sites.[9] And (or) they press for the expanded judicialization of nonjudicial sites by, for example, claiming that people have procedural rights of due process even in nonjudicial settings.[10] Such causes seem obviously worthy of support. In 2008, civil libertarians won important victories in the Supreme Court on behalf of detainees in Guantanamo. Historically, however, even when courts have maintained jurisdiction, they have tended nonetheless to suspend their jurisdictional autonomy in deference to executive branch claims of emergency, a tendency still metaphorized for most Americans by the name Korematsu. More to the point, proceduralization itself does not set ends or judge them. Alan Dershowitz has called for the proceduralization or judicialization of torture, proposing that government interrogators who use torture be required to seek the issuance of a warrant by a magistrate "authorizing nonlethal torture." When we require government torturers to get judicial approval, we risk domesticating torture, Dershowitz concedes. But, he goes on to argue, since torture will go on anyway, we may as well bring it into law's fold and secure both for ourselves as a society and for those being "interrogated" the protections and benefits of judicial procedure.[11] Proceduralism by itself cannot be made to speak against a proposal to ensure the fair and transparent practice of torture.

Thus, for those who want to put human rights and the dissenting politics they are meant to protect onto more certain ground, participating in the to and fro of judicialized processes versus administrative discretion will not be adequate. It may be necessary, but it will not be sufficient. The two poles operate in an oppositional yet partnered relation, and the terrain they together stake out is too formal to grapple fully with the political issues at stake.

Enacting or exacting accountability is one of the essential responsibilities of democratic citizenship. Citizens, always already interpellated by government powers and perspectives, assert their own vision of governance over that of the institutions that frame their lives. Their counter-interpellation may mirror or support existing institutions with affirmation or may expose patterns of inequity and protest them. Accountability was enacted, and a counterinterpellation issued by Louis Post, assistant secretary of labor under Wilson, when Post was called by Congress to account in public for his use of discretionary power to release hundreds of aliens rounded up for deportation in the Palmer Raids. Post responded by enacting a counteraccountability, calling on Congress to live up to the democratic ideals it had abandoned in the context of the First Red Scare. For Post, survival itself was at issue: The mere life of democracy was not a fair trade for the mere and more life of equality and justice that he valued and on which democracy's mere life was deeply dependent.

Because he fought for procedural rights and due process during the arbitrary round-ups of the Palmer Raids, Post is often lauded as a principled proceduralist who anticipated later Court rulings on the rights of noncitizens. But Post was no mere proceduralist. He began his career in post–Civil War South Carolina, documenting the testimonies of Ku Klux Klan members detained under President Grant's suspension of habeas corpus. About Grant's decision to suspend habeas corpus in order to break the Klan, Post never protested. For Post, a champion of proceduralism in 1919–20, proceduralism was not a good in itself—it was simply one of law's many mechanisms whereby all sorts of political aims could be pursued.

Louis Freeland Post and the First Red Scare

On April 28, 1919, a homemade mail bomb arrived at the office of Ole Hanson, the Seattle mayor who had crushed a strike by shipyard workers just three months earlier. A day later, another bomb arrived at the home of former Senator Thomas Hardwick, exploding and maiming the unfortunate person who opened the package on Hardwick's behalf. Postal authorities located thirty-two other bomb packages before they were delivered. (Sixteen had been held back for insufficient postage, an oversight that also stalled some of 2001's anthrax mailings). These had been sent in a likely bid for May Day delivery to, among others, John D. Rockefeller, Postmaster General Burleson (who had used his powers to censor newspapers and other organs of opinion that were critical of the U.S. war involvement), Judge Kenesaw Mountain Landis, and other enemies of organized labor as well as immigration restrictionists. Some with more liberal leanings were also on the list of addressees: Senator Hardwick, Justice Holmes, Secretary of Labor William B. Wilson, and others.

The April bombings were followed by another round six weeks later in June when a new series of bombs exploded in eight different cities at the same hour. One of these—a suicide bomber, an Italian anarchist from Philadelphia—damaged Attorney General Palmer's house hurting no person but himself. Even with the technologies of communication and transportation of the early twenty-first century, it is a great feat of coordination to get a series of bombs to explode in eight different cities at the same time. How much more impressive is such a feat, and more terrorizing, in a time in which communications and transportation are primitive by comparison with ours? It seems hardly surprising, then, that a sense of vulnerability overtook the nation. As one historian puts it,

> Terrorism had come to America's own doorstep. . . . There had been terrorist attacks in the United States before, but nothing so coordinated and menacing. Most of the previous attacks were isolated bombings, conducted by self-proclaimed anarchists. This was different. During the latter half of 1919, the threat of terrorism sent Americans into a frenzy of fear.[12]

We can understand this, perhaps, by analogy to 9/11. There had been previous terrorist attacks on the United States as well—the attempted World Trade Center bombing in 1993 and the attack on the USS *Cole*. Both of these were troubling and yet neither really "prepared" people for what happened on 9/11.

The villains of the First Red Scare[13] are still relatively well-known but one of the period's heroes is all but forgotten. Louis Freeland Post, assistant secretary of labor, defended the rights of the foreign born against those like Attorney General Palmer and J. Edgar Hoover (a mere twenty-four years old at the time and already head of Palmer's General Intelligence Division, also known as the antiradical division), who sought in wholesale deportations a solution to the anarchist threat and the problem of dissident action in the United States. Mindful of the recent Third International, the aim of Palmer and Hoover was "to destroy the Union of Russian Workers and the new Communist Party."[14] From late 1919 to early 1920, a series of raids known as the Palmer raids swept up five to ten thousand (estimates differ) aliens and lined them up for deportation under the Sedition Act of 1918.[15] Outraged by the Justice Department's actions, Post took action when the opportunity arose.

Until 1920, John W. Abercrombie, solicitor general for the Department of Labor, worked in tandem with Commissioner of Immigration Caminetti, going so far as to issue five thousand blank deportation warrants for use by Palmer's agents. When in March, Abercrombie left the Labor Department to run for the Senate, Post took charge of deportation oversight and stopped the Labor Department's cooperation with Caminetti's Immigration Bureau and Palmer's Justice Department Taking advantage of the language of the Act that created the Department of Labor, Post usurped, in accordance with the law, the de facto power of the Commissioner of Immigration to decide the fates of detained aliens. Post "asserted the right to decide deportation cases without prior briefing [i.e., by Caminetti or his agents] and ordered that all records be sent to Washington for his personal review."[16] This move was continuous with earlier efforts made by Post, ever since he took up his position as assistant secretary of labor in 1913, to consolidate the power of the Labor Department over its bureaus.[17]

Having claimed jurisdiction and the power of decision, Post then began to whittle away at the category of deportability. First, he got Labor Secretary Wilson to rule that membership in the Communist Labor Party was not a deportable offense. A "student of radicalism," Post persuaded Wilson that the Communist Labor party was more moderate than the Communist Party of America. Since only the latter did not disavow the use of violence, it could only be membership in the latter that was, strictly speaking, a deportable offence.[18] This directly contradicted the less nuanced position of J. Edgar Hoover, who insisted that "both organizations have arbitrarily pledged themselves to overthrow the Government of the United States . . . therefore . . . the Communist Labor Party and persons who are members thereof fall within the provision of the Act of Congress approved Oct. 16, 1918."[19]

Second, Post decided, again contra Hoover, Palmer, and Caminetti, that what he coined "automatic membership" was not grounds for deportation. Automatic membership meant that a person was taken to be a member of the Communist party if his name was found on their rolls. But the party padded its rolls, listing inactive or unpaid former members and borrowing names from lists of other related but nonidentical organizations. Post insisted that no one could be deported simply for having his or her name on a list. Some evidence had to be shown that the person in question consented explicitly to membership in the outlawed party.[20] This requirement substantially raised the evidentiary bar.

Third, and most radically, Post applied to administrative cases standards of evidence and due process that normally would have been thought at the time to obtain only in judicial settings, not administrative ones.[21] "Since deportation was not a criminal proceeding, and the prisoners were not citizens, Caminetti, Palmer, and Hoover claimed that the constitutional guarantees of right to counsel, to confront one's accuser, reasonable bail and habeas corpus were not applicable."[22] Post took the opposite view, repeating over and over that aliens facing deportation deserved constitutional protections of habeas corpus no less than citizens, and that protections traditionally thought of as attached to criminal investigations should apply also to administrative processes if not as a matter of law then simply as a matter of fairness. Fairness, after all, is what those protections were designed to capture or secure; or, in more purely procedural terms, those protections are proxies for an otherwise elusive fairness. Deportation—even if it is an administrative matter—must be fairly administered, Post argued, and so it made sense to follow those existing rules and procedures (such as the criminal law's due process) that, in other venues, serve as proxies for fairness.[23]

In short, Post bound himself by law. He subjected himself to the rights/powers of others. Claiming he had no choice because he was bound by rights that he himself attributed to those whom others (including some of the courts) thought rightless, Post used his discretionary power to limit his discretionary powers again and again. For example, he ruled that aliens' self-incriminating statements could not be used against them if those statements had been made without benefit of counsel.[24]

Finally, Post used all his powers of reasoning and all of the law's resources to find in favor of aliens marked for deportation whenever possible. He employed the distinction between political and philosophical anarchism to the benefit of those charged (only the former was actionable under the law). And he second-guessed the self-incriminating statements of detainees. Here is his account of his decision in the case of a self-professed anarchist, a well-known activist from Mexico named Flores-Magon:

When asked about his political beliefs, Flores-Magon said he was a "communist anarchist." But Post did not take him at his word. He read further:

> I considered what his saying he was an anarchist meant. And if I had stopped there I should have been obligated to deport him. . . . I should have done as I did in the case of Emma Goldman, whose case stood wholly on that one word. She said she was an anarchist and I deported her and I should have done the same in his case. But I found on reading further [the record of Flores-Magon's interview] his meaning of the word did not tally with the definitions of anarchism as anyone who has investigated the subject knows; and because it did not tally, I came to the conclusion he was a man in favor of government and not opposed to government and that determined the case. . . . I decided to cancel [the warrant] because he was not an anarchist within the meaning of the law.[25]

It will be apparent from this line of reasoning that almost anyone (with the exception of the unfortunate Emma Goldman) could in such a way be found not to be an anarchist, or at least not to be in violation of the law. Post found in the law and the rule of law's procedural requirements technicalities that undid or counteracted the Sedition Act's intended (at least its deniably intended) and unintended effects.

In this way in three months Post and two assistants, working ten-hour days and deciding as many as one hundred cases per day, managed to free two to three thousand or perhaps even as many as six thousand (estimates differ) detainees. One historian refers to Post's actions as an "insurrection against Palmer." Indeed it was and Palmer knew it.[26] When, by the spring of 1920, Post had canceled the warrants of most of the detainees and released them, Palmer was livid: He charged Post with abusing his discretionary power and "demanded that Post be fired for his 'tender solicitude for social revolution.'"[27]

Post was not fired but he was called before the House Committee on Rules to answer Palmer's charges.[28] Was Post implementing the Sedition Act or was he using his discretionary power to undo it?[29] The public's impression and that of the members of the Committee was that when Post canceled a deportation warrant, he was in effect freeing an "alien after he was found guilty and ordered deported." Indeed, one of his antagonists at the hearing of the House Committee on Rules snipped: "We have given you time to empty the jails as far as you could."[30] Post countered with the legally more precise claim that "Cancelling [sic] a deportation warrant is nothing more than finding a verdict for the defendant." That is, a warrant (which is all Palmer and Hoover could issue) was merely a charge, not a finding. It began a process of investigation, rather than marking the end of one. This clarification turned the tide of public opinion in Post's favor.[31] The Committee was not so quickly won over, though, and moved to take issue with Post's most radical invention: the rules under which Post decided the cases of the charged aliens.

A Democratic Administrative Power?

Post's discretionary decision to apply the more stringent criminal procedure rules to an administrative process was one of the core issues before the Committee on Rules. Post defended himself, deploying ideals of Americanism, constitutionalism, separation of powers, and limited government, appealing to an ideal of self-limiting administrative power that could otherwise be limitless in its reach, arbitrary in its application, despotic in its actions.

> My contention is that when the executive department of the Government is the absolute judge of whether a man shall remain in this country or not, *and the courts will not interfere*, we should see to it that no injustice is done to the

man. . . . And that is the reason—not that I am applying absolutely criminal law to administrative process, although I think the principles of criminal law, the protections of criminal law, ought to be accorded; yet I know that we cannot accord them as criminal law. But I can take from the criminal law its humane, its just, its American, its constitutional principles of protection to the liberty of the citizen and apply it when I am acting for the executive department of the Government. And I doubt if the Senate of the United States will condemn that attitude. . . . I have drawn from the criminal law its principles which recognize the rights of the individual and especially his right to a fair trial, to a fair decision as to whether he is guilty or not, before he is penalized in any way. And to send a man who has been here 10 or 15 or 20 years—to take him away from his family and send him out of the country on an administrative warrant, a mere police warrant, until it gets to the Secretary of Labor, is to penalize him and to penalize him in a very drastic and very un-American way.[32]

Post emphasized the administrative character of the warrant to underline the finality of the judgments involved:

[W]e should be all the more careful in judging these cases because he [the alien who has lived here ten or fifteen years] has no redress in the courts when an administrative judgment is given. And therefore I say that there are principles of the criminal law which ought to be applied by the administrative department of the Government unless there is the strongest reason, in each individual case, for not applying them.[33]

Post's appeal to an ideal of a self-limiting executive power did not move the committee, at least not right away. One questioner, in particular, could not fathom why an executive branch administrator possessed of broad discretionary power would bind himself by judicial rules and procedures that, in the absence of such self-binding, would be inapplicable.

Mr. Garrett. "Congress has passed this act; it has made it administrative; and it has put it in the hands of executive officers to enforce. . . . I would say that it was a fair presumption that Congress intended, in the passage of that act, irrespective of the differences between the rights of aliens and the rights of citizens under the Constitution of the United States, to eliminate the rules that would be applicable in court.

To this Post responded (in what must have been at least partly mock horror): "In other words, the United States Government—because this is the exact point—when a complaint is made against a man under this law and the case comes before the Secretary of Labor, he must deport the man, whether the man is innocent or guilty? You did not mean that?" Garrett demurred, of course, but Post went on: "That is the issue, however. . . . The issue is: Not whether those who violate the law shall be deported, for we are deporting them . . . but whether those who have not violated the law shall be deported."[34] With criminal procedures acting as a proxy for fairness, and with a commitment in place to the imperfect proceduralism presupposed by the rules of criminal justice, there was no extraprocedural place from which to call "guilty" those who were not legally deportable according to the legal and procedural lines drawn and followed by Post.

And then there were the borderline cases. Throughout, Post admitted that although his own decisions were fully within the law, another might have decided the same cases another way, even using the same criteria.[35] He knew and owned up to what Wittgenstein would soon after say about adding by twos: It is almost as if "a new decision was needed at every stage."[36] Wittgenstein's point was that a rule does not provide for its own application nor does any external criterion independent of the rule secure the rule's specific application. Human agency is postulated by the very idea of a rule that both contains the expectation of pattern and upholds the possibility of some deviation from the expectations set in place by prior behaviors.

Post understood the political implications of such a view. Having usurped the power of decision, and having legally defined the boundary of decision as narrowly as possible and embraced the ensuing "constraints," Post took full responsibility for the decision that remained, even owning a certain inclination to favor people facing hardship. For example, in cases where the person in question was, say, the father of dependent children born in the United States, Post said that person should be given "the benefit of the doubt": "I think that some humanity should come into the trial of these cases when there is some doubt as to guilt." This led to another typical exchange:

> The Chairman (interposing). "Yet if there had been enough men of that kind in the country to endanger the country, the fact that they had children born here that they would have to be separated from if they were deported, would not be any mitigation of the offense, would it?" Mr. Post. "Did you understand me to say anything to the contrary?" The Chairman. "No; and yet we should be keen to detect those who are keen to overthrow the Government of the United States."
>
> Mr. Post. "I said I was not keen to do it on flimsy evidence, and where there was any doubt. I never refrained from doing it in any case where the membership in the organization was clear, no matter what the hardship was. I could not sleep at night for thinking of some of the cases where the man had to be sent out. They were good, hard-working and useful men, who would have made good American citizens; but it was proved that they were members of this organization, even though they did not know what its purpose was; even

though they thought they were joining an organization of men from their own country; even though they thought that they were going to school. I have deported such men, because the evidence showed that it was clear that they belonged to the organization."[37]

With such oratory, delivered in a public venue and reported on daily in the nation's newspapers, Post sought to (re)humanize those whom Palmer and Hoover had successfully demonized. But Post knew that humanism, counter-Americanism, and oratory were not enough (either to change the nation's path, or to save himself and the ideals—and calm—he represented). They were necessary but not sufficient to his cause. Their resources were not powerful enough to undo the effects of his opponents' demonological politics, at least not right away. Post was a lawyer, though he had practiced only briefly and thirty years before. He knew the law well and exploited its resources to the best of his abilities, which were considerable. Reviewing thousands of cases in a matter of weeks, he almost always found the detail, technicality, or doubt that might warrant a detainee's release.

Palmer and Hoover cast Post as an arbitrary, untrustworthy administrator whose aim was to undo the law. They claimed, by contrast, to be law's servants, operating in adherence to the requirements of the Sedition Act and the will of the legislators who passed it. Post responded by casting himself as law's strictest adherent and casting his opponents as arbitrarians and securitarians whose own decisionism was poorly cloaked by pseudolegality. The success of his strategy depended largely upon whether Post's use of technicality would persuade or enrage the public and the members of the House Committee on Rules.

Recurring to Wittgenstein's image of the machine as symbol versus the actual behavior of the machine, the question that hovered over Post was whether his actions were contained in the congressional act that Palmer took to authorize the roundups, or amounted, by contrast, to a distortion, a bending or breaking of the legislation. Post responded to the questions in two ways, both of which find some support in Wittgenstein. First, Post in effect split the difference between the two options by resorting to technicality. And second, he solicited through his publicly addressed testimony a public that could rise from the constraints of survival politics as mere life to champion a bivalent democratic commitment to mere and more life.

The Politics of Technicality

Post's use of technicality to limit the range of the Sedition Act is reminiscent of the strategy whereby rabbinical interpreters in effect abolished the death penalty in Judaism. Working with biblical law, divinely authored, the Rabbis could not simply change the law. They had to be more subtle and creative than that. So instead, they *legalized* the death penalty out of existence, creating such demanding procedural requirements that no one could be sentenced to death under the law. Here is a summary of their reasoning:

> They required that the culprit be warned by two witnesses immediately before he committed the unlawful act carrying the death penalty (after all he may not know the act is illegal or punished so severely and how can you hold him liable for death for transgressing a law that he never knew?); that he respond, "Even so, I am going to do it" (because he may not have heard the warning), that he commit the act within three seconds of hearing the warning (for otherwise he might have forgotten the law he had just heard and therefore could not be held responsible); that the witnesses not be related to each other or to the culprit; and that there be at least one judge on the court who votes to acquit him (for otherwise the court might be prejudiced against him. . . .).[38]

These requirements are familiar to any student of the rule of law: publicity, intentionality, evidentiary requirements, impartiality, and so on.[39] But the Rabbis extend them, comically, cartoonishly. Here interpretation, the substitution of one expression for another, upon which the law depends for its animation, preservation, and application, is (also) used to undo the law.

Without interpretation, law which is general and broad can never be applied, implemented, or understood.[40] Without interpretation, law is insensitive to particularity and nuance. Such sensitivity, however, can lead to the creation of technicality, which is a product of working in law's nuances. And technicality seems to violate the basic premises of the rule of law: Technicalities are rarely public because they are usually the products of arcane professional knowledge that makes sense only to lawyers and judges (or rabbis). Technicalities tend to be discovered or invented post hoc, they are not normally broadcast in advance as the rule of law requires.[41] Often they apply only to an individual case, and not to a general class of cases and so they violate the rule of law's generality requirement. In short, technicality, a necessary postulate of the rule of law (an outgrowth of interpretation and implementation), also threatens to corrupt or undo the rule of law.[42]

This doubleness of technicality is explored weekly (actually, now daily, no—hourly) on the U.S. television show *Law and Order*, whose title suggestively both couples and severs the relation between its two terms—law and order. The "and" severs and couples. The title's doubleness is apt because the show's recurring theme is the district attorney's office's efforts to outwit defendants by creatively finding in law hitherto unsuspected traps, resources, and incentives—technicalities—by way of which order (but perhaps not law, at least not in the rule of law's usual sense of the term) can be maintained and the guilty punished. The ample literature on overcharging documents such practices in the real world.[43]

The ambiguous tactics of *Law and Order*'s infinitely creative and sometimes unprincipled (or overly principled) D.A. are presented as heroic, for the most part. In popular discourse, however, the term technicality still has a bad name. It is a term that brings to mind not a mechanism whereby order or justice might be secured but rather a mechanism whereby law's good aims are subverted by sly criminals or their lawyers, as in: "He got off on a technicality." But note how this phrase, now a popular synecdoche for all the ways in which technicality—by implication, a cheap lawyerly trick—betrays the rule of law, actually turns on an assumption that Louis Post did not share and to which the rule of law does not commit us: It assumes or invites us to assume a coincidence between the rule of law's procedural ideals and its substantive rightness. The phrase's force relies on the assumption that the law's proceduralism is perfect, that the rule of law, if only unhampered by crooked devices such as technicality, will imprison only the guilty and free only the innocent. When we say "he got off on a technicality," we imply he is guilty but has been found not to be so under law not because the law errs, but rather because the law erred in this instance only because it was exceptionally corrupted by a lawyerly device.

However, if we step out of the ideological prejudice that leads us to assume a match between procedural and substantive justice (that is, if we insist that in law, procedural fairness is in John Rawls's terms at best imperfect or pure but never perfect),[44] then we should be able to see that technicality, no less than proceduralism itself, is a device available for capture by parties from all sides with a wide variety of agendas, a device whereby all sorts of ends, just or unjust, might be sought, as indeed they are on *Law and Order*. The instrument itself (technicality) does not prejudge or predetermine the worth of the end in question. In Post's hands (and in those of the Rabbis), technicality was used, in my view, to worthy ends. And administrative power, about which the rule of law's advocates tend to be wary, often for good reason, was made to serve laudable political goals. As it happens, those goals in this instance coincided with the larger goals of the rule of law: the protection of vulnerable individuals from arbitrary state power.

Moreover, as it happens, those larger goals could not in this instance have been secured by the rule of law, per se. The humor, cleverness, idealism, humanism, prerogative, and administrative decision that Post (no less than the Rabbis who preceded him and in whose company he in some strange way belongs) brought to the rule of law were its necessary supplements (in the sense of both supporting and undermining it). As aliens subject to administrative power, the detainees lacked the rights Post attributed to them. Post used his administrative powers to grant them rights they did not have juridically. He also advised them to invoke the writ of habeas corpus while in detention, even though he knew no court would likely side with them.[45] He understood the power and powerlessness of law. He knew that law cannot be pressed into new directions unless claims, even—or especially—illicit ones, are made in its name and using its terms. And then Post (before the Committee, in his practice at the Labor Department, in relation to the Justice Department) acted as if these rights, which had no juridical existence apart from his own contestable administrative rulings, bound him. That is, Post acted as if he had not granted those rights, as if they existed ex ante, as if they bound him, and as if he merely deferred to the force of those rights or channeled them, acknowledging their power to limit the range of his discretion—the very discretion whereby he granted or acknowledged the rights in the first place. He worked the paradox of politics, acting as if he was already living in the world he sought with his own action to bring into being. All by itself, the rule of law did not secure nor mandate that outcome. And Post never implied that it did.

Thus, when one of Post's more antagonistic questioners asked (a question that might well have been posed in some form to the rabbinical reformers of Judaism's death penalty):[46] "You realized, of course, Mr. Secretary, that all of these rules that you had laid down—or the imposing of these deportation regulations—that every one of them operates to make it more difficult to deport the alien?" Post not only accepted the implied criticism, he embraced it: "Every rule in the interest of personal liberty makes it more difficult to take personal liberty away from a man who is entitled to his liberty."[47] That entitlement, possessed even by the most vulnerable alien, secured in this instance by one man's discretionary administrative power and further legitimated by way of the device of technicality, was the check used by one executive agency to force itself as well as other loci of executive power to pause and be humbled.

Of course, the fact that the Justice Department had by then failed to "find more than four firearms and a few tons of propaganda pamphlets in the possession of the four thousand supposedly violent revolutionaries they arrested" did not hurt Post's case that aliens were people too and perhaps even good Americans (even if not citizens).[48] The bombings of 1919 had been real and devastating in their coordination; they had induced in most Americans a real and not unwarranted sense of vulnerability. But fears of cabals and networks of anarchists poised at the ready to attack the United States were waning in the face of little evidence to support them and in the face of doubts, prompted and fed by Post and his supporters, regarding the arbitrary administrative powers used by the Justice Department to fight those specters.

*   *   *

It is often said that the First Red Scare ended when the country chose hedonism over politics, shifting its focus from Italian anarchists to American flappers, from homemade bombs to homemade whiskey.[49] But it matters how we tell the story.[50] Often, antipolitical scripts govern our reception of these events. Did Americans abandon Palmer because they preferred to party? Or because they were disgusted by his methods? Or both? Couldn't we just as well say, shouldn't we just as well say, that the Red Scare ended when the country—and even a hostile congressional committee—chose democracy over despotism, and fairness over arbitrariness in the exercise of governmental power? The Committee on Rules found in Post's favor. Soon after, Palmer's political career was destroyed (he had been planning to run for the presidency) when he testified less effectively than Post before the Committee regarding the Justice Departments handling of what Post and many others came to call the "deportations delirium."[51] It was a huge victory for Post. But J. Edgar Hoover survived and went on to thrive.[52]

It is tempting to think the whole history of the American state's development into a national security state over the course of the twentieth century can be summed up by simply doing the math: Post was seventy-one years old at the time of these events; Hoover was twenty-four and lived for a half century after Post, perfecting the policing and surveillance techniques he first developed as head of Attorney General Palmer's antiradical division. Hoover was in this period already keeping files on various liberals, including Post, Brandeis, and Frankfurter, as well as black leaders like Marcus Garvey and labor leaders as well. It would be only four years until Hoover got the opportunity he needed to institutionalize his techniques and the demonological perspective that animated them. In 1924 Hoover was made head of the Federal Bureau of Investigation. Post died just five years later, and his initiatives, by contrast, were never institutionalized. They passed out of the Department of Labor with him, months after the hearings, when the president he served left office. It is ironic that, of these two administrative exercisers of discretion, the man who stood up boldly for the rule of law never succeeded in institutionalizing his ideals so that they could survive, lawlike, in his absence, while the man who stood for discretionary executive power eventually succeeded in creating an institution that would, even well after his own death and for a very long time to come, exercise power arbitrarily, in ways consonant with his own personal, often paranoid, vision.[53]

Until now, I have treated Hoover and Post as villain and hero. But my aim is not to write a history of great men. If Post and Hoover are of interest to us now, it is not only because the story of their engagement may inspire us to act well in challenging settings, but also because they name and order twin impulses in American political culture that may be in conflict but nonetheless together drive national responses to emergencies (real or imagined). American political culture has within it elements that are both demonological and inclusive, particularistic and universalistic, securitarian and willing to take risks, in favor of both discretionary and proceduralized power, and oriented toward both a centralized powerful administration and a fractured, divided, plural, or chastened sovereignty. The challenge for democratic activists is how to mobilize the energies of the latter in each of these pairings, in order to offset and balance the former, which will never be entirely overcome. The problem is that the contemporary political scene is dominated largely by impulses personified by Hoover, not by Post. We are living in an era that is, as it were, *post*-Post in part because of the particular way the two impulses traced here played themselves out. The rights-centered future of American politics won out in the period after Post's victory, a period in which Post was blackballed from the public lecture circuit by supporters of Palmer and Hoover. It was not the chronological facts of the matter (Post's age, Hoover's youth) but rather the political battles won and lost after Wilson's departure from office that paved the way toward that future—our present. We are left with the civil libertarianism that animates the courageous rights-centered arguments of people like David Cole, but without the Progressivism and Henry George-ism that breathed life into Post's.[54] We are left, in short, with only the shadows of the rights for which Post fought. Some of those rights are now more firmly entrenched juridically than they were then and this has led many to talk about how much "progress" the last century witnessed regarding rights. There is truth in that. But it is also worth noting that none of these rights is lodged in anything like what Post had—a visionary counterpolitics that sought to stand up to executive power overreaching in the settings of everyday as well as emergency politics.[55] Denuded of such a context, contemporary liberal or, better, neoliberal rights—fought for by lawyers, legal elites, and decided upon by courts—are important but, insofar as they operate on the register of democracy's mere life, they are inadequately able to generate or even respond to the forms of collective action needed to counter and go beyond the color-coded, securitarian, emergency politics of governance with which democratic citizens in the United States have been confronted and by which they have been interpellated since 9/11.

Law's Agency

Louis Post is said by one historian to have "anticipated Supreme Court rulings of half a century later."[56] Noncitizens facing administrators (in nonemergency settings) do now have some of the procedural rights that Post discretionarily granted to the Palmer Raids' detainees in 1920. But the term "anticipation" credits law with all the agency (phenomena—like rights—are not real until the law says they are) and leaves to people like Post only the perspicacity or good fortune to line up on the right side of the law before (or after) the law has spoken (or in anticipation of its one day doing so).[57] The implication is that law only steps forward and never back, that it is not dependent upon activist agencies to propel, redirect, and re-create it. Finally, to identify Post's struggle as an *anticipation* of what came later is to misidentify the "rights" for which he struggled as the same things as the rights for which others struggle now. Why is this a *mis*identification? Because the rights valued by Post were embedded in a quasi-Progressive politics quite different from the liberal politics in the context of which contemporary rights operate now.

Post did not anticipate the law. He worked in the paradox of politics. He used all the law's resources and even creatively invented some in order to render the actually existing constitution more democratic, that is to say, to render it more responsive to the needs, rights, and views of the actually existing people over whom government power was brought to bear.[58] If he was able to do this and to resist the pull of American demonological politics, it may be because he knew some of the people whose loyalties were at issue. But such knowledge is not enough. Familiarity, as we know, can also breed contempt. Post cultivated empathy for those under suspicion and made himself vulnerable to their proximity on behalf of his democratic ideals. He took up what Franz Rosenzweig in this same period would call the cause of "the neighbor." And for better or worse, the law—through the agency of other interpreters, administrators, judges, and activists—eventually was made to support some of the democratic commitments and ideals that so moved Louis Post.

Post pursued many substantive Progressive goals while at Labor. Specifically, he sought to develop labor arbitration procedures so as to diminish strike violence and to improve the Labor Departments services to black labor. His innovations were short-lived. They were swept aside when he was pushed into the defense of proceduralism—as we all are—by the demands of emergency and demonological politics, which made survival as mere life rather than the more life of world-building a priority. Or, better: In the context of demonological politics, proceduralization *is* world-building, albeit what is built is a barer world than we might otherwise seek. In the realm of proceduralization, a dangerous realm in 1920, as now, Post took advantage of the ambiguity that left others in doubt as to whether it was he or the law that was the primary agent of his controversial administrative decisions. In short, Post was in the same position as Rousseau's lawgiver/charlatan who acts on behalf of the people while simultaneously seeking to solicit a people out of the multitude. Post enacted solidarity with alien residents of the United States, he humanized those accused of anarchist sympathies, and sought to solicit from members of Congress and the American public an alternative orientation to democracy—from the (in)securities of mere life to the risks and promises of mere and more life. If some concluded that the "law made him do it," then so much the better for both him and the law.

But the question of whether Post made law or acted at law's behest can only take us so far. It is important also to pose the critical questions that lie beneath it: What is at stake in depicting Post as either bound by law or as law's author? In other words, for those who turn to it, what problem is law's independent agency supposed to solve?

Attributing agency to law is a way to secure the distinction between the rule of law and the rule of man. Faced with the undeniable impact of variable human agency on the rule of law's supposedly univocal, predictable governance, scholars of law and legal historians may seek to excise or domesticate those elements of the rule of law that appear dangerously decisionistic (e.g., interpretation, implementation, technicality). One solution is institutional: Authorized or sanctified in one way or another, or legitimated by their norms or practices, institutions like the rabbinical Sanhedrin or the American Supreme Court interpret or make law through authorized processes, forms, and norms that are said to transcend and bind the agency of any mere human.[59]

Lucy Salyer takes this institutional approach in her book, *Laws Harsh as Tigers*, which seeks to explain why hostile, nativist lower-court judges decided cases in favor of Chinese petitioners seeking entry to the United States at the turn of the century. Salyer casts law as possessed of an agency of its own—the judges were "'captives of law,'" she says—but she also locates that agency in particular institutions: The judges were constrained by "the court's norms and traditions" and moved by their "institutional mission."[60] That judges with nativist views rule in favor of petitioners they might rather exclude speaks to the force of law. Legal institutions set expectations, generate grammars, and set out norms that are internalized by their members or work to constrain them.

Salyer's emphasis on the courts' institutional mission solves the puzzle with which she begins, but her argument exceeds the question posed and meets up with others intent upon a different effort: to shore up and relegitimate judicial power, insulate it from the charge of decisionism, and direct that charge instead at administrative power. Diverse proponents of

procedure (e.g., Martin Shapiro, Andrew Arato, Jurgen Habermas) operate with a lexicon that identifies *the rule of law* with law-disciplined judges,
norm-bearing lawyers or legal elites, and rights-bearing clients, juxta-
posed to *the rule of man*, which represents arbitrary power exercised
over rightless persons by unaccountable administrators with too much
discretion and a focus on efficient outcomes not justice.[61] The critique of
those who exercise power unaccountably, deporting the powerless or refusing to hear their cases and appeals, is absolutely important but it also
plays into the ideological self-image of the rule of law by representing,
rightly enough, such arbitrary acts as betrayals of the rule of law and its
aims—justice, equality, fairness. Yet, the rule of law as a system of governance postulates both judicial and administrative power.[62] And the binary distinction between rule of law and rule of man is overdrawn and
misleading.

To highlight the binarism of the distinction between the rule of law and
the rule of man as it operates in contemporary scholarship is *not* to deny
important differences between administrative and judicial settings. People
have access to a wider array of procedural rights and protections when
confronting state power in judicial arenas than when confronting state
power in administrative arenas. Those procedural rights and protections
may be nugatory or they may be invaluable; it depends on the political
and legal context in which we try to claim or (re)take them.[63] Either way,
the differences between administrative and judicial settings do not under-
write the longer list of binaries that structures the arguments of those
who champion the rule of law over its demonized, administrative other:
efficiency versus justice, outcome versus process, decision or discretion
versus norms, caprice versus regularity. These do not map neatly onto
administrative versus judicial power. Some unholy mix of all these considerations informs administrators and justices alike in their exercises or
easements of state power. Administrators can be nuanced, careful, and
even self-limiting, while judges can be brutal, ambitious, and overreaching. Proper judicial procedures do not secure just outcomes. And courts
are not the only public institutions guided by norms. Public administration (particularly as practiced by the Progressives) is no less structured by
ideals, norms, and grammars than are courts. True, the ideals, norms,
and grammars that motivate the two institutions may differ (hence the
different rights and privileges possessed by their respective petitioners)
but those differences exceed and confound the binary demands of the hi-
erarchical opposition—rule of law versus rule of man.[64]

Something like what Michael Rogin calls demonological thinking seems
to be at work here:[65] Legal scholars and political theorists see something
that is unsettlingly inside of the rule of law (variable and fallible interpretation, application, implementation, invention, and technicality) and cast

it outside in its extreme form, calling it decisionism and thereby keeping the ordinary rule of law free of its delegitimating taint. Decisionism is identified with emergency politics, the state of exception, and its very foreign proponent, the legal theorist turned Nazi jurist, Carl Schmitt; or it is identified with the other "other" of the rule of law, administrative power, whose partnership role with more judicialized institutions in the United States is largely disavowed and whose position in relation to the rule of law is (re)cast as simply adversarial, rather than supportive or supplementary. That is to say, the rule of law presents itself as somehow a condition of no-rule, disavowing its implication in institutions of governance, despite the fact that the term—"*rule* of law"—implies governance. Similarly, the so-called state of exception is disavowed, rendered exceptional, marked as a suspension of law rather than seen as part (even if an extreme part) of the daily rule-of-law-generated struggle between judicial and administrative power.

A sense of the alienness of administrative power in relation not just to the rule of law but also to the United States as such is underlined by those like Tocqueville and Woodrow Wilson who see the United States as relatively ungoverned by comparison with France.[66] Wilson (president at the time of the Palmer Raids and responsible for the appointment of Post and other Progressives to executive-branch agency positions), in particular, saw administration as a foreign practice guided (if guided at all) by principles developed elsewhere and in need of Americanization.[67] The contrast Wilson drew with France's centralized bureaucracy, in particular, is striking. But the contrast is also misleading insofar as it suggests that although the United States has some administrative machinery, it is really a rule-of-law state, not (also) a bureaucratic one.[68] Or better, it suggests that one can have the rule of law without being implicated in mechanisms of governance: administration, implementation, and decision.[69]

Unfortunately, efforts to insulate law (and the United States) from the "others" of decision and administration themselves contribute to the rule of law's undoing, for the rule of law is partly legitimated by its claim to be an instrument of self-rule, after all, and so it depends upon, or as Oakeshott would say, it postulates the very human agency that many of the rule of law's proponents are committed to disabling or marginalizing for the sake of the equity, regularity, and predictability that the rule of law is also said to require and deliver.[70] With the disavowal of all that goes by the name decisionism, with the quest to bind ourselves everywhere by law, we disavow something else too: our human inaugural powers, which law *refuses but also offers* to its subjects: It refuses human agency when it aspires to regulate, command, and police us while also, of course, remaining dependent upon us, its subjects, to *do* the regulating, commanding, and policing that the rule of law postulates and requires. We interpret and implement and even undo the law (perhaps even as its [co]authors). Lest this promisingly undecidable dimension of law be obscured, liberal democratic regimes need a third way, or perhaps a better way of thinking about the two that we have. Perhaps somewhere between the rule of law and the rule of man, or on the terrain of their jurisdictional struggle, we might, together with Louis Post, find or enact the rule of men or people: plural and riven, plainspoken and arcanely technical, lawlike and lawless, all at the same time.

We may be supported in that quest by Ludwig Wittegenstein who in his consideration of rules and rule-following did his best to resist the idea that the power that patterns human behavior comes either from the rule (or its essence) or from its follower(s). For Wittgenstein, what mattered was the same as what matters to democratic theorists and activists: the collective practices whereby understanding and meaning are made and out of which patterns emerge. Notably, what Wittgenstein argued against, over and over again, were the misunderstandings and confusions created by philosophical isolationism. In their solitary introspection, philosophers could subject to doubt practices in which doubt would never arise in the practices' usual operations. Of course it is always possible to doubt, Wittgenstein frequently concedes. (Conversely, Rosenzweig, as we shall see in the next chapter, concedes to the philosophers that it is always possible, though not necessarily desirable, to explain—to erase doubt or wonder.) But this philosophically produced possibility does not speak as volubly to us as the fact that, for the most part, we do not doubt; we simply go on.

The collective life and practices that made sense of Louis Post's actions have largely disappeared from American public life. Without their animating power, there is ever greater room to disagree about how to tell Post's story today. I end by granting, as Post himself said of his own discretionary decisions, that another might have decided differently and told the story otherwise. Indeed many have. It matters how the story is told and retold. In isolation, we may doubt any particular telling of the story. As actors in concert, we may well find in the story of Louis Post as I have told it here some of the sustenance needed to move beyond mere life to promote the mere/more life, the overlife, of democracy.

Chapter Four

Orientation

MIRACLE AND METAPHOR IN THE
PARADOXICAL STATE OF EXCEPTION

> For the word is mere inception until it finds reception
> in an ear and response in a mouth.
> —*Franz Rosenzweig*

WHEN TRAVELING THROUGH ITALY, Goethe observed a trial and took note of its peculiar timekeeping practices. A man seated at a desk held in his hand a glass sand bottle, a timepiece. It was not immediately clear what his purpose was. But Goethe soon noticed that when the prosecutor spoke the man kept the bottle lying on its side with its sands inert but whenever the defense began to speak the man would turn the bottle upright and restart its sand flow. When the state spoke, time stopped. The defense, however, was subject to time.[1]

The story accords well with the views of state sovereignty propounded by Carl Schmitt who identifies sovereignty with the power to legally suspend law for a time by declaring the state of exception. For Schmitt, as for Giorgio Agamben who works in his wake, the state of exception is that paradoxical situation in which the law is legally suspended by sovereign power. The ensuing condition is one in which we or, rather, sovereign powers are neither subject to law nor free of it but rather both, since the state of exception is itself a legal condition of alegality. Grounded in paradox (the legal suspension of law), and seeming well positioned to explain elements of the current political landscape that liberal and deliberative democratic theorists seem only able to criticize, Schmitt and Agamben's "state of exception," I think it is fair to say, has captured the imagination of contemporary political theory.

In this chapter, I seek to loosen its hold on our imagination by pluralizing the particular political theology on which Schmitt's account is based and from which it draws sustenance. I do so in order to highlight the dependence of the so-called state of exception upon democratic energies and to mark its vulnerability to democratic action and resistance.[2] At the center of this effort is Schmitt's metaphor for the state of exception—the miracle. I note that we may accept his metaphorization and yet be drawn by it to very different conclusions. For this alternative, I turn to Franz

Rosenzweig's theology. Rosenzweig, a contemporary of Schmitt's, develops a conception of miracle that points not to singular sovereign ruptural power but rather to popular receptivity and immanence. The Rosenzweigian miracle postulates not divine command but rather human orientation to divine sovereignty in everyday life. With the help of Rosenzweig's "new theology," we may rethink emergency politics in the state of exception in more democratic terms. The idea here is to focus less on the prerogative of the timekeeper at the trial observed by Goethe and more on the agency of those grains of sand that ran through his glass bottle.

Agamben keeps our gaze on the timekeeper, however. His account posits, in Nietzsche's terms, a being behind the doing: the sovereign, singularly constituted by its power to declare or invoke the state of exception. What if instead of the sovereign as "he who decides the exception" we thought about sovereignty as a set of circuits, contingent arrays of diverse forces and powers that, like grains of sand that sometimes run smoothly and sometimes clump up, fall into place as they contest or produce (and are produced by) the declaration of a state of exception? From such a vantage point, which I here develop with Rosenzweig's help, sovereignty is not simply that which decides the exception. It is a contingent formation that might get relocated or redistributed in contests over whether a state of exception should be instituted, in what such a state of exception should consist, and about when it should end. When the people (who, as Rousseau knew and as we saw in chapter 1, are always also a multitude) resist or affirm or call in all their plurality for the institution or end of a state of exception, they reenter the paradox of politics and act as sovereign in order to become who they already need to be in order to act as they are.

Agamben stumbles on something like this idea but skips past it when in his book, *State of Exception*, he quotes Meuli regarding festivals of reversal as a kind of state of exception. "Chariveri," Meuli says,

> is one of many names for an ancient and widely diffused act of popular justice. . . . A close analysis shows that what at first seemed simply to be rough and wild acts of harassment are in truth well-defined traditional customs and legal forms by means of which from time immemorial the ban and proscription were carried out.[3]

Here is Agamben's interpretation of that passage:

> If Meuli's hypothesis is correct the "legal anarchy" of the anomic feasts does not refer back to ancient agrarian rites which in themselves explain nothing [that is, the feasts are not, as Wittgenstein said against Fraser on the fire festivals, explicable by reference to a supposed referent]; rather it brings to light in parodic form the anomie within the law, the state of emergency as the anomic drive contained in the very heart of the nomos.[4]

We can see here the extent to which Agamben is captivated, captured, by his model. What Agamben describes strictly as "legal anarchy," Meuli also casts as "well-defined traditional customs and legal forms." Where Agamben see emergency within the law, Meuli says there is here justice. Where Agamben sees anomic drive, Meuli notes a roughness that in fact turns out to be ritualized. Of course, roughness and ritual may coexist as, indeed, may legal anarchy and legal form.[5] Or there may be plural legal forms, one of which decries the others as anarchic.[6] But Agamben does not explore these possibilities here and so he seems to miss what Meuli sees at work in this festival of reversal: popular law and popular justice, both formed and formless. These are elements of a democratic state of exception whose undecidability, contra Agamben, comes not simply or entirely from its paradoxical logic of legal illegality, but from the fact that it is performed by the people, the multitude—both formed and formless— in the paradox of politics.

Agamben's account of the state of exception is anchored in his specula- tion that there was what he calls a "secret conversation" between Schmitt and Benjamin on the topic of emergency in which Schmitt failed fully to acknowledge Benjamin. I add to that the possibility of another such se- cret conversation, between Schmitt and Rosenzweig, in which neither side acknowledged the other and the stakes were also high. When we put Schmitt into dialogue with Rosenzweig on the topic of the miracle, we switch our gaze from sovereign to popular power or to sovereignty *as* implicated in and dependent upon popular power.

A Secret Conversation?

In his book, *Political Theology*, Carl Schmitt, the soon to be lapsed Cath- olic legal thinker who would later become jurist to the Nazi party in 1930s Germany, claimed that *all* significant political concepts are rein- habitations of theological concepts and should be treated as such.[7] In *The Enemy*, an intellectual biography of Schmitt, Gopal Balakrishnan points out this is an overstatement: The only such reinhabitation to which Schmitt really devoted attention was that of sovereignty. Balakrishnan is partly right; but only partly, because Schmitt's theorization of juridical politics is also grounded in the miracle. In *Political Theology*, the state of exception is metaphorized by the divine miracle of the theological world: Both display sovereign or divine power by interrupting or suspending the order of normal or natural law.

But the metaphor of miracle has a further function as well. Schmitt turns to political theology to find a way to secure political sovereignty, something he thinks modern constitutionalism fails to do. That potentially agonistic pairing, political + theology, is sutured together by the metaphor of miracle in his work or, better, the pair is sutured together by the miracle of metaphor. Metaphor posits its plural, contested ground ("miracle," in this instance) as an apparently uncontroversial simple (miracle simply means sovereign suspension of law) and presents as the problem for scrutiny its effect or figure (state of exception: What is it [like]? It is [like] . . . the miracle). Thus, the miracle of metaphor is its naturalization of its ground, its removal of its ground from scrutiny. In Schmitt's political theology, this means theology's concepts are treated as if they possess clear and univocal meanings—we *know* what miracle is—such that they can serve as the ground for unclear or contested political concepts that we are unclear about: the state of exception.

However, "miracle" is itself the object of intense philosophical reflection and theological debate in the period in which Schmitt wrote. The fraught nature of the concept is hidden from view when Schmitt presses miracle into service as the ground of his metaphor. This is one of the miracles of metaphor. By analogizing the state of exception to miracle Schmitt was not only participating in political debates about constitutionalism and authority in which the question is: What is the state of exception? He was also intervening in ongoing theological debates about the status and place of miracle in belief after the Enlightenment, in an age of deism and secularism. He may have been deliberately intervening in debates about the merits of Christian versus Jewish theology. That is, he may have been as interested in subtly securing the meaning of "miracle" in the theological sphere as he was in staking out the meaning of the "state of exception" in the juridical sphere.

In this, Schmitt was not alone. The reconstruction or rehabilitation of "miracle" was the project as well of the Jewish theologian and philosopher, Franz Rosenzweig, who wrote at roughly the same time as the early Schmitt.[8] Rosenzweig's concept of miracle is difficult and vague but it functions more like a sign than a command and so points toward the popular receptivity and interpretation upon which signs depend. Rosenzweig and recent Rosenzweig scholarship provide democratic theory with an opportunity to assess the implications of Rosenzweig's concept of the miracle for thinking beyond Schmittian sovereignty and its state of exception to more democratic alternatives. These are not Rosenzweig's terms, however. The idea of popular prophecy with which this chapter concludes is not his. But it is invited by him and by some of his readers and it comes out of a kind of self-overcoming warranted in my view by Rosenzweig's own emphasis on the undecidability of the sign and the importance in everyday life of orientation to the eternal.

Rosenzweig claimed the *Star of Redemption* was not a Jewish book but rather a work of philosophy. Still, he remains a difficult thinker for contemporary democratic theory because of his providentialism, in particular his stress on the importance of Judaism as a blood community, on Jewish exceptionalism, and on Judaic anti-idolatry as Judaism's special gift to the world, not to mention his dismissal of Islam and all other world religions, apart from Christianity. For some, these obstacles can be overcome. Hilary Putnam says that when Rosenzweig says god, he only means to be talking about the name as such, that which calls upon us to respond, as ethical subjects.[9] Eric Santner, deals with this challenge by funneling Rosenzweig's thought through psychoanalysis, reading him with and against Freud to great effect in *On the Psychotheology of Everyday Life* and in "Miracles Happen." Santner generously reads Rosenzweig's emphasis on kinship and the community of blood not as an embrace of blood kinship over other forms of community but rather as a metaphor for the fate of a deterritorialized people who have nothing *but* kinship to define them. Leora Batnitzky charts a different, also effective and important path in *Idolatry and Representation*, situating Rosenzweig in the tradition of hermeneutics, with Gadamer, and in relation to the neo-Kantianism of Cohen. She decenters Rosenzweig's belief in Jewish election or downplays it in the first half of her book in order to open up the contemporary reader to his hermeneutics.

Such creative recraftings seem necessary and I engage in my own. But I also try to preserve Rosenzweig's alienness, partly because of Rosenzweig's own insightful insistence that only an alien past has any existence for us. This point comes up when Rosenzweig argues against rationalists who dismiss the past and against modern theologians who seek to reclaim the past for their postrevelatory theologies. These projects necessarily fail, he says, because they insist on the necessary place of the past in a larger progressive trajectory that deprives the past of its potential power and meaning for us. We might say the same of Rosenzweig himself. I am drawn to Rosenzweig because he understood that the only way to combat the problematic otherworldliness of theology was not by way of a this-worldly antitheology but rather through an alternative theology, a this-worldly theology.[10] If we render him less alien in order to learn from him, we undo our own quest: If he is less unsettling, he is also less able to point us toward a different future.

In Rosenzweig's theorization of the miracle I find important resources for thinking our way out of the apparently irresistible implications of Schmitt's influential claim that the state of exception is like the miracle. If the state of exception is like the miracle but like Rosenzweig's version of the miracle rather than Schmitt's, then we are invited by miracle to think about forms of sovereignty that postulate not just ruptural power, imposition, or governance but also receptivity, openness, and a future, not community defined by its opposition to the other as enemy, but community defined by its openness to the other as divine.[11] From Rosenzweig we might learn that just as the Enlightenment's tactic of opposing the miracle with rationalism must be inadequate, so too the tactic of opposing the state of exception with more law may be inadequate.[12] It may be necessary but it will not be sufficient. Where Rosenzweig calls on a different conception of miracle (in which I see intimated something I call the people's prophecy), political theorists today wrestling with Schmitt's legacy may do well to call on a different state of exception: a democratic state of exception.

In the end, I part ways with Rosenzweig, finding another alternative in the same tradition that inspires him to theorize miracle in relation to popular orientation and prophecy. Through a critical reading of Rosenzweig and one of his commentators, Eric Santner, I find intimations in the Hebrew Bible of a popular prophetic voice that speaks in agonistic relation to divine sovereign power and that of the lawgiver. Might this be a trace within Judaism of what Santner calls the metaethical subject, by contrast with the superego of Freudian psychoanalysis? Here my focus is not, as in psychoanalysis, on the lawgiver and his individuated divided subject but rather, as in radical democratic theory, on the people/multitude and their counterpowers, not just on their resistance or obedience but on their actions in concert and their collective communal insight such as it is.

Rosenzweig's importance stems also from the fact that others to whose work I am here indebted may be themselves indebted in subtle ways to him. When Hannah Arendt theorizes a posttheological politics using the metaphor of the miracle, she surely works in the wake of Schmitt and Rosenzweig. While Arendt calls action a miracle, she is actually as concerned as Rosenzweig to theorize what he calls the "*possibility of experiencing* a miracle," that is, to think about the sociopolitical, symbolic, and cultural conditions under which people are open to the miraculous, to receive, perceive, and perform it. In what might well have been a deliberate effort to counter Schmitt, Arendt in *The Human Condition* associates the miracle with rupture, but specifically with the ruptural power of a form of political action that is immanent not transcendent. Hers is a nonsovereign rupture that inaugurates a new limitedly sovereign order rather than suspending an existing order in a way that delineates or exhibits decisive sovereign power.[13]

Arendt's miracle decenters sovereignty, which in her work reigns more in the realms of the predicative "what" of reproductive labor and productive work than in the honorific and excessive realm of the "who" in which transformative human activity may inaugurate new political powers that also elude sovereign power's grasp. Her miracle is a metaphor for action in concert rather than for the identity-forming division of friend-enemy. She identifies action with promises kept, rather than with betrayal or the suspension of promise-keeping. When she theorizes promising, a normally ordinary practice, as an extraordinary act, she does not err (as a theorist of ordinary language philosophy might infer), but rather shows an awareness of how ordinary practices might take on a heroic cast when performed in the context of exceptional circumstances like political transitions or revolutions, police states, martial law, or under conditions of deep alienation.[14] And through her account of action, she endows talk, speech acts, and political writing with the power to create and sustain social fabrics and political realities, in contrast to Schmitt who took a dim view of political talk, which he cast as impotent and associated with the Weimar parliamentarism he criticized harshly. Indeed, in a passage that reads like a direct rebuttal of Schmitt on this point, Arendt says:

> Without the disclosure of the agent in the act, action loses its specific character and becomes one form of achievement among others. It is then, indeed, no less a means to an end than making is a means to produce an object. This happens wherever human togetherness is lost, that is, when people are only for or against other people, as for instance in modern warfare, where men go into action and use means of violence in order to achieve certain objectives for their own side and against the enemy. *In these instances, which of course have always existed, speech becomes indeed "mere talk," simply one more means toward an end* [or toward no end] whether it serves to deceive the enemy or to dazzle everybody with propaganda.[15]

That the miracle recurs in a pivotal role in the thinking of Rosenzweig, Schmitt and Arendt, three early and mid-twentieth-century German (two of them German Jewish) thinkers suggests that a subtle conversation is occurring among these members of the world of political theory and existential philosophy in pre- and postwar Germany. What if Hannah Arendt, in taking the idea of the miracle as a metaphor for her account of political action in which the actor does not know what he is doing, herself *knew what she was doing* and was writing in direct perhaps deliberate counter to Schmitt, who appropriated the miracle for his decisionistic sovereign, the very model of sovereigntist politics Arendt was writing against?[16] And, what if we read Schmitt as if he himself was writing in direct and even deliberate counter to Rosenzweig?[17]

The Miracle of Metaphor: Schmitt, Rosenzweig, and Political Theology

Schmitt and Rosenzweig (one a soon to be lapsed but formerly devout Catholic, the other an almost lapsed but then returned Jew), began from similar concerns: Both worried that deism had banished the miracle from the human world under the benighted belief that this banishment constituted progress.

Both thinkers saw that the miracle had become an embarrassment in modernity, outlawed by Enlightenment rationalism, deism, and liberalism. For Schmitt:

> [T]he idea of the modern constitutional state triumphed together with deism, a theology and metaphysics that *banished the miracle from the world*. This theology and metaphysics rejected not only the transgression of the laws of nature through an exception brought about by direct intervention, as is found in the idea of a miracle, *but also the sovereign's direct intervention in a valid legal order. The rationalism of the Enlightenment rejected the exception in every form*

—and in every sphere (theological and also juridical).[18] Schmitt's response to the problem (a problem of atheism, too) was to reaffirm the importance of decision, to show its indispensability to a politics of friendship and enmity that always operated below the tamed surface of liberal constitutional politics. But what was it that Schmitt was reaffirming?

For Schmitt, the miracle on which the exception is modeled is an interruptive force that suspends the ordinary lawfulness of the world and thereby exhibits divine power and sovereignty. For Rosenzweig, however, it is precisely this construal of the miracle as interruptive and illustrative of a naked sovereign power that is the problem that must be solved. The notion of *miracle as rupture*, Rosenzweig suggests, is part of the apparatus that *sidelines* miracle; it is complicit with the deism it opposes. Where the miracle is rupture, the deity appears mercurial. God can make anything happen, if he wills it.[19] Deism and atheism banish that mercurial, willful deity for the sake of a rational, rule-governed, and less personality-centered theology. A real alternative, however, would seek to suspend such logics of rule-exception in which Schmitt's decisionism and the deism/atheism he opposes are both stuck.[20] One way to do this might be, as I argued in chapter 3, to recontextualize the decision, to demote the "decision" from extraordinary sovereign prerogative to more ordinary administrative discretion upon which the rule of law is in any case dependent. Another sort of alternative is what Rosenzweig himself aims at in his development of what he calls "the new thinking."

In *The Star of Redemption* and *On Understanding the Sick and the Healthy*, Rosenzweig seeks to recast the holiday from a suspension of the ordinary to an intensification of the ordinary. Rosenzweig reads the cycle of holidays and the Sabbath in relation to and not in their apartness from the workaday. He emphasizes the role of the holiday's liturgical and material practices in orienting subjects to the divine. "The difference between prescribed prayer and spontaneous prayer is that the latter is born out of the need of the moment, while the former teaches him who prays to feel a need he might otherwise not feel."[21] Belief alone is not enough.

Liturgical practices and the cycle of holidays prepare the community
to receive and experience belief. These material cultural practices ap-
proximate and double the ordinary, the workaday.[22] They do not interrupt mere life, they elevate mere life into more life.[23] Most important,
they insert us into a communal and theological context (dubbed "co-
existentialism" by Rosenzweig's commentator, Nahum Glatzer) in which
the will to mastery is undone.[24] This prepares us for what Rosenzweig
calls "the possibility of experiencing miracles."

Cyclical, liturgical practices open us up to the miraculous, says Rosenzweig; they are not, as Kant would have it, dead or deadening rituals that
block access to the real sublime. Instead, they render us receptive to miracle. But receptivity does not guarantee right interpretation. Rosenzweig's
god of miracles is also a god of human freedom. His signs are underdetermined lest they impinge upon the freedom of his subjects to decide
their meaning. God's own sovereignty, miracles, and prophecy cannot
be a matter of brute facticity (missed only by the most recalcitrant and
perversely unbelieving), for Rosenzweig's god does not seek to compel
belief. Rosenzweig says in *The Star*:

> A rabbinic legend tells the tale of a river in a faraway land that is so pious that
> it stops flowing on the Sabbath. . . . But God does not give such signs. Obvi-
> ously, he shudders at the inevitable result: that then precisely the least free, the
> most fearful and the weakest would be the "most pious." And God obviously
> wants only those who are free for his own.[25]

For Rosenzweig, miracle is not a ruptural divine decision; that is a
remnant of earlier theologies and the by-product of their rationalization
(in which miracle is that which must be expelled from a rational theology). Instead, Rosenzweig argues, miracle is an ambiguous sign that
thrusts upon humans the responsibility to receive it. That responsibility
presupposes and requires a readiness and preparation provided by community membership, neighborliness, liturgical practice, material preparation, and study.

Rosenzweig on the Miracle

In *The Star of Redemption*, written mostly while Rosenzweig, a soldier in
the German army, was on the Macedonian front during and after the
First World War, Rosenzweig aimed not as Schmitt would do two years
later to reassert the centrality of miracle (or state of exception) but to
philosophically reconstruct miracle for a new this-worldy theology. In a
chapter called "On the Possibility of Experiencing Miracles," Rosenzweig begins as follows:

If miracle really is the favorite child of faith [referring to Goethe], then, at least for some time, faith has been seriously neglecting its parental duties. For at least a century, the child [miracle] has been only a source of great embarrassment for the wet nurse dispatched by its parent, theology: she would gladly have got rid of it somehow or other, if only—yes, if only—a certain consideration for the parent [faith] had not held her back while the child was alive. But time brings counsel. The old parent cannot live forever. And the wet nurse will know what to do with the poor worm [miracle], incapable as it is of living or dying on its own. She [theology] has, moreover, already begun making the preparations.[26]

That is, when belief dies finally, theology will toss miracle overboard.

The new theology, dubbed by Rosenzweig "atheistic theology," broke free from the traditionalists' commitment to the rule of the past over the present as well as from the Enlightenment's rejection of the past for the sake of the improved present. Instead the new theology posited a faith in progress and replaced the belief in "the historical objectivity of miracles" with, as in Schleiermacher, "the present intensity of religious feeling as the crucial warrant of faith."[27] But that present intensity was not durable and its subjectivism would not long survive the empiricist scrutiny of modernity. Miracle had to undergo a philosophical reconstruction in order to be delivered in good health to a new this-worldly theology. Rosenzweig aimed to move beyond historicism and neo-Kantian rationalism (from Kant to Cohen) but without lapsing into historicism's supposed other—"irrationalism."[28]

Where for Schmitt, the decisive feature of the miracle and the decision is their interruption of the everyday, their sovereign suspension of normal lawfulness, for Rosenzweig this interruptive quality is not essential to the miracle at all. Rosenzweig aligns himself with a tradition of Jewish thinking in which the interruptive miracle is seen not as confirmation of the perfection of God's order, but as its negation. A world that requires the saving supplement of a miracle is a world that was not perfect to begin with, and how could that be true of a divinely created world? If interruptive miracles were necessary, that might mean that something was occurring in time that god did not will, or about which, as it were, he had changed his mind. That could be true only of an imperfect god. It could not be true of a perfect divinity to whom all was revealed instantaneously and simultaneously.

Moreover, Rosenzweig argues, what appear to be interruptions of natural order are hardly a certain sign of miracle in any case. Signs are, as we just saw, underdetermined, and in any case others could produce such suspensions—the Bible is full of stories of sorcerers whose magical acts violate the laws of nature. But these are not miracles. The miracle is not, pace Hume, about the contravention of everyday patterns of existence or laws of nature. It is a sign of divine providence that is experienced as such and that opens us up, both to providence and to the everyday. It allows or solicits us to experience the everyday as miracle, the ordinary as calling for acknowledgment, or receptivity or gratitude; it calls us to experience the apparently steadfast as contingent and as could have been otherwise. And it calls for us to experience the apparently contingent as steadfast, as fated, willed, foreseen or, at least (in more secular terms) significant. It calls for what we might now call mindfulness.

For Rosenzweig, not interruption but prediction is a predicate of miracle.

> [F]or us, today, miracle seems to need the backdrop of natural laws, for it is only against this that it stands out as it were as a miracle. [If there is a pattern, then its interruption, as it were, "speaks" to us.] But in so doing, we see only that, for human consciousness at that time, the miraculous character of miracle rested on a completely different context: not on its divergence as regards the course of nature predetermined by laws, but on the fact that it was predicted.[29]

That is, it was not the miracle's rupture of divine and natural order that as an event recemented the people's relationship to god by revealing him in all his power to them. It was rather that the event followed a certain arc: It was predicted, prophesied, and the event then occurred. Thus, on Rosenzweig's account, the event's character as a miracle is tethered to the event's function as a sign or portent of divine providence (rather than, say, its manifestation of power).[30] That is why Rosenzweig says in *Star* that "[m]iracle and prophecy belong together."[31]

With this argument, Rosenzweig shows his unease with the "magical" or ruptural miracle. But he is also uneasy with the opposite rationalist take on the miracle, which stresses miracle's conformity with natural law. Says Paul Mendes-Flohr,

> Referring to [the rationalist] Maimonides' oft-cited explanation of the parting of the Red Sea, Rosenzweig noted that "the east wind has probably swept bare the ford in the Red Sea hundreds of times, and will do so again hundreds of times." . . . [W]hat is actually miraculous about miracle is that "it comes when it does." . . . [The Red Sea] parted the very moment when the fleeing Israelites set foot in its waters.[32]—"What only a moment before was coveted future, becomes present and actual. The enriching of a present moment with the past, with its own past . . . gives it the power to continue as a present not past moment and thus raises it from the stream of all other moments, whose companion it remains nonetheless.

So the miracle is neither purely exceptional nor purely temporal. It occurs in time but also out of time. It exceeds the rationalists' explanation of it and it must always do so since, as Mendes-Flohr puts it: "Every miracle can be explained—*post eventum*."[33] But such post hoc explanation is possible, as Rosenzweig says beautifully, "[n]ot because miracle is no miracle, but rather because explanation is explanation."[34] Thus miracle, whatever it is, demands an orientation other than explanation. Hannah Arendt showed she understood this point when she argued against the efforts by behaviorism to "explain" human action.[35] Kant, in his critique of miracles showed an acute understanding of the shift that is here evident, when he claimed (albeit critically) that where once miracle had propped up faith, now faith (a certain orientation) is required for miracle to be, a description with which Rosenzweig would agree but an implied judgment from which he would depart.[36]

Rosenzweig supplemented and revised the Maimonidean strand of Jewish thought. What makes a miracle is not its defiance of explanation (magical), or its capacity to be explained in accordance with laws of nature (Maimonidean rationalist). A miracle may be (in)explicable but that is not what makes it a miracle. For Rosenzweig, miracle is a sign, and an invitation, quite like prophecy, on which it depends, and to which it is linked.[37] Thus, to understand miracle we need to understand prophecy, which Rosenzweig explains by juxtaposing true prophecy to its opposite: sorcery.

Sorcery and Prophecy: or, What Happened at Meribah?

Rosenzweig specifies the difference between sorcery and prophecy at length in Star of Redemption.

> [M]agic and sign are on different planes. . . . The magician actively intervenes against the course of the world. . . . He attacks God's Providence and wants to snatch, bully and force from it, by trickery or by force, that which is unforeseen and unforeseeable of it, that which is willed by its own will. The prophet, however, unveils by foreseeing that which is willed by Providence; by telling the sign—and even that which would be sorcery in the hands of the magician would be sign in the mouth of the prophet—he demonstrates the hand of Providence, which the magician denies. He demonstrates it; for how would it otherwise be possible to see the future ahead of time if it were not "provided" for? So it is necessary to go beyond the pagan miracle, to curb its spell that carries out the command of man's own power, through the sign that proves God's Providence.[38]

The binary, oppositional structure here is thorough: prediction not intervention, divine providence versus heathen miracle or man's might, prophecy versus magic, unveiling versus audacity, guile, or coercion, speech versus force, mouth versus hand, in short postoedipal versus oedipal demands and satisfactions. Elsewhere the same binary structure is repeated when Rosenzweig contrasts true and false prayer: The latter, he says, is willed and is comparable to the "magic practiced by the medicine man." Mendes-Flohr concludes, "Fundamentally distinguished from the theurgic practices of pagan magicians," the Rosenzweigian miracle is intrinsic to "the new concept of God introduced by revelation."[39]

Rosenzweig here writes as if there is a distinction of kind between sorcerers and true prophets. But, as with Rousseau whose distinction between true lawgiver and charlatan slips into undecidability, we can see here slippage rather than distinction, a site of undecidability or tension rather than opposition.[40] To make clear the slippage and mutual implication of Rosenzweig's binary oppositions, I develop here in detail an example used by Eric Santner to unpack Rosenzweig's distinction between sorcery and prophecy, magic and miracle. Here is Santner's parsing:

> [Rosenzweig's] distinction between magical and providential miracle, between sorcery and sign-event, plays a crucial role in the so-called waters of Meribah episode recounted in Numbers 20. There, one will recall, Moses and Aaron are once more faced with the rebellious lament of the Israelites who complain of the hardships of their wanderings: "and why have you made us come up out of Egypt to bring us to this evil place? It is no place for grain, or figs, or vines or pomegranates, and there is no water to drink.'" Moses and Aaron withdraw from the assembly and supplicate God who thereupon tells Moses: "'Take the rod and assemble the congregation, you and Aaron your brother, and tell the rock before their eyes to yield its water; so you shall bring water out of the rock for them; so you shall give drink to the congregation and their cattle.'" What Moses, does, however, amounts to a rupture of this arc of promise and fulfillment [the arc of the miracle, on Rosenzweig's account]; instead of bearing witness to the providential sign of God, he . . . performs a purely magical miracle: "And Moses and Aaron gathered the assembly together before the rock and he said to them, 'Hear now, you rebels; shall we bring forth water for you out of this rock?' And Moses lifted up his hand and struck the rock with his rod twice, and water came forth abundantly, and the congregation drank, and their cattle." It is against this background that we can understand the otherwise perplexing extremity of God's punishment. 'And the Lord said to Moses and Aaron, 'Because you did not believe in me, to sanctify me in the eyes of the people of Israel, therefore you shall not bring this assembly in the land which I have given them.'"[41]

Moses is barred from entry to the Promised Land because of this incident at Meribah. He will die in Moab, able to see the Promised Land from the mountaintop, but not able to enter the land. This moves one contemporary commentator to note wryly and movingly: "Like many people, Moses doesn't get the reward he has been working toward his whole life."[42] Why not? Why is Moses so harshly punished? What did he do wrong?

For Santner, Moses was called upon to prophesy, to predict, and to witness, along with the assembly, the realization of prophecy. He was told to "*tell* the rock before their eyes to yield its water." But, rather than say, "Behold!" he hits the rock. Moses uses force not speech, thus resorting to sorcery not sign, a point made in psychoanalytic terms by Robert Paul, upon whom Santner here draws: "'At the waters of Meribah,' Paul explains, 'Moses disobeys the paternal injunction to speak, to use language, and reverts to a pre-oedipal demand for the breast and its withheld bounty. It is thus for a symbolic incestuous infraction of the oedipal law of the father that Moses is punished.'" Santner explains, "The 'regression from sign to sorcery is correlated here with one from oedipal to preoedipal modes of demand/desire and satisfaction.'")[43]

Many others have also commented on this episode, seeking to explain the harshness of god's punishment, its "extremity," although the wry commentator quoted above shows it is not an extremity, when he says, with pathos, "Like *many* people, Moses does not get the reward he has been working toward his whole life." Perhaps what is so startling to most commentators is precisely the fact that Moses is subject to a fate not unlike that which befalls *many* people. He is not exceptional.

Rabbinical interpreters point out that when Moses hit the rock not once but twice, he showed mistrust in god,[44] striking a second time when, after the first strike, the water did not flow out right away[45] (in effect acting like those people [of whom I am one, but I am working on it] who punch the elevator button repeatedly, not just once, and so exhibit an interventionist rather than a witnessing or prophesying disposition—a predilection for force over finesse). Others suggest that Moses stole god's thunder—showing *himself*, hubristically, to bring out the water with his rod rather than speaking and then *witnessing*, along with the Israelites, god's work in a more self-effacing way.[46] Another way to put this point would be to say that, in Santner's terms, Moses shows himself here to be subject to the rule of talents (or is perhaps in this scene experiencing a crisis of investiture, depending on how one reads his resort to magic: as self-indulgent, or the product of a crisis of faith?).[47]

What is important here, however, as Santner shows, is the fact that regardless of which of these interpretations one adopts, it is clear that, in Rosenzweig's terms, one way or another Moses acted as sorcerer not prophet; he used force not finesse, hands not speech.[48] He slipped from prophet to magician, he performed the magic but not the miracle, and so the event occurred without the invitation that miracle is supposed to extend. But there is more: Worse yet, I want to suggest, beyond Rosenzweig,

Santner, and Paul, what if Moses did what he did because he thought that was what the people wanted? He saw them as rebels—he calls them by that name. And he pandered to their baseness, or so he thought, rather than solicit their spirits. Moses saw the Israelites as stuck in their appetites; he thought they could be satisfied only by magic, not lifted up by miracle. In his eyes, they wanted their thirst satisfied, not their souls extended; they were subject to the demands of mere life, not open to the promise of more life. But what was it they were thirsting *for*?[49]

Once we pose the question, it becomes apparent that Moses may have underestimated the people; indeed the text itself (Numbers 19:1–22:1) suggests it. First, when the people complain to Moses, they do say, "Would that we too had perished with our kinsmen in the LORD's presence!" suggesting they have no appreciation of the heights they have ascended (biblically speaking) as a people, since liberation and exodus. But they also say, "And why have you made us come up out of Egypt to bring us to this evil place?" They know it is *up*, so their questioning is not fundamental. They are not asking, as on earlier occasions, to return to Egypt. This suggests Moses should have trusted them more.

Instead, Moses and Aaron withdraw from the assembly upon hearing the people's complaints. Moses Mendelssohn, the great Jewish Enlightenment thinker, says in his biblical commentary, *Biur*, that this withdrawal is the real cause of Moses's punishment.[50] Moses's sin, says Mendelssohn, was that when the people began to complain of thirst, he and Aaron fled from answering them directly and went to the tent of meeting to speak to God.[51] Moses's sin was not his failure to obey god but rather the fact that he turned to god at all, and away from the people. Mendelssohn's interpretation invites rumination on what it would have meant to "stay" with the people. This, as I argue below, is the most necessary thing to ruminate upon in this context.

Had Moses trusted the people and stayed with them, he might have been able to ascertain their rightness. For the people are right when they say they have been brought to an evil place. It is an evil place not only because nothing can grow here, not only because it lacks figs, pomegranates, and water, but also because here it will come to pass that Moses will fail them. Here, the people prophesy, "evil will happen." "This will turn out to have been an evil place." And sure enough, here Moses gives in to the Israelites' supposed need for magic; he does not trust them. He does not hear their prophecy. They see that this place's nonfecundity is a sign and so they prophesy that this place is evil. Like all prophecy on Rosenzweig's account, so too the people's prophecy is an invitation. Moses can make Meribah a place of wonder, not evil, by registering the people's prophetic power and responding to it. But he does not. He assumes their speech act is constative. This *is* an evil place. And he thinks they are wrong. He can bring water to them, even here. But he hears them on the wrong register; unbeknownst to him, their utterance signifies as performative as well. "This will be an evil place, if you are not careful," is another way to hear: "This is an evil place." To hear it the latter way, one needs to assume the speech is uttered by prophetic voice.

Where Moses fails, God succeeds. God shows his own faith in the people when he says to Moses, "Therefore you shall not bring this assembly into the land that I have given them [but not you]." The land is for them. Not for Moses. This is not because he disobeyed god and hit the rock (or not just for that reason), but because he did not see the people as they need to be seen, as the people to whom this land has been given—as a free people, capable of giving and receiving prophecy, as bearers of mere *and* more life. Moses's failure, in short, is his failure (and Aaron's too) to see the people as they need to be seen for their promise to be fulfilled. As anyone undergoing change knows, a sure obstacle to transformation is the continued presence of those who persist in seeing you the old way and continue to interpellate you in those terms, in terms of your predicates, not your yearnings, in terms of your past, not your future.

Thus, the real issue is that Moses gives the people what they want at Meribah, or what in his eyes they appear to want or deserve. He reads their demand in a way that turns him from prophet to sorcerer. Or, better: He (mis)reads their demands as a demand that he be a sorcerer to them rather than a prophet. Unbeknownst to him, the people are not only interested in the demands of mere life (water, figs) but also in the promise of more life (spiritual connection). And for this error, he must die or, if Freud is right, for this the people kill him. If they do so, that is because they seek to claim or reclaim their own prophetic powers, which according to Spinoza they had renounced at Sinai in their moment of terror at witnessing the Shechina, the presence of the divine. Spinoza says that in their fear, the Israelites elected Moses their king, abdicated their democratic power, and told him to go talk to god on their behalf. Hardt and Negri take Spinoza to mean that at Sinai the people create their own prophet, but Spinoza saw here not an exercise of democratic power but rather its abdication.[52] On the other hand, Spinoza treats the Israelites' renunciation as final, but it need not be so treated. There may be democratic energies here yet, post-Sinai, in need of daily reinterpellation or available for resurrection.

We are made alert to the people's prophetic powers by the opening lines of this critical chapter. Chapter 20 of Bamidbar begins *not* with the people's cries of thirst and disappointment, but rather with a report, really a mention, of the fact that Miriam, Moses's sister and the Hebrew Pentateuch's only female prophetess, has died. One midrash says she prophesied Moses's birth and arrival as a liberator and she is even said to be responsible for his birth, having encouraged her parents to resume marital relations after they desisted in response to Pharaoh's edict against Israelite male babies. If so, she may be seen as one of those who refuse to be reduced by emergency (Pharaoh's edict) to a narrow focus on mere life.

The first sentence of the chapter reads: "And the people of Israel came, all of their Assembly, to desert Tzin, in the first month, and they sat there and Miriam died there and was buried there." The *very next sentence* *says:* "As the community had no water, they held a council against Moses and Aaron. 'Why did you raise us out of Egypt, only to bring us to this wretched place which has neither grain nor figs nor vines nor pomegranates? Here there is not even water to drink!'" Surely in this context, the referent of the Israelites' plaint, "nothing can grow here," is not only the lack of water and food but also the death of Miriam, whose name can be interpreted as meaning from the water or the sea.[53] She led the women in dance at the Red Sea escape, and it was she who put the infant Moses's basket into the water, as well, so the association with water is one of long standing. This reading works to strengthen rather than weaken Robert Paul's claim that the Israelites long for the breast (as it were). But it also gives a more serious, less spoiled cast ("Ye rebels!" Moses says to them) to the Israelite characterization of Meribah as an "evil" place. The people are not merely appetitive, though they are that too. When they long for water, they don't long just for water. They also mourn a prophetess. Or better, when they thirst for Miriam, they long not just for mere life but also for more life. Their cries are both rebellious and funerary, appetitive and spiritual. The people mourn Miriam and say, "This is a place of death. It is an evil place for a reason, for that reason." On this reading, the episode at Meribah is one of many, from Classical Athens' Antigone to 1970s Argentina, to 1980s South Africa, in which what turn out to be political demands flows out of funerary practice and mourning, where mere life's needs open out onto more life's promise.[54] Indeed, this reading confirms but also puts some pressure on Rosenzweig's claim noted above that there are two kinds of prayer: spontaneous prayer that responds to human need (mere life) and other prayer that exists to create a need in humans (more life). In their demand for water, the Israelites respond to human need but also create a need in themselves: They express the needs of mere and more life, both. But their leaders hear only the former, the biological not the aspirational.

Interpretation is one function of the prophet. Prediction, another: "This is an evil place" means—it is an evil place (interpretation): Here Miriam died. But it is also predictive. When the people say "this is an evil place" in the mode of prediction, they mean that it might depend on how Moses responds to this new challenge. Miriam's death and the people's thirst for her and for water create opportunities for Moses. She was his rival. "Does the Lord speak only through Moses?" she had asked earlier in the exodus story, challenging Moses's hierarchy on behalf of more plural, popular, prophetic practices. For this, she was punished. The official story is that god struck her with leprosy as punishment for her dissension (her leprosy is said by rabbinic interpreters to be a sign of the corrosive effects of gossip and mistrust) and so she had to be confined, separated from the people. But the chronology, I have always imagined, was more likely in the reverse: She had to be separated from the people, and so was said to have been struck with leprosy. Whatever happened, she did not challenge Moses so directly again. With her death, Moses has an opportunity to revisit his earlier engagements with rival claims to prophecy and to respond differently, to grant the people their power, to heed their prophecy, to permit plurality. The people approach him in their own prophetic voice. But he is not up to hearing their prophetic solicitation. If he hears them at all, it is just on the register of mourning. They are thirsty? They long for Miriam? Then he will give the people what in his view Miriam gave them—not authentic prophecy, but sorcery. Not the more life of their aspirations, but the water of mere life that they seem to ask for. Because he mis-takes Miriam and the people, because he sees them only in terms of their attachment to mere life, he loses his leadership. And the people's predictive prophecy to which Moses was deaf comes to pass: This is an evil place, the place in which Moses's reward is undone, Miriam's legacy is occluded, and Aaron also dies. His death is mourned officially, for a month, by contrast with Miriam's, which is only mentioned, not mourned, at least not officially, only subtextually, and in a way most readers miss. This important chapter marks the beginning of the end of the leadership of these three siblings.

In Moses, in this episode, we see the slippage that Rosenzweig's binary distinctions occlude. We need not plot that slippage in a psychotemporal narrative that casts it, as Freud would, as a *regression* (in Santner's and Robert Paul's language). It is a slippage to which, I want to say, all prophets and their peoples are prone (although Moses may be more vulnerable to it once Miriam dies; she is not there to balance him; he may even be mourning her; hence perhaps his own vulnerability or impatience).[55] Prophets and their people test each other and slip and slide, from multitude to people, from prophet to sorcerer, and back again. That is what prophets and peoples do. As we saw in chapter 1, Rousseau knows this. Although he positions the miracle of the lawgiver's soul as his security, Rousseau goes on in bk. II, chap. 7 of the *Social Contract* to document, even as he tried to halt it, the slippage between lawgiver and charlatan and between people and multitude and between true signs and mere sorcery.[56]

Seeing the dynamic in relational terms switches our gaze from lawgiver-charlatan to the people/multitude *in relation* to the lawgiver/charlatan by whom they are solicited. In the end, as Martin Buber says of the *navi*, the prophet, prophecy is given in predictive form, but it is only a possible future, not a certain one: The people must then decide.[57] When the people decide, they do so in a context that may (or may not) acknowledge or open them to the power and experience of miracle or lawgiver. But the fact is, it is part of the structure of prophecy or miracle that the people do indeed do so; that is, the prophecy or miracle cannot happen if it is infelicitous, if it fails to be received. Like the proverbial tree falling in the woods, if no one is there to hear it, it will not make a sound.[58]

Foregrounding the people's own prophetic powers points to the importance of receptivity and agency, qualities that Rosenzweig highlights. When Rosenzweig says that "miracle and prophecy belong together," he does not equate them but he does call attention to this commonality. What Rosenzweig himself saw as the importance of miracle is its character as a solicitation, its postulate of orientation, its staging, in short, of a possible event—an encounter between human and divine.

Bilaam's Ass

Even while he insists on their fundamental connection, Rosenzweig is at pains to distinguish prophecy and miracle perhaps because the former offers only a mediated relation to the divine while the latter stands for a more direct revelation. But both share a dependence upon their audience, who need to be prepared to receive them.[59] These dimensions of prophecy and miracle are brought out by him in response to a student who asked Rosenzweig if he really seriously believed in the story of Bilaam's ass, a biblical miracle in which an ass reproaches its master, Bilaam, a non-Israelite prophet, for unjustly beating him when the animal refuses to go where Bilaam instructs him, because the animal sees what Bilaam does not—an angel of god blocking their way: "Then the lord opened the ass's mouth and she said to Bilaam, 'what have I done to you that you have beaten me these three times?'" (Numbers 22–28; two chapters after the Waters of Meribah story).

The story of Bilaam's ass is a long story, worth recounting in this context not least because the speaking ass seems so well to combine the pre-oedipal and oedipal desires already mentioned here.[60] But I allude here only to Rosenzweig's response to his student's question in a letter written to colleagues at the Frankfurt Lehrhaus. "All the days of the year," said Rosenzweig, "Bilaam's talking ass may be a mere fairy tale, but not on the Sabbath wherein this portion is read in the synagogue, when it speaks to me out of the open Torah." What it is on that day, Rosenzweig says he cannot say. He can say that it is "certainly not a fairy tale, but that which is communicated to me provided I am able to fulfill the command of the hour, namely, to open my ears."[61]

Notwithstanding the voluntaristic phrasing, "provided I am able to fulfil. the command to open my ears," Rosenzweig here and elsewhere means to point to the conditions under which such receptivity or audibility arise. These conditions recall Rousseau's material conditions of shared living as well as J. L. Austin's conditions for felicitous speech acts—in this instance, that the hearer be in synagogue, on the Sabbath, on the specific Sabbath in which the portion of the Torah that is supposed to be read is the one containing the story of Bilaam's ass, that the hearer be one of at least ten community members, in a community of similarly oriented hearers, that the reading not be theatrical, citational, or ironic, and so on and so forth. If these conditions are met, miracle may happen, which is to say, an event may be staged in which the human encounters the divine. If not, the hearer hears what can only strike him as . . . a fairy tale.[62]

The People's Miracle

In Rosenzweig, as in Rousseau, the prophet or the lawgiver tries to interpellate the people but can never succeed wholly in doing so. The leader's decision is not decisive. It fails, to some extent . . . even when it succeeds, to some extent. Santner rightly says this is because there is always a remnant that is ex-cited by the interpellation and resists its enclosure: The "people" when solicited do not respond unanimously, partly because their receptivity varies, I have focused analogously on a remainder of sovereign power (contra Schmitt and yet working within the frame of his metaphor), on sovereign power's dependence upon the decision-power of the people, on something like what Jason Frank has called the democratic state of exception.[63]

If the undecidability and/or slippage between prophecy and sorcery, miracle and magic means the people have to decide, then we have here an invitation to refigure the decision. If the Rosenzweigian miracle rather than the Schmittian one is the metaphor's ground (the decision is like the miracle, yes, but it is like Rosenzweig's miracle not Schmitt's), we see the "decision" in terms of popular orientations to the decision, its uptake, its impact, the plural, iterative effects and chains of actions begun by it, and its success, or not, in staging an encounter between a people and sovereign or prophetic powers that (as with their prophecy at Meribah) could be the people' own powers. From this angle of vision, the decision testifies to an unsettling encounter with that which disrupts the binary of ordinary-extraordinary. Sovereignty looks more contestable than in Schmitt and Agamben, more democratic, more fraught, more fragile.

From a Rosenzweigian view, we might say, sovereign are *they* (prophetic are they) who declare the exception or refuse to and/or resist its invocation in the name of an openness to something beyond or apart from the norm-exception binary, something that might disturb or unhinge that binary. Here, we are perhaps aided by a site of apparent overlap between Rosenzweig and Schmitt: Schmitt says that the exception is the power of real life breaking through the torpid crust of ordinariness. Rosenzweig would agree—but for him the exception that revitalizes must itself break through the norm-exception binary and the conception of vertical sovereignty that anchors it; it must be an exception, in short, that (as in the title of the 2006 Cornell conference) "takes exception to the exception."[64]

Beyond the binary there are intimations of alternative conceptualizations of sovereignty. Again, informed by Rosenzweig and contra Schmitt and Agamben, we can see how talk of sovereign decisionism can give the false impression that sovereign power is more dominative than it is, that it does not take its bearings from its subjects or from the contexts in which it operates, that it does not depend on uptakes of its performatives. William Connolly says that Agamben

> sometimes acts as if an account of the "logic of sovereignty" discloses ironclad paradoxes, paradoxes to be resolved only by transcending this logic. His mode of analysis engenders the eschatological logic with which it closes. Politics and culture, however, do not possess as tight a logic as Agamben suggests. They are more littered, layered and complex than that. The dense materiality of culture ensures that it does not correspond neatly to any design, form, pattern of efficient causality, or ironclad set of paradoxes.[65]

Connolly gives a pointed example of that dense materiality, illustrating sovereignty's location in a "zone of instability," when he writes about how during the Supreme Court's "deliberations" on *Bush v. Gore*, Court members and Court watchers were aware of the many Bush supporters expressing their expectation in the streets of a decision favoring Bush, and television news stations were covering that story, "frequently report[ing] that there would be a vitriolic response by Republicans if the official count went against George W. Bush."[66] (Since Connolly's writing, the HBO film *Recount*, makes the same point, powerfully.) This constellation of players—candidates, judges, social protestors, viewers—forms part of the assemblage of sovereignty, on Connolly's account. And since, as he puts it, sovereignty is always in the making and only comes into being after it claims to have performed sovereign acts (there is no "doer

behind the deed," as it were), this assemblage of players is both constitutive and invisible. It is always (almost) catching up with itself and is itself
not immune to paradox (this is a way of marking its openness or vulnerability to what Santner calls "crises of investiture" and to what Connolly
and I explore under the term the paradox of politics). This approach to
sovereignty breathes life into Agamben's otherwise tightly closed paradox of the logic of sovereignty.

One task of democratic theory is in some ways like that of Franz
Rosenzweig's liturgical practice: to prepare us, to help identify or imagine
or attune us to the openings and solicitations and limits of sovereign
power. Democratic theory identifies obstacles to such openings, like the
work of logics that seem to clarify matters but actually or also freeze action. Opening up alternatives, Connolly says: What would have happened to the *Bush v. Gore* decision

> if a militant electorate [all by itself that term—"militant electorate"—enlivens
> the democratic imagination, packing activism and accountability into repre-
> sentation in a powerful way], insisting that the essence of democracy requires
> a concerted effort to count the votes accurately in a close election, had boycot-
> ted work, blocked expressways with cars and trucks, refused jury duty and
> otherwise interrupted everyday life?[67]

Such an interruption would interrupt the Schmittian-Agambenian binary
of norm-exception itself.

If the exception is like the Rosenzweigian miracle not the Schmittian
one, then the miracle serves not as an imposition, not as an exemplifica-
tion of top-down sovereign power, not as a source of political unification
and cohesion, not as a rupture in the normal order; or perhaps it is better
to say, it risks being all these things but not only these: For it is also an
invitation for which diverse members of the assemblage of sovereignty
need to be differentially prepared and rightly or well oriented. Or else, it
will turn out to have been that the sovereign decision in any moment was
not a miracle, but a fairy tale (as Rosenzweig said of Bilaam's ass). And
fairy tales, as we know, can be pretty scary.

In place of such fairy tales, a different story has been told here: a story
of popular prophetic power. Schmitt may have aimed to undermine precisely this option when he metaphorized the decision as miracle qua sovereign prerogative. He not only cemented a certain notion of sovereignty
thereby, he also occluded one thing to which miracle also points even if
inadvertently: the people's role in popular prophecy and the central importance of their receptivity to power. The role of the people has been
missed because it is usually cast as "stiff-necked resistance," a casting
taken at face value by readers of the exodus story for generations. This,
however, is the Mosaic perspective on the matter. Even Freud adopts it;

so does Michael Walzer. But what if we exodus that exodus and abandon thereby or at least rework what Santner calls Egyptomania? What if what looks like resistance to Mosaic or divine law might also be a struggle to establish a different law, a different sovereignty—one that, like Rosenzweig's miracle, might seek to break rather than merely inhabit the torsion of norm-exception by which all sovereignty seems to be marked in various ways?

The figure of the would-be sovereign assemblage, bearer of a counterlaw, issues an invitation to identify not with Schmitt's oedipal father-sovereign but with some hitherto unappreciated implications of the Mosaic family romance. Freud's Moses, an Egyptian, imports into the Israelite community a notion of rule that is vertical and monotheistic and alien.[68] It is alien, in any case, to an alternative that was certainly also indigenous to this people, an alternative represented by a tradition of popular prophecy personified by Miriam on my reading here and later represented by Rosenzweig as a trait of post-Mosaic communal Jewish life in the Diaspora. Michael Walzer, who does not subscribe to Freud's retelling of the Moses story, sees a hint of that alternative within the Mosaic tradition itself when he notes Moses's wish that all the people should one day become prophets.[69]

Unlike the divine sovereign ruler of Rosenzweig's providential universe who does not deal in univocal signs lest he impinge on the freedom of his creations (as I noted above), the would-be sovereign rulers of our own political world are not so self-limiting.[70] Sovereign power does not normally accede to its own overcoming, does not delight in the freedom and resistance of its subjects. Here the contrast between the realities of politics and the fantasies of theology is striking. Several rabbinic tales tell the story of the people's resistance to god and end with god's satisfaction at being beaten, outfoxed, or outreasoned yet again by these stubborn headstrong people he chose. Moses called them "ye rebels." God does on occasion threaten to wipe them out and begin anew. This is his Leninism. (Michael Walzer *contrasts* the exodus model of liberation with the Leninist model of revolution but there is *in* the exodus story this Leninist moment. Walzer notes the moment, he concedes that purges have a role in reshaping the people from a slave population to a free nation, but he stops short of seeing the continuity here with the Leninism with which he elsewhere in the same book contrasts the exodus story).[71] Moses, playing good cop here to God's bad cop but they take turns in these roles, talks him out of it by arguing that if God wipes out the people he will have to also erase Moses's name from his Book. God gives in—outfoxed this time not by his people but by their lawgiver.

But in the post-Mosaic world of rabbinic Judaism, God is said by the Rabbis in some such instances (not all!) to cherish these impossible people in their very impossibility as "my children." Perhaps the most famous episode in which this occurs involves the meaning and status of miracle, and it is therefore with this story from the Talmud that I end this chapter.

Rabbi Eliezer and the Sages debated a point of law regarding the ritual purity of a certain type of oven. Rabbi Eliezer declared it clean, and the Sages declared it unclean.

> Rabbi Eliezer went to great lengths to persuade his colleagues, but failed. Finally, he gave up persuasion and resorted to demonstration, saying: "If the law agrees with me, let this carob-tree prove it!" The carob-tree moved a hundred cubits out of its place. (Others say, four hundred cubits.) Said the Sages: "No proof can be brought from a carob-tree."
>
> Again he said to them: "If the law agrees with me, let the stream of water prove it!" Whereupon the stream of water flowed backwards. Said the Sages: "No proof can be brought from a stream of water." Said Rabbi Eliezer: "If the law agrees with me, let the walls of the study hall prove it!" Whereupon the walls inclined to fall. But Rabbi Joshua rebuked the walls, saying: "When scholars are engaged in a halachic dispute, what have you to interfere?" Hence they did not fall, in deference to Rabbi Joshua, nor did they resume the upright position, in deference to Rabbi Eliezer; and they are still standing thus inclined. Finally, Rabbi Eliezer said to his fellows: "If the law is as I say, may it be proven from heaven!" There then issued a heavenly voice which proclaimed: "What do you want of Rabbi Eliezer? The law is as he says!" Rabbi Joshua stood on his feet and said: "The Torah is not in heaven! . . . We take no notice of heavenly voices, since You, God, have already, at Sinai, written in the Torah to follow the majority."[72]

This story does not deny revelation in the abstract but rather, as it were, to its face on behalf of human self-sovereignty and the goods of proceduralism as laid out in the Hebrew Bible by God. (As I noted above, Rosenzweig elsewhere comments on the irony of human autonomy as a gift from God. There seems to be less irony in it when the gift is proceduralism but the aim here, no less than there, is autonomy.) This resistance may not be the best model for a theology that, Rosenzweig insists, seeks not a domesticated proceduralized divinity but rather an alien god for the sake of revelation. But is it a good model for a democratic politics?[73] That all depends on how we read the ending: For that is not the end of the story. How could it be? Were the story to end here, we might be left with a sense of unease about this legalistic coup d'etat, the rabbinic declaration of a state of legal exception to the divine rule of god, the victory of the ethical over the metaethical subject, all concerns that would apply equally well to the rabbinic strategy, discussed in chapter 3, to put an end to Judaism's death penalty by way of hyperlegality. Here, however, the story continues, perhaps seeking to reassure or put us at ease.

Years later, in the afterworld, Rabbi Nathan subsequently met Elijah the Prophet and asked him: "What did God do at that moment?" [Elijah] replied: "He smiled and said: My children have triumphed over Me, My children have triumphed over Me."[74]

This is the Rabbis' version of the Freudian story, in which the sons kill the father and eat him. In the rabbinic version, the father takes pleasure in the son's violence against him. A projection to be sure, perhaps even (to recall Rosenzweig) a fairy tale, but then democratic politics depends upon such projections and tales.[75] And as projections go this one may not be a bad one for democratic politics, in which the people must often counter their infantilization by sovereign power and somehow engage or democratize sovereign powers that present themselves at least some of the time as divinelike, beyond engagement, beyond the reach of the people and immune to their prophetic powers.

Resisting the irresistible, demanding accountability from those who present themselves as beyond such demands, taking exception to the exception, enacting collective life otherwise: These are elements of democratic political practice. They do not occur in a vacuum. On Rosenzweig's account as on Rousseau's, they depend upon immersion in forms of life that orient people toward alien pasts and promising futures. So immersed, we may find that we, the people, *are* the sands of time. Those grains that slipped through the court timekeeper's glass in Goethe's Italy could do so only one at a time. Bound together, they would have stopped time. Similarly, the *people* when bound together can arrogate to themselves the rights of states: The people can make time stop too. The *people*, always also a multitude, may even begin a new time in which we can see clearly that what is most decisive is not, contra Schmitt, the decision, but our orientation to it, and most important of all, our (non)complicity in it.

Chapter Five.

Proximity

PARADOXES OF LAW

AND POLITICS IN THE NEW EUROPE

> If a "not yet" is written above all redemptive union, the only
> result can be that, for the end, it is, at least to begin with . . . the
> neighbor [the well-nigh nighest] who is precisely there. . . .
> [W]here someone or something has become the neighbor of the
> soul, a part of the world becomes what it was not before: soul.
> —*Franz Rosenzweig*

IN *Another Cosmopolitanism*, Seyla Benhabib promotes the idea that recent developments in international institutionalism evidence the growth
of what she calls cosmopolitan norms. She turns to an emergency to set
the stage: Genocide serves as her synecdoche for several new legislative
and normative trends in human rights, especially in Europe. Noting the
lack of appropriate institutions with which to try Adolf Eichmann in
1961, Benhabib presses upon her readers the need to support international tribunals now. But the lens and mood set by Eichmann and genocide set us up to relate in a certain way—in a mode of dependence and
felt need of rescue—to the project of interstate law and cosmopolitan
norms that Benhabib here seeks to promote. It is problematic in a way
that recalls the question posed by Bernard Shaw to Mike Dukakis in the
1988 American presidential election campaign: (something like) "what
would you want done to the perpetrator, if your wife was raped and mur-
dered?"[1] Dukakis's dispassionate response, in which he said he would
want the perpetrator to be tried, underscored for the electorate what was
seen as his passionless bureaucratic character. But the problem was with
the question, not the answer. One is thrust by the specters of genocide,
rape, and murder into extremes of (il)legality: passionate vendetta or
sober, fair judicial process.

If Benhabib begins and ends *Another Cosmopolitanism* with the concern about genocide and the need for institutional accountability for it,
that may be because she senses greater consensus on that particular issue
than on some of the more intractable issues of multicultural politics that
she discusses in the pages in between. She hopes the divisions of multicultural politics may become less intractable if they are adjudicated by way

of the universal norms that condemn genocide and to which, on Benhabib's account, the new International Criminal Court gives expression. In short, Benhabib's intention is to enable widespread acceptance of new developments in EU law that she sees as expressing moral condemnation of intolerance from genocide to multicultural politics. But, although universal outrage against genocide may seem a promising ground for a new cosmopolitanism, Benhabib's universal norms also insulate us from the urgencies of contingency and contiguity out of which solidaristic progressive politics often arise. If those who happen to be here have no more claim on us than those far away, or if their being here can only "count" once it has passed a test of universalizability, then the impulse to act in concert with them simply because they are here is attenuated and indeed delegitimated. The same goes for those who are distant, physically, but with whom we feel neighborly in the sense of sharing a common cause. Here, Rosenzweig's idea that in "the just present moment, the universal and highest [is represented] by the approximately proximate" is potentially very powerful, as I will suggest below.

The politics of genocide has not, in any case, always produced the unanimity Benhabib seeks. Benhabib opens and closes *Another Cosmopolitanism* by invoking Hannah Arendt, the democratic theorist to whom she and I are in different ways indebted. The Hannah Arendt with whom she opens is in dialogue with Jaspers in 1960 regarding the need (shared by Jaspers and Arendt but felt more keenly by him) for international institutions to try Eichmann for war crimes. Arendt expressed hesitations about the "impaired" quality of the justice meted out at Nuremberg and then at the Eichmann trial in Jerusalem. Her hesitations are overcome by Benhabib who casts the establishment of the new International Criminal Court in 2002 as itself a fulfillment of the promise of those initial, partial efforts and as an instance of the sort of inaugural action that Arendt theorized and praised in *The Human Condition*, *On Revolution*, and elsewhere. This is the second Arendt, the Arendt with whom Benhabib closes *Another Cosmopolitanism*, the theorist of revolutionary beginnings who sees politics as an opportunity for actors to inaugurate a "*novo ordo saeclorum.*"[2]

But would the Arendt who expressed concerns about the impaired quality of the Eichmann trial have agreed with Benhabib's endorsement of a new normative and juridical universalism? True, Arendt bemoaned the absence of appropriate institutions with which to try Eichmann. And she did criticize the Israeli court for trying Eichmann on the wrong charge —crimes against the Jewish people rather than crimes against humanity. This may be why Benhabib believes that the new international court along with the new moral fact—prohibiting crimes against humanity— together answer to Arendt's earlier concerns. But Arendt's analysis of the

Eichmann trial did not stop there. These two criticisms are part and par-
cel of a third, in which Arendt not only noted the imperfections of the
trial, she also tracked the trials's political impact or effects. She asked not
only, "How are they trying Eichmann?" but also always, "What are they
doing by trying Eichmann? What political ends is this trial serving?" The
urgency of the moment, the need to do justice in response to the Holocaust, did not obviate these political concerns. For this she was seen, perhaps predictably, as insensitive or even treasonous. And in some ways,
she was. Her portrait of the Eichmann trial is unforgiving in its detail, and
the acidity of her judgments is to this day sharp.

Her readers were offended by many things, especially by her sugges-
tions that Jewish complicity was an issue in the genocide. This seemed to
undermine Nazi culpability while also manifesting a deep failure to understand what people do when pressed to focus in the barest possible
terms on survival as mere life. Many readers were also offended by Arendt's relentless insistence on the politicality of the trial. For Arendt, the
Eichmann trial, in spite of the fact that it was needed and not completely
invalid but only impaired, nonetheless was a way also for the still new Israeli state to establish its own legitimation as a nation state by casting itself as protector of international Jewry and seeker of justice for the crimes
of the Holocaust. It is in this context that Arendt's other two criticisms—
wrong charges (crimes against the Jewish people), wrong setting (Israeli
court in Jerusalem)—are significant. The trial provided the State of Israel
with an opportunity to further nationalize itself as a state, and this dealt
yet another blow to Arendt's already dashed dream of a binational state
of Israel in which Palestinians and Jews would share power. This is the
reason for Arendt's scathing criticisms of Gideon Hausner in the early
pages of *Eichmann in Jerusalem*. Indeed, her halfhearted wish for an international criminal court, expressed in the form of a lamentation of its
impossibility, was not simply a wish to escape from politics as such into
a really neutral or just realm of law.[3] Or that's not all it was. It was
(whatever else it was) a way to highlight and criticize the part played by
the Eichmann trial in a larger politics of state-building to which she was
opposed.

So the question is: Would Hannah Arendt—if she were writing now—
have any less political an analysis of the formation of the EU and the use
therein of law, courts, and bureaucracy to promote and consolidate a
particular conception of Europe as a political form? Would she be any
less likely now than then to ask not just "what can we accomplish through
law on behalf of human rights?" but also "what new political formations
are advantaged and legitimated thereby?" Her example suggests not. It
suggests that she would assess new international norms, laws, and institutions not simply as good or bad solutions to an earlier problem, but

also always as political maneuvers in their own right. In this particular instance, I imagine she might see the developments tracked by Benhabib as signs of welcome developments in human rights. But Arendt would not stop there. She would also, I believe, ask whether these developments might not also be part of an effort to consolidate a certain conception of Europe and promote it over other contenders. Thus, rather than treat the Arendt who wished for appropriate international institutions to judge Eichmann as if she were fulfilled or satisfied by the inauguration of to-day's new norms and institutions, we might do better to see in Arendt's example a demand that we assess emerging new orders in the most relent-lessly political and critical terms. Arendt offers a valuable example of the double gesture often called for in political engagement when she criticizes the politicality of the Eichmann trial while nonetheless affirming its im-perfect justice.

Working from a perspective that owes much to Arendt's political analy-sis in *Eichmann* and is indebted as well to the work of Jacques Derrida, I look at recent developments in Europe focused on by Benhabib. Benhabib works her views out by way of Kant's idea of a right to hospitality. I begin with Derrida's own reading of that right, for it motivates an alternative to Benhabib's neo-Kantian cosmopolitanism. That alternative is often termed "cosmopolitics," and, as I argue here, it is better served by Rosen-zweig's idea of neighborliness than by neo-Kantian universals over which the neighbor, as such, famously has little claim.[4]

Hospitality and Rights

As with many of the concepts he deconstructs, including the gift, justice, forgiveness, and democracy, Derrida casts hospitality as belonging to two discontinuous and radically heterogeneous orders, conditional and un-conditional, whose conflict and asymmetrical necessity render ethical-political life (im)possible. There is no question of a choice that must be made between one order and the other, between the conditional and the unconditional. Nor is there a fundamental compatibility between the two such that, for example, one is legal and one is moral or one is specific and the other generic, in which case the latter could subsume the former and make sense of it or complete it. Rather, the two orders or concepts coexist in "paradoxical or aporetic relations . . . that are at once heterogeneous and inseparable."[5]

Unconditional hospitality postulates a giving without limit to the other, an infinite openness that both enables and jeopardizes one's capacity to host another.[6] Conditional hospitality, by contrast, postulates a finite set of resources and calculable claims. It is "the only one . . . that belongs to the order of laws, rules, and norms—whether ethical, juridical, or political—at a national or international level."[7] In this second order of hospitality, distinctions must be made and limits set, lest hospitality be extended to or demanded by everyone and encompass everything to a point at which the would-be host would be dispossessed of the very property and scope that enable him to offer hospitality to the dispossessed other.

Kant delimited hospitality (to the right of those washed ashore to be permitted visitation or offered refuge) precisely in order to avert this risk of dispossession and thereby secure, by limiting it, the duty of (conditional) hospitality. Derrida, by contrast, insists we see what the averted risk itself intimates, that against which we cannot inoculate ourselves: That those who claim a right to hospitality are positioned inevitably in an ambiguous and undecidable terrain marked by both hospitality and hostility. Elsewhere he also notes that the French term for hosts (*hôtes*) is the same as the term for guests, denoting another register of undecidability.[8] The undecidability of host/hostility and its ethicopolitical implications are erased, not expressed, by an analysis like Benhabib's that identifies *hostility* with one singular principle—ethnos, or republican self-determination, or state nationalism—and *hospitality* with another that is distinct and apart: Enlightenment universalism. The division of host/hostility into two distinct and opposed binary options cleanses hospitality of its fundamental undecidability and misleadingly casts the threat to universal hospitality as something that always comes to it from some distinct and unrelated outside.[9] The mutual implication of host/hostility, by contrast, illustrates the persistent trace even in our own most cherished ideals of that which we seek to overcome.[10]

Any right to hospitality is caught in the aporia signaled by the two orders, the one heterogeneous to the other, and yet necessary in some way to it. And Derrida points out, although "*unconditional* hospitality [is] impossible . . . heterogeneous to the political, the juridical, and even the ethical . . . the impossible is not nothing. It is even that which happens, which comes, by definition."[11] One way to think (part of) this thought might be as follows: Any particular right to hospitality takes its motivation, its energy and animation, not just from a finite economy of right, a moral law, universal human rights, or a particularist ethics, but also and problematically from the infinitude of the unconditional hospitality that is both expressed and betrayed by any proclaimed table of values or by any enacted right to or gift of hospitality as such.

The distinction between the unconditional and the conditional might illuminate from a new angle Arendt's famous call for *the right to have rights*.[12] This is a call in the name of an unconditional order of rights, something that is quite distinct, as she herself makes clear in her reading of *Billy Budd* and elsewhere, from such tables of rights as universal human rights, the Rights of Man, or EU charters.[13] The right to have rights is itself a double gesture: It is a reproach to any particular order of rights (albeit certainly to some more than others) *and* a demand that everyone should belong to one such order.[14] A double gesture is necessary because, paradoxically, we need rights because we cannot trust the political communities to which we belong to treat us with dignity and respect; however we depend for our rights upon those very same political communities.[15] Are we helped out of the paradox by locating the ground of rights in a different, higher order of belonging, such as international institutions? Yes and no. Having another place to go to, to appeal when you lose in one venue, is a good thing. But being able to so appeal still presupposes a belonging whose fragility those very same rights are supposed to protect us against. In the international arena no less than in the national, rights still presuppose belonging, now not only to states but (as in Benhabib's depiction) also to a legal, bureaucratic and administrative order or to the EU.

The unconditional—Arendt's right to have rights—is a way of marking the fact that no venue and no armory of rights (conditional, contingent), no matter how broad or developed or secure can represent the subject's absolute value in economies of rights-adjudication that are at once contingent, communal, legal, judicial, bureaucratic, moral, administrative, governmental, and discretionary. And there is no way out of the paradox of rights, though awareness of it can inflect our politics in useful ways. Indeed, Arendt's right to have rights—a polemical, political call—directs our attention repeatedly to the need for a *politics* whereby to express and address the paradox as it is experienced by minorities, the stateless, the powerless, and the hapless.

Benhabib also wants to endorse a politics in response to a paradox that she wants *not* to resolve but to ease. For this she turns to what she calls "democratic iterations," particular culturally or politically inflected enactments of universal or cosmopolitan norms. One way to assess the differences between her approach and that developed here is by comparing each one's distinct diagnoses of the current situation. From a vantage point shaped by awareness of the conditional/unconditional and modeled on Arendt's own call for the right to have rights, things look more ambiguous than in Benhabib's account.

For example, although Benhabib is right to point out the great promise for democratic citizens in the development of Europe's newly porous borders, in new recognitions of extracitizen human rights and alien (but still membership-based) suffrage, and in extrastate fora to which state-based injustices can be appealed, it is also the case that a focus on these developments misleads as does the casting of these developments as signs of an increasingly capacious normative universalism.[16] The new porousness of territorial borders among EU countries has been accompanied in recent years by the erection of new, not at all porous borders inside the EU. The hosts are not only welcoming; they are also hostile.

And this is no accident. In France, for example, as postcolonial immigrants exercise their option in recent years for French citizenship or legal residency, those who do not fit the profile of the proper citizen are subjected by formal and informal state agents to police or administrative control and informal intimidation. When policed postcolonial subjects, only some of them *sans papiers*, are constantly asked for their papers, this renders fraught and fragile the place of all postcolonial immigrants, residents and ethnic minorities in the territory to which some of them are now said to belong, in some sense under French and EU law. Is it not significant that at a time of new economic pressures a new class of worker is created, an always already criminalized population that is unable to access the resources of law and rights that are at that moment expanded? Criminalized populations are often quiescent. But they sometimes take the risk (riskier for them than most) of politics, as the *sans papiers* movement has demonstrated. What that movement also demonstrated is that in practice if not in law, French residents are now repartitioned not along the formal juridical line—undocumented/documented—but along racial lines. Many are moved by the situation to joke cynically that their *cartes d'identites* are their faces, their skin/color. Etienne Balibar names the new racialized political order "apartheid in Europe."[17]

In this Europe, formal law lives side by side with, but is also both aided and undercut by, an administrative police state apparatus and a xenophobic public that legalists disavow at their peril. (These points may ring familiar to readers of Arendt's insightful analysis of the situation in interwar Europe.)[18] Benhabib, however, in the second lecture of *Another Cosmopolitanism*, "Democratic Iterations: The Local, the National and the Global," focuses for the most part on formal law—state and regional powers, commissions' rulings and court decisions.[19] She has a formalist's understanding of law as independent of and prior to politics:

> The law provides the framework within which the work of culture and politics go on. The laws, as the ancients knew, are the walls of the city, but the art and passions of politics occur within those walls and very often politics leads to the breaking down of those barriers or at least to assuring their permeability.[20]

Although Benhabib's call to break down the barriers between law and politics by way of politics seems to attenuate law's autonomy, it does the opposite. It posits a chronology in which law is, first, prior to politics and capable therefore of providing a framework for it; then, second, law is corrupted by politics; and finally law is brought into the political arena in order to wrest from law (in its limited democratic or republican form) payment on its universal (context-transcendent, i.e., extrapolitical) promise:

> It is only when new groups claim that they belong within the circle of addressees of a right from which they have been excluded in its initial articulation that we come to understand the fundamental limitedness of every rights claim within a constitutional tradition as well as its context-transcending validity.[21]

A view of rights as always pointing beyond themselves is deeply attractive. But to what do they point? Not to an open futurity dotted by new or emergent rights that may generate new forms of life, such as that explored in chapter 2. Rather, Benhabib assesses new rights in terms of their fit with molds and models already in place, incomplete, but definitive in their contours. Notwithstanding her commitments to reflexivity and revisability written about in detail elsewhere, what changes in Benhabib's practices of democratic iteration is the subject's relation to universalistic categories, not the categories themselves: The universal stays universal, the particular stays particular. Benhabib notes:

> [I]t is clear that all future struggles with respect to the rights of Muslim and other immigrants will be fought within the framework created by the universalistic principles of Europe's commitments to human rights, on the one hand [but what evidence could put their universality in doubt? What principle?], and the exigencies of democratic self-determination on the other.[22]

Although she treats the universal and the particular as two moments in a dialectic, the two are not equal. One overcomes the other: Universality represents a *principle*; democratic self-determination an *exigency*.

With Europe's commitments cast as universalistic (in theory if not in practice, Benhabib might concede; but then something in her theory prevents the practice—racial stratification, police-state style policing, and so on—from being seen as significant evidence regarding the theory), there is little room to take seriously the sort of concern aired by Derrida in *Of Hospitality*: "the foreigner who, inept at speaking the language, always risks being without defense before the law of the country [or region] that welcomes or expels him; the foreigner is first of all foreign to the legal language in which the duty of hospitality is formulated, the right to asylum, its limits, norms, policing, etc." Here the paradox of politics reemerges, for, "He has to ask for hospitality in a language which by definition is not his own."[23] For that request to be heard, for it to be audible, the hospitality in question has to always already be extended to the speaker. It has to be given before it is asked for or in spite of the fact that (and, indeed precisely *because*) the request for hospitality is incomprehensible, or dangerous. This is hospitality's unconditionality. It is risky.

That is why it is always partnered with its conditional, risk-assessing, partner: conditional hospitality.

The unconditional makes no promise about our future, and it inspires and haunts every conditional order of rights. From its vantage point, we wager that every political-legal settlement generates remainders, no matter how progressive or expansive that settlement aims to be. This is in no way to suggest that all orders are equal from this perspective; only to suggest that even those that are better than others still depend upon the supplement of a politics that is different from Benhabib's dialectically iterative politics. From the vantage point of the unconditional but not from that of Benhabib's universal, for example, even a full realization of universal human rights on earth would be seen to necessitate further political work, generating new claims, each of which would make its own universal appeal, perhaps on behalf of those forms of life remaindered by the order of universal human rights, which would itself be in its instantiation a conditional order.[24] Benhabib by contrast would see such further claims as coming from a particularity in need of education or adjustment, one in want of appreciation for that full achievement of universality. Put a different way: If we expect hospitality always to harbor a trace of its double—hostility—then proponents of hospitality will always be on the lookout for that trace and its remainders. The same goes for universalism or cosmopolitanism. And that wariness will surface in our politics, often in the form of a double gesture, in which the promises *and* risks of a particular conditional order of hospitality (and universalism or cosmopolitanism) are named and confronted.

The Double Gesture's Paradox

Benhabib's idea of democratic iterations is her response to paradoxes that afflict her cosmopolitanism. The paradox of democratic legitimation, key to Benhabib's critical reading of Rousseau and her turn to Kant as we saw in chapter 1, reappears in her later work on cosmopolitanism, but it shifts. The paradox of democratic legitimacy slips into the paradox of bounded communities when Benhabib says the paradox of democratic legitimacy is "the necessary and inevitable limitation of democratic forms of representation and accountability in terms of the formal distinction between members and nonmembers."[25] In fact there are two paradoxes or, as Benhabib puts it in her first lecture, "The Philosophical Foundations of Cosmopolitan Norms": "On close examination, we are dealing with a dual paradoxical structure." She restates the paradox of democratic legitimacy so that it again resembles the version we looked at earlier in chapter 1: "that the republican sovereign should undertake to bind its will by a series of precommitments to a set of formal and substantive norms, usually referred to as 'human rights.'" This is a paradox between liberalism (universal human rights) and democracy (republican sovereign). The problem of membership is now cast as a different distinct problem, not between democracy and its others but rather "internal to democracy, namely that democracies cannot choose the boundaries of their own membership democratically." This "paradox of bounded communities" is an "anxiety that must be faced by any serious deliberative democrat."[26]

The paradox of bounded communities is actually a product of the deliberativist commitment to a certain universalism, though Benhabib would not put it that way. "Because the discourse theory of ethics articulates a universalist moral standpoint, it cannot limit the scope of the moral conversation only to those who reside within nationally recognized boundaries; it views the moral conversation as potentially including all of *humanity*." Boundaries themselves require moral justification, since "membership norms impact those who are not members precisely by distinguishing insiders from outsiders, citizens from non citizens." The problem is: "[E]ither a discourse theory is simply irrelevant to membership practices in bounded communities in that it cannot articulate any justifiable criteria of exclusion, or it simply *accepts* existing practices of exclusions as *morally neutral* historical contingencies that require no further validation."[27]

The second paradox captures a somewhat different problem than the first. The first worried that a majority could betray its legitimacy by willing the wrong thing, that democracy could be immoral by failing to will only universalizable legislation. In the second, the concern is that those defined as the majority by the happenstance of boundaries are arbitrarily relevant from a moral point of view. The focus here is not on what is decided but rather on who is doing the deciding. This shift in focus is welcome because it calls us to consider more centrally than did the paradox of democratic legitimation the politics of membership and solidarity. It also calls attention to a problem with universalism. In the first paradox, universalism solves the problem (or tries to) by insisting that the people's will must be universalizable. Here in this second (version of the) paradox, universalism is *causing* the problem: It is from the perspective of universalism that proximity, community, territory, and boundary are morally *ir*relevant. So a world in which these contingencies still define life chances, as indeed they do in our world, is subject to the paradox of bounded communities if we take a universalist perspective: How can a people morally constrained to will universalizably premise that willing on nonuniversalizable contingencies of membership? The answer, Benhabib says, is that the conflict between particularity and universality, between membership and cosmopolitan norms must be mediated by democratic iterations and by international and national law with the aim, she says, not of exiting the paradox but rather of relaxing it. As sovereign states adopt increasingly cosmopolitan constitutions, and citizens internalize cosmopolitan norms, the paradox will be further eased.[28]

I favor a different, two-pronged strategy that does not draw for its solution on the very thing—universalism—that is causing the problem. First a democratic politics should be committed to diminishing international inequalities so that it would matter less from a moral and material point of view where one was born. Such a response highlights the power relations that govern the international sphere and subject some nations and nationals to the will of others. But since this first strategy can never be entirely successful and there will always be differences of power and privilege associated with different locations, a second strategy is needed to respond to that inevitability. The second strategy seeks not to ease but rather to embrace the paradox of bounded communities by supporting action on behalf of those contingent neighbors who just happen to be here for no good universalizable reason (though they are often "here" for known reasons of political history—as the slogan goes: They came here because we went there). At the same time, of course, we must realize that proximity and neighborliness are no longer dictated alone by spatial nearness. We have global neighbors as well. Democratic activists enter into coalition with those near and far. Some become our neighbors as a result of the way pollution, consumerism, and capital cross borders. Shared challenges make neighbors out of us, putting us into common cause with those who might otherwise have been distant. Recall the discussion in chapter 1 of how the American colonists and revolutionaries cannily *expanded* the distance between themselves and the king by pretending never to have received sovereign instructions sent from England. Here, too, we see that distance is not a fact, as it were. It can, conversely, be shortened by way of political work as well.

It matters whether we relate to those near or distant under the sign of universality or under the sign of the neighbor. Indeed, I suggest, those who move to universalizable norms to ground a sense of moral connection and obligation may find that the promise of contingent connections of geography or common cause are undone not solidified by a universalist morality and politics that attenuate such connections and insulate us from the call of the other. Universalism may seek to ground human rights, but human rights also postulate the very memberships and proximities with which universalism is ill at ease, as Hannah Arendt knew. This second strategy points to the need for a "double gesture" that both affirms the values of universal human rights (the equal dignity of persons) while calling for forms of action that may seem to violate that universality at the same time, as when we act on the basis of geographic or political proximity in solidarity with those who are near just for that reason— because they are near.

Such double gestures are necessary because, in any case, rights are not enough. When Benhabib points out that over time second-class members of democratic regimes, like women and African Americans, have been brought into full possession of formal rights, she does not note that these subjects have still never come to bear those rights in the same way as their original bearers. Her optimism is supplemented by her assumption of progressive, evolutionary time, as when she characterizes the second-class status of colonial American Jews as "transitional" (en route to what?).[29] This is a tempting narration, and a familiar one, in which supposed systems of rights are (to borrow Habermas's term) "tapped" as liberal democracies take the protections and privileges they first limited to propertied white males and then spread them outward to encompass all classes, races, and genders. It is from this perspective that the status of colonial Jews looks transitional. But that is not how colonial Jews would have described their status. The speaker here, unlike those in the moment, speaks as if she already knows that the human rights side of the democratic legitimation paradox will in the end win, even though we are not yet at the end of the story nor could we ever be and so cannot ever know who or what wins in the end.

In Benhabib's text, the constitutive tension central to her argument is a bit more past than present, with universality positioned toward a (cosmopolitan) future and particularity toward a (Westphalian) past. Discussing the French veiling controversy, for example, Benhabib says of the girls who stood up for their "cultural rights" that having learned to "talk back to the state," they will likely one day learn as well to "talk back to Islam."[30] Here Benhabib's cosmopolitanism seems to be firmly in the paradox of politics. Does it not both presuppose and promise citizens who do not yet exist? These citizens negotiate state and cultural powers on behalf of universal human rights that are themselves (again) both the condition and the goal of liberal democratic statehood in a cosmopolitan setting. But Benhabib breaks the vicious circle, first by staging it as a conflict between universality and particularity (returning us to the paradox of democratic legitimation as she has recast it here in her lectures) rather than between or within democratic freedom and democratic (self-)sovereignty, and then by inserting the amended paradox into a time sequence: She wagers that these young women will likely "talk back to Islam" too one day and thereby show in the course of historical time that they have learned democratic and cosmopolitan citizenship. The prediction

of eventual Islamic cultural self-overcoming confines the paradox of politics to a particular historical moment, not to a past moment of founding
perhaps, as we saw in chapter 1 was the move attributed by Connolly to
Rousseau, but to a present precosmopolitan moment whose eventual,
promised, overcoming is what underwrites *our* affirmation of *their* cultur-
alism now.

Whether or not this wager is right (a great deal depends upon domestic
and international developments in France, Europe, and the Middle East,
not simply on the trajectory of rights) is less important than the work the
wager does. The wager privileges the backward-looking gaze of a still future cosmopolitanism. We assess the present from the perspective of a
posited future in which the particularities of the present are overcome.
That temporality anchors the chrono-logic of rights, the quasi-logical unfolding of rights in accordance with the sequencing demands of linear,
normative progress (*Das Weltgeschichte ist das Weltgerichte*), and it also
occludes from view impositional and violent processes that help secure
such developments when they do occur. Benhabib is aware of current xenophobic policies but she does not worry that any coming cosmopolitanism may be not just obstructed by them but itself partly produced by
them. She does not worry that cosmopolitanism might carry the traces of
beliefs and practices it is said to oppose. That is, she does not ask whether
such policies might both violate and also help to produce the projected
coming of a (post-)cultural cosmopolitanism.

From the perspective of Benhabib's history of democratic (trans-)statism
as a history of expansion and increasing universalization, we simply do
not see that which does not fit its linear time trajectory: for example, the
history of disenfranchisement. In the Jim Crow South, newly won juridical rights were rendered nugatory by local political intimidation and a
failure to secure and enforce the political and material conditions of
rights-taking. In the United States and Canada resident alien voting was
once an uncontroversial practice, but it was ended by World War I–era
xenophobia. Historically, it is worth noting, alien suffrage occurred without all the things that Benhabib sets up as necessitating it now: border attenuation, pressures on state sovereignty, and extranational institutions.[31]
Faced with the prior practice of alien suffrage, it is hard to think of recent
EU gains in alien suffrage as the latest in a line of serial expansions earned
by our progressive tapping of the system of rights.[32]

For example, it is hardly insignificant that when the idea of alien suffrage appealed to the province of Schleswig-Holstein in 1989, the aliens
to be empowered to vote were all citizens of northern European countries
while the new minorities putting the most pressure on traditional German conceptions of citizenship at the time were from the more liminal

borderland of Turkey. And it is significant that recent debates in Europe about the social rights of aliens, specifically about whether "we" should share our social welfare with "them," have occurred in the last two decades at the very moment at which European social welfare rights have been downsized. Depictions of foreigners as those who want to come "here" to take "our" welfare have worked to reassure western Europeans that they still have social welfare worth taking (which they may, by comparison with others, but which they do not by comparison with themselves thirty years ago). This is one of the ways in which xenophobic politics is not just negative but also productive.

Where the unconditional focuses our gaze on the remainders of new and established orders, Benhabib does see those remainders but does not assess them as such, that is, as *remainders*. She knows that at the very moment in which "the entitlement to rights is" expanded, "the condition of undocumented aliens, as well as of refugees and asylum seekers . . . remains in that murky domain between legality and illegality," but she does not read this remnant as a *remainder produced in part by* the conditional order of universal hospitality (as I myself have been suggesting, though other forces are at work too).[33] Instead, her language suggests, the problem is that some people have been left passively behind by an imperfect but still progressive cosmopolitan law, in which case appeals to human rights commissions and exercises of cultural political interventions may correct the wrong and result in a truer universalism. She subtly puts us onto a temporal register in which this limit is always already about to be overcome. From that register, we are in no position to ask whether these remainders are the direct products of the political project of Europe-formation which is, we might note, not only a vehicle whereby national belonging is transcended, but also a way to resecure national belonging: In a time when claims to national belonging, say, in France, are being made by non-Europeans, the political (re)formation of Europe as a site of belonging is surely a way to resecure and not just attenuate or transcend national belonging. As Derrida points out in *The Other Heading*: "I am (we are) all the more national for being European, all the more European for being trans-European, and international."[34]

The challenge then is to see the situation in all its ambiguity and from that vantage point to intervene in ways that claim Europe for a different present, for different futures, for different constituencies, for a different politics. The challenge is to open up room for the much-needed double gesture: For example, one might oppose the constitutionalization of the EU in the name of an alternative, locatable, and accountable rule of law, to counter that future with another in the name of the very democratic and human rights that constitutionalization has historically *claimed* to entrench, and to do all this without being cast as a mere agonist or defender of national particularity, or as a member of the National Front, as if these were the only options (naysayer versus lawgiver, NF or EU).[35] Or one might argue in favor of such constitutionalization while seeking to embed in it counters to its own gravitational pull to centralized sovereignty, as the U.S. founders thought they had. We know however, from that very example, that no charter can deliver on its promises of stability and accountability without an activist politics to risk and secure them.

The same challenge of the double gesture is incited by Benhabib's treatment of sovereignty. Here the very same evidence that allows her to speculate hopefully but cautiously that "the conflict between *sovereignty* and *hospitality* has weakened in intensity" could also suggest that sovereignty is on the contrary in the process of being shored up, transformed into something altogether new.[36] The new openness Benhabib endorses can just as well be a sign of sovereignty's adjustments, accommodations, and relocations—from visible peripheral borders to less visible internal ones (city/suburbs, French/Algerian, Catholic/Muslim/Jewish/secular), from states to regions or from states weakened by globalization to states reempowered by their new, sometimes fraught membership in regional associations, like Europe, that restore nationalist fervor or salvage it while also perhaps attenuating or redirecting it and working to secure the continent's peripheral borders in ways that mime old state sovereignties.[37] Just as the problem of refugees to which Benhabib briefly alludes may not be (just) a *problem* for state sovereignty but rather *or also*, as Nevzat Soguk argues, an *occasion* for the refinement and enhancement of state power, so too the problem of refugeeism in Europe, testified to by the many refugee camps lined up on both sides of Europe's old and new borders, may serve as a sign of the new continental sovereignty of the EU.[38] Here, Giorgio Agamben's suggestion regarding state sovereignty may motivate a new analysis as well of the EU: What if refugees, rather than (or in addition to) being the exceptions of the juridical state (or continental) system, are metaphorically its norm, the exemplary objects of the sort of power that the state system and its sovereign legalism represent but hide—bio-power and its rule overall as bare life?[39] The risk of such an analysis, as I argued in this volume's introduction, is its disempowering interpellation of citizens into the (for many of them, imagined or exaggerated) subjection of emergency sovereignty. But there is also a gain to be had: Agamben does not allow camp existence to be dismissed as an exception to the human rights rule but rather insists on the disturbing possibility that in the camps we find what Hannah Arendt said was perversely postulated by universal human rights as such: the biopolitics of, in Agamben's language, bare life or, in my language, the mere survival of mere life.

New Facts, Old Norms

Benhabib says she is led to cosmopolitanism by the new empirical facts of state sovereignty attenuation in the late twentieth century. A lot *has* changed in recent years. But the "facts" are not univocal; they are subject to widely varying interpretation, as I have been demonstrating here. Indeed, Benhabib's turn to cosmopolitanism seems to me to have been in some sense overdetermined by other factors. Long before cosmopolitan norms were on their agenda, Habermas and his followers sought a solution to the paradox of democratic legitimation (what happens when the people on whose will the legitimacy of a regime rests will the wrong thing?), another version of which serves as Benhabib's point of departure. They found that solution in various forms of statism (including the rule of law), which they relied upon to preserve deliberative democratic norms and procedures from the caprice of the people, or local majorities. Concerns about the undemocratic nature of the statist solution got vented in the 1990s by way of analyses of the paradox of constitutional democracy that I discussed at length in chapter 1, a paradox that in failing to name the state, as such, as a problem for democracy, covered over the real concern while also giving some vent to it.[40] Because there are now concerns about the state's caprice—most especially about state-sponsored violence and injustice—a new paradox of democratic legitimation, a new version of the one discussed in chapter 1, which pits cosmopolitanism norms against republican self-determination, surfaces as the problem that has to be solved in these lectures. (All of Benhabib's examples in her second lecture, "Democratic Iterations: The Local, the National and the Global," are of state-based injustices agitated against by local and transnational agents and agencies.) But although it surfaces as a problem, the new paradox of democratic legitimation is really also working as a solution, the solution to the last paradox's now problematic solution: statism. In short, at each register, universalism seeks a new harbor: liberalism, constitutionalism, state institutions, and now—cosmopolitanism. But no harbor is safe. (Sound familiar? It is the story Hegel tells in the *Philosophy of Right*.) That is, of course, because the universal is never really as we imagine it to be: truly unconditional, context-transcending, and unmarked by particularity and politics.

In the end, statism is not really overcome. Benhabib applauds three girls from Creil for having learned to "talk back to the state," but the applause is to some extent contingent on the likelihood that they will therefore learn also one day to "talk back to Islam" and therewith affiliate better with the proper universalism of the French state and the EU. But those three girls from Creil did not act alone; they were fronts for an organization, a social movement represented in Benhabib's text by M. Daniel

Youssef Leclerq, head of Integrité and former president of the National Federation of Muslims in France. This is for Benhabib an indication that the girls' gesture was a "conscious political" one.[41] That may be. But it also indicates something else: The girls appeared in the public realm as the effects of a social movement no less than Rosa Parks did when she supposedly spontaneously one day out of the blue simply refused to move to the back of the bus.[42] It is a trick and a victory of statist law and politics in liberal democracies to ascribe to individuals those significant actions that are products of a concerted politics. Rival sovereignties, oppositional movements, and political dissidence are thereby erased from view and we are left only with small individuals (three girls) or large phantoms (Islam, radical particularism, etc.).

Benhabib does not dwell on the role of social movements in these cases of "democratic iteration," and absent that, it is hard to tell what's democratic about them. It is also hard to tell what's "iterative" about them. The term, in the hands of Derrida whom Benhabib cites here, signifies a drift and residue, a ruptural quality of language as such; hence "iteratibility" (not iteration) is his term, connoting something different from the subject-centered practice suggested by Benhabib's term "democratic iterations." Derrida meant to call attention by way of iterability to a quality of language and practice that pushes terms and concepts always to exceed and undo the intentions and aims of any particular speaker in time; this would include the languages of law and even universality itself.[43]

Iterability, as Derrida theorizes it, is not inconsistent with the notion that the women in the French veiling controversy should have been "given more of a public say in the interpretation of their own actions."[44] This is Benhabib's suggestion in response to the concern that "the meaning of [the girls'] actions [was] dictated to these girls by their school authorities."[45] I do not disagree. But the suggestion does highlight the agent-centered quality of Benhabib's view of political action and performativity. For, unlike iteration, iterability presses upon us awareness that such public say cannot control the semantic field. If the veil looks "backward" to some French citizens, appears offensive to others and legitimate to still others, that is the shape of the political battle, a battle in which the girls should of course take part. By privileging the girls' interpretation of their actions because the actions were "their own," Benhabib rightly seeks to enhance their agency and correct for their exclusion from the interpretative field. What Benhabib does not note is that such inclusion, while necessary and perhaps promising, is also fated to replay the conflict.

Indeed, one of the issues for the school authorities was precisely whether the girls' action was "their own." This concern cannot be allayed by moving from action to justification; it will rather almost certainly be replayed. The same questions that were posed about the false consciousness of the girls' action will now be posed about their post hoc account of themselves: Is their explanation their own? Their interpretation authentic? This is one of the key points in dispute for the players, after all: Were the girls pawns or were they autonomous actors?[46] Benhabib herself slips into the morass when, in order to argue that the girls' act was a "conscious political" one and not a manifestation of false consciousness, she points out that they were working with the head of Integrité, M. Youssef Leclerq. She infers from their involvement with Integrité that the girls' actions were consciously political and autonomous. But this fact also allows observers to come to the opposite conclusion, that the girls' actions manifest not autonomy but heteronomy, because their association with Leclerq implicates the girls in his agency and agenda, not their own. This is a problem for a politics of democratic *iterations* but less so for an analysis focused on iterability. Iterability has us focus not on the autonomy of the players but on the play of meanings and dissemination. That the girls should have a voice in that and that they can and should *claim* their actions as their own is indisputably clear. But agonistic political theorists more focused on diagnosing the stuckness of such situations than in generating norms to govern them see that something more than the equal inclusion of all players is needed—movement politics, action in concert, new coalitions and pressure groups—if we are to move beyond this conflict and its eternal return.

Agonistic Cosmopolitics

An alternative cosmopolitics oriented by the unconditional order of hospitality prizes proximity and might join Benhabib on several fronts, including her endorsement of the reinhabitation of the French Marianne by postcolonial (im)migrants. But a cosmopolitics might also unsettle elements of her universal human rights agenda. For example, it might adopt a hyperlegalist critique of state violence in the name of the rule of law while also resisting the legalists' project of constitutionalizing the EU. These seemingly contradictory moves would be made in the name of those human rights more likely to be attenuated than secured by the EU's constitutional order and in the name of a more engaged, accountable democratic politics than that thus far identified with the EU, hampered until now by the famous "democratic deficit" that is unmentioned by Benhabib.[47] Such a double gesture is characteristic of an "agonistic cosmopolitics" by contrast with Benhabib's normative cosmopolitanism. In chapter 2, I discussed an example of this—the battle by Slow Food, an activist food politics group that ably plays the globalization game, to support sustainable food production by creating global markets to local producers. With that same goal in mind, Slow Food also resists EU standardizations that harm local food producers and privilege the largest players in the mass food and agriculture industries. Slow Food never loses sight of questions like Arendt's: What interests are advanced or advantaged by certain institutional innovations? And, more broadly, what new worlds are brought into being thereby? What will we lose if we win?

An agonistic cosmopolitics locates itself squarely in the paradox of politics—that irresolvable and productive paradox in which a future is claimed on behalf of peoples and rights that are not yet and may never be. Arendt's unconditional right to have rights is as good a motto as any for that project, as long as we understand rights to imply a world-building that is not incompatible with the project of building juridical institutions and safeguards but also reaches beyond that project because it is wary of how power and discretion accrete in such institutional contexts. In the name of such a right to have rights and motivated by the doubly gestured diagnoses developed here of in/formal law and politics as they are operating in early twenty-first-century Europe, an agonistic cosmopolitics might call for: the enactment of underground railroads devoted to the remainders of the state system, such as refugees (Michael Rogin); or the designation of some spaces as cities of refuge (but not camps) such as Jacques Derrida called for (following the recovery of them by Emmanuel Levinas, who commented on the biblical injunction to establish six of these in Israel); or we might stand up for *droits de cité*, a demand to extend full hospitality to refugees and other nonimmigrant border crossers simply because they are here.[48]

The phrase "Simply because they are here" rejects the legitimationist demand that some justification be given for privileging those who are proximate. The Habermasian concern on this front is with "the paradox of bounded communities" that Benhabib says must be attended to by any "serious" deliberative democrat. The worry encapsulated in this paradox is that it is an arbitrary matter who is in and who is out of this particular community that now has to hold itself responsible for universalizable legislation that will apply, however, only to this contingently bounded community. But there is in fact no problem of logic here, only a political problem introduced by the particular form of the demand for universality made by Habermas and his followers. Another way of thinking universality might see proximity not as a problem but as an opportunity, not as an artifact of the contingency of boundaries, but as a device for their attenuation. This or something like it is what Franz Rosenzweig is after when he thematizes neighbor-love which he characterizes, in Eric Santner's parsing, as a process of "ensoulment" in which we "by acts of neighbor-love—small miracles, as it were, performed *one by one*[—]mov[e] from one neighbor to the next (rather than by way of a love directed immediately to *all* humankind)."[49]

In a passage quoted at the head of this chapter, Rosenzweig himself richly puts the point:

> If a "not yet" is written above all redemptive union, the only result can be that, for the end, it is, at least to begin with . . . the neighbor [the well-nigh nighest] who is precisely there. . . . [W]here someone or something has become the neighbor of the soul, a part of the world becomes what it was not before: soul.[50]

Here the neighbor presents not a moral problem to be solved (Why him and not someone else? What justifies that?), but an ethical and political opportunity to be acted upon. The former justifies, as Bernard Williams points out, or it paralyses, as does all philosophy on Rosenzweig's account (as on Wittgenstein's), but the latter propels.

Thus, qua acts of neighbor love, we can enact *droits de cité*—by taking people in, harboring them, offering them shelter, finding sympathetic agents of discretionary power who are willing to look the other way—while also risking the reauthorization of law's authoritative institutions by working through them to win papers or amnesty for those who are here—simply because they are here; then the poor migrants and refugees living in that murky space mentioned by Benhabib will not be so dependent on law to position them with more clarity in its network. Then they will not have to wait for their time to come, and a good thing too—because it won't. For even when our time seems to have come, time can nonetheless still subject us to its trickery.

"This is a story about the trickery of time," is the first line of an article about Ibrahim Parlak, a Kurd from Turkey and a would-be immigrant to the United States who was held for almost a year in detention and was almost deported to no-country as a result of the recasting of his past by post 9/11 politics and by likely abuses of discretionary power that postdated his previously approved applications for asylum in the United States. Post hoc, Parlak was cast as a terrorist but this has not yet erased from his neighbors' memories his decade-long membership in a Michigan community.[51] The activism of his many friends and supporters—his Michigan neighbors—prevented him from becoming one of the disappeared, a casualty of policing and immigration policies that we now think of as post-9/11, even though they were also pre-9/11: The Antiterrorism and Effective Death Penalty Act of 1996 played a role in his recasting, though again, due to time's trickery, even that legislation, a response to the Okalahoma City bombing, is now often assumed to be part of our post-9/11 landscape, in which the emergency is *foreign* terrorists, not

domestic ones. A federal court ordered Parlak set free on bond on May 20, 2005. Two years later, Parlak was preparing to appeal his deportation by the Department of Homeland Security's Immigration and Customs Enforcement Office, and the Department of Homeland Security had appealed the federal court's decision to free Parlak on bail, and lost, and was filing a motion to vacate the judge's order on a technicality.[52] Meanwhile a group called Free Ibrahim formed. Their slogan? "Ibrahim for Citizen." They succeeded in getting Senator Carl Levin and two representatives to introduce two bills in the House and Senate to make Parlak a permanent resident should he fail to prevail in the courts.[53]

In this set of events, I discern a connection hinted at by Rosenzweig one hundred years ago. In his remarks on neighbor love quoted above, Rosenzweig took advantage of a pun in German and put proximity and urgency into connection. As Santner points out: The German for neighbor, *der Nachste*, is shifted in the passage from Rosenzweig's *Star* to *das Nachste*, as in the well-nigh *nighest,* a term that connotes now not proximity but urgency. The pun is apt, not because urgency is never distant but because when it is proximate, we often find ways to reason our way out of action. The need is greater elsewhere; what justifies my actions here? Or, their proximity to me here is illegitimate and illegal. Why should they gain from breaking the immigration queue when others wait legally? Or, we must work through the proper channels. These concerns are not wrong. These worries about consistency and principle are important. But they undo the compelling call of the neighbor. That is their troubling remainder.

An agonistic cosmopolitics would approve of movements like Free Ibrahim and of those that demand alien suffrage for coresidents—"because they are here." They made their own "lucky break" (language I borrowed in chapter 2 from Lear via Santner) and can serve as ours and we as theirs. But an agonistic cosmopolitics requires also that we at the same time work to prevent the energies of our political movements from being lost once our state-centered and state-affirming goals are won: Thus, such a politics postulates ongoing activisms. We might join with those working to diminish the desperate global inequalities that are among the reasons people are set in motion; we might work globally to sustain local economies that can thrive, a goal set as well by Slow Food. Or we might declare our cities to be sister cities in solidarity with cities from other nation states, thus inaugurating all sorts of extrastatist relief, aid, trade, and learning between us.[54] Or within the juridical domain, we might see more citizens of privileged nations marrying, instrumentally, those who seek to live among them in order thereby to enable their fellow world-dwellers to stay on as their neighbours and, as a nice by-product, thereby deromanticizing *two* institutions insistently romanticized and still claimed by most states as their monopoly, both marriage and citizenship.[55] Practices such as these and others are designated by Étienne Balibar, who draws on Bodin, as "marks of sovereignty," in a move meant to take Bodin and democratic sovereignty back from the state sovereigntists.[56] Such practices are jurisgenerative in Robert Cover's sense perhaps more than in Benhabib's because, although she does not mention it, the jurisgenerative in Cover's account is always partnered with the jurispathic.[57] Generativity without destruction is no more possible for Cover than is hospitality without hostility for Derrida.

Were all this to happen and be visible to us (for it does happen but it is often not visible) through lenses that do not *privilege* (although they do take note of and seek to engage, improve, and democratize) formal legal, state, statelike, and interstate institutions, then we might see more worldliness, in Hannah Arendt's sense of care for the world. For, contra Benhabib, Arendt is no "Kantian in moral theory." Arendt's Kant is that of the Third Critique, not the Second. Moreover, Arendt is not nor are postmodernists (so-called) "*skeptical* that political norms can ever be judged in the light of moral ones."[58] Arendt has a critique of that.[59] Arendt did have a juridical moment in relation to Eichmann; who wouldn't? Benhabib is not wrong to suggest that there is in Arendt a persistent legalism that is on display in her *Eichmann in Jerusalem*.[60] But the limits of that trait in Arendt's thinking are also on display in *Eichmann in Jerusalem*, perhaps most when Arendt derisively dismisses the survivor, K-Zetnik, for his inability to testify coherently before the Israeli court. In Arendt's cutting portrayal of this man's failure, the ruthlessness of her legalism is as apparent as its tone deafness, its inalertness to context.[61]

For Arendt, the chief political virtues are worldliness and care for the world; and these are in danger of being marginalized and sidelined, in my view, by versions of cosmopolitanism in which law, states, statelike and interstate institutions are our principal addressees (in all of Benhabib's examples), our guardians, ventriloquizers, impersonators, shapers and censors of our voice, our desires, our aspirations, our solidarities. Under the sign of worldliness, however, and in the name of neighborliness, potential commonalities might emerge between a normative cosmopolitanism like Benhabib's and an agonistic cosmopolitics. They may share a common motivation and a common cause: to work through the paradox of politics in order to combat the abundant forces of inequality in our world. Committed to the view that all institutional settlements generate remainders, an agonistic cosmopolitics is committed to the perpetual generation of new sites of action in concert on behalf of worlds not yet built or on behalf of those still emergent and in need of activist support and sustenance.

Thus, some differences remain even when the differences between Benhabib's position and my own seem to disappear:

> The democratic dialogue, and also the legal hermeneutic one, are enhanced through the repositioning and rearticulation of rights in the public spheres of liberal democracies. The law sometimes can guide this process, in that legal reform may run ahead of popular consciousness, and may raise popular consciousness to the level of the constitution; the law may also lag behind popular consciousness and may need to be prodded along to adjust itself to it. In a vibrant liberal multicultural democracy, cultural-political conflict and learning through conflict should not be stifled through legal maneuvers. The democratic citizens themselves have to learn the art of separation by testing the limits of their overlapping consensus.[62]

These are Benhabib's words. To "the art of separation" I would marry *"the craft of recombination."* Against and together with the idea of raising popular consciousness to the level of the constitution, I would promote the need for an aconstitutional politics as well, to raise constitutions to a new consciousness. What each of us might mean by rearticulation of rights surely differs, as I have argued in detail here.

Postscript

In a response to my response to her Tanner Lectures, Benhabib attributed to me an antistatist governmentality-centered Foucaultianism: "For Honig, neither the state and its institutions nor the law and its apparatus can be sites of democratic iteration and emancipatory politics." I am said to endorse "movement politics" and to manifest "hostility toward institutions."[63] The charge of antistatism is also a charge of nonseriousness.[64] The latter charge is made explicit later—"political struggles which address the state and its institutions . . . mean *getting serious* about the political by engaging with it at all levels of state, law and civil society."[65] To ignore the state is, perforce, to be lite, marginal. It goes to the heart of what we think we are doing as political theorists. Do we aspire to write constitutions for emerging democracies, influence sitting judges with amicus briefs, map out agendas, be part of the action, point the way forward? Or will we editorialize from the sidelines, write critiques, diagnose our stuckness, and call for the double gestures that best engage the complexities of the current situation?[66]

The precise phrasings in my original reply to Benhabib belie the charge of antistatism.[67] The state and its institutions are always our addressees. They wouldn't have it any other way. But when they are our addressees, when they self-privilege as our most important addressees, we are called—

indeed interpellated—into and by their perspective and we lose hold of our capacity to imagine politics otherwise. There is nothing "holier than thou" about pointing this out, surely.[68] It is one of the many double binds of political action in the contemporary world.

To use the term interpellation is risky. It is, Benhabib says, "old Althusserian language."[69] But for me, it continues to capture something no newer term does: the ways in which our entire being is swept up in the address of the state and its agents, even in anticipation of such address. Not just that of the police, though they are pretty good at it, but also immigration agents, passport control, transportation safety employees, the internal revenue service, health insurance agents, and so on. One of the things progressive democratic activists must do is to join those swept up in those interpellations, as Louis Post, the subject of chapter 3, did and called others to do, and help engage these institutions: Elect different representatives, protest institutional injustices, educate members and demand accountability, and strive for better legislation and demand better court appointments.

Engaging the state is a feature but not the essence of democratic politics. The choice between social movements and a more juridical politics focused on state and transnational institutions is a false one. To focus on institutions of governance without a foot in movement politics and critique is perforce to perform juridical politics differently than would otherwise be the case, without the balancing perspective of a life lived otherwise. It is to be left vulnerable to the self-privileging perspective of statism and its formalisms. Louis Post, assistant secretary of labor under President Wilson, proceduralist and antisecuritarian foe of J. Edgar Hoover, was also a Henry Georgeist Progressive with professional, personal, and political connections to anarchist politics. Post had had occasion to meet, talk, and work with communists and anarchists well before the First Red Scare and was able to resist Hoover's securitarian perspective partly for that reason: Post was acquainted with those Hoover wanted to demonize and Post had imagined the world otherwise, living out an alternative in the world of dissident politics.

Juridical politics is always in need of the support and orientation of life lived in political movement. In addition to engaging state and transnational institutions directly, democratic actors must also, and not as a secondary matter, in some ways begin living now as if we had already succeeded in that first endeavor. This is the lesson of the paradox of politics. Otherwise we get locked into the eternal agon of small (or even large) institutional victories and never do what we want those institutional changes for and what can and must happen even in advance of those victories—live otherwise or, better, move from mere life to more life. Better to get on with the business of what Franz Rosenweig might have called neighborliness and what Hannah Arendt called action in concert. In so doing, we do not ignore or sideline the state. But we insist—and we remind it and ourselves—that it does not exhaust life. Louis Post's story illustrates how the practice of neighborliness can be undone by the need to engage the state in its politics, in order to survive its politics. Post's battle to survive took the place and usurped the energies of his progressive political agenda. Here survival, as mere life, conflicted with the aspirations of survival as more life. That this is a valid concern is one of the insights buried in Arendt's controversial distinction between labor, work, and action. In *The Human Condition*, Arendt details the threats posed by labor and work to the honorific action. In *On Revolution*, however, she sees less of an opposition between ordinary life and extraordinary politics.

In chapter 1 we saw how, on Hannah Arendt's account, the most revolutionary thing that the American revolutionaries did they did long before the revolution occurred. More important than their protests and challenges to the king, more weighty than any tea party, was the experiment in living they undertook alongside sovereigntist politics, an experiment whose reverberations moved from the margins to the center of an empire and succeeded in becoming an institutional revolution because the form of life it presupposed had somehow been magically, through the daily work of life, brought into being *avant la lettre*. Some changes do need to be argued and fought for on judicial or formal institutional terrains. But they also need to be lived. From a democratic theory perspective, neither tactic is more serious or central or important than the other and both carry risks. The work of institution-building simply cannot succeed without the support and perspective of life lived otherwise, without the supplement of orientation promoted by Rosenzweig and the undecidable, difficult gift of proximity.

Benhabib, in her reply to me, claims Derrida for her argument:

> Ironically, Derrida himself is far from splitting the political into the unholy realm of the state and its institutions and the angelic realm of social movements. He states: "[T]he political task remains to find the best 'legislative' transaction, the best 'juridical' conditions to ensure that, in any given situation, the ethics of hospitality is not violated. . . . To that end, one has to change laws, habits, phantasms, a whole 'culture.'"

Benhabib concludes: "Changing 'laws, habits, phantasms and a whole culture' is not contradictory to seeking the best legislative and juridical practices."[70] She is right; there is no contradiction here and I have nothing against seeking the best legislative and juridical practices nor do I think social movements are "angelic." A lot of them scare me. But in seeking the best legislative and juridical practices, we must be mindful of how such endeavors press us to make our cases and envision ourselves and our political futures in terms quite different from those we might otherwise imagine and seek to vouchsafe. That is a concern that Benhabib simply does not share. She sees law as regulative not productive. I note here that Derrida, but not Benhabib, places the terms "culture," "legislative," and "juridical" all in scare quotes. Why? Perhaps it is the "phantasms."[71]

Still skeptical of Althusser, Benhabib says, "Honig practices the method of ideology critique and shows that every universality is afflicted by particularity and difference which, in turn, it must repress. But if this is an ideological truism, how does its repeated deployment help?" It is not an ideological truism, however. Rather it is a conclusion drawn again and again from the study of particular would-be universals in action. As we track the work of Benhabib's universals in her neouniversalist cosmopolitanism, we can see through a close reading of her work how the universal operates in a way that does not simply mediate the political but also triumphs over it in ways she seems to approve.[72] More important, however, throughout this book I mean to be arguing *in favor* of something like the repeated deployments dismissed here. The repetition of critique could be a symptom of repetition compulsion, which is what Benhabib implies with her criticism. But it could also be a sign that the critique bears repetition, that in spite of the claim that we have moved on, we in fact continue to repeat our old errors or remain stuck in our old habits, a point made by Nietzsche who mourned the fact that although we have killed god we continue to dwell in his old houses.[73] What choice do we have, in such instances, but to repeat and redeploy our critiques? Besides, we need not assume that repetition is like dead ritual. If we repeat our criticisms and engagements as Rosenzweig counsels us to repeat daily liturgy, we may find we ourselves are reshaped by the exercise. If we repeat our concerns always in new ways with new resources in relation to new texts or new political events, we do so not in order to win the argument but rather in order to illustrate again and again the stakes of winning or losing it and to reshape ourselves as subjects into its proper bearers.[74] In other words, one way to assess the merits of a political theoretic position is by inhabiting it for long enough to see the world through its perspective and assess that world. This is what I have tried to do here.

Aftermath

And afterward? What happened afterward? What should I write
about now? About the way that a great experience comes to an
end? A melancholy topic, for a revolt is a great experience, an
adventure of the heart. Look at the people who are taking part in
a revolt. They are stimulated, excited, ready to make sacrifices.
At that moment they are living in a monothematic world limited
to one thought: to attain the goal they are fighting for. Everything
will be subjugated to that goal: every inconvenience becomes
bearable: no sacrifice is too great. A revolt frees us from our own
ego, from that everyday ego that now strikes us as small, non-
descript—alien. Astounded, we discover in ourselves unknown
energies and are capable of such novel behavior that we ourselves
look on with admiration. And how much pride we feel at being
able to rise so high! What satisfaction at being able to give so
much of ourselves! But there comes a moment when the mood
burns out and everything ends. As a matter of reflex, out of
custom, we go on repeating the gestures and the words and want
everything to be the way it was yesterday, but we know already—and the discovery appalls us—that this yesterday will
never again return. We look around and make another discovery:
those who were with us have also changed—something has
burned out in them, as well, something has been extinguished.
Our community falls suddenly to pieces, and everyone returns to
his everyday I, which pinches at first like ill-fitting shoes—but we
know that they are our shoes and we are not going to get any
others. We look uncomfortably into each other's eyes, we shy
away from conversation, we stop being any use to one another.
—*Ryszard Kapuściński*

THE ABOVE QUOTATION from Kapuściński's book on the Iranian revolution captures one version of the "lucky break" in which the everydayness
of life is overcome or decentered and something great happens. But in the
end, this particular event was more "break" than "lucky," a democratic
rupture that lacked staying power. Kapuściński's passage, which seeks to
describe the melancholy mood of the aftermath of revolution, is itself
melancholic. Ordinary life reasserts itself, with a bit of a vengeance, as it
were, and the thrilling moment of non-egoic life is over. Here the melan-

choly tone is added to by the reader's knowledge of what came to pass since the toppling of the Shah: the erection of an oppressive theocracy.

The end of the moment of action, as Kapuściński describes it here, is true. From his prose, one can feel (really, one recognizes with a certain discomfort) the sense of embarrassment that permeates a community that knows it can do better because it just did do something great even though it has given up its aspirations, its dreams, and—in Kapuściński's memorable image—put its old, ill-fitting shoes back on. Decades of acculturation are not easily undone. Political action is both thrilling and exhausting, and although it energizes its bearers, at some point the energies for it run out. At that point, we need a lucky break—a piece of contingent good fortune, a miraculously decent lawgiver, an infrastructure that happens already to be in place, an event not dependent on our own spent energies. Somehow we are sometimes visited by a dividend not a deficit, more life not just mere life. If it comes, and if we are lucky enough to receive it rightly, some experience of democracy may be ours for a more prolonged moment. If not, we will have experienced what we may come to call a miracle, but only the ruptural kind. That is not the sort Rosenzweig had in mind when he identified the miracle with *freedom* and hoped it might launch us into more life, knowing that only if we were already so launched could we experience the miracle as such.

The task of democratic theory is to identify such breaks where we can, explore the conditions of orientation and preparation by way of which best to receive or agitate for them, diagnose the reasons for our frequent unavailability to such breaks when they do occur, and work to prolong them and make them part of our everyday. This was Rosenzweig's project with the holiday.[1] Although he was not exactly a democratic theorist, I take these to be among the aims of his philosophy. The reasons for our reluctance or inability to pursue democratic intimations may include material interests, which may run counter to greater democratizations. Other reasons may also include felt isolation as well as various practical limitations or failures of imagination. Emergency settings only aggravate and accentuate the ordinary ways in which we retrench from the more life of democracy into the mereness of mere life. Thus, the standpoint of emergency casts into sharp relief issues of long-standing concern to democratic theory and action.

The preceding chapters have tracked some of the conceptual resources seen by many political theorists to offer great promise to democratic theory and practice (universal human rights, the agency of law, faith in progress), while identifying the ways in which their promise also constrains the democratic imagination in regrettable ways, limiting opportunities for progressive democratic practice, pressing us in conservative directions. This does not mean that we should reject universal rights, agentic law, and faith in progress. It does mean, however, that reliance on these resources must be located in a (counter)politics of more life and must be part of a "double gesture" that is attentive to their remainders. In the space of the double gesture's both-and we are located in a necessarily paradoxical politics. Hence the importance of sensitizing ourselves not just to the stuckness of paradox and the mere life of emergency but also, as I have sought to do in this volume, to the potential generativity of paradox and the mere and more life of democracy.

Notes

Preface

1. Carl Schmitt, *Political Theology*, 5.

Introduction

1. Williams, "A critique of utilitarianism," in *Utilitarianism: For and Against*. I have elsewhere discussed these examples in detail, focusing on their productive differences, noting in particular that the one resolvable dilemma is set by Williams in the homeplace of England while the other more truly tragic and irresolvable dilemma is set in an unnamed country in South America. I argued that the two examples together work to produce in us a sense that if we stay home, geographically and morally, we will be less prone to encounter tragic situations. The political processes whereby home is constructed as a safe space are occluded by the two examples in tandem, which work to encourage moral agents to stay home rather than put themselves at risk—politically, morally, and geographically. Home is thereby naturalized, as is its corollary in the agent: integrity, the chief consideration in light of which, Williams argues, moral agents in tragic situations should decide what to do. Here I offer a different reading of Williams's examples than on my earlier account, enabled by my application of the theory to democracy rather than the self. I here treat the two examples as staging a developmental moral psychological education that is germane to a democratic self-understanding. For my earlier critical engagement with Williams's treatment of tragic situations, see my "Difference, Dilemmas, and the Politics of Home." For a heartfelt critique of my earlier argument, see Iris Marion Young, *Intersecting Voices*, chap. 7: "House and Home: Feminist Variations on a Theme."

2. Honig, "Difference, Dilemmas, and the Politics of Home."

3. Williams, "A Critique of Utilitarianism," 117. When Williams counsels George to stay home, it is worth noting, Williams both partakes of and stands against the comforts of home. Home insulates us against the violence of its maintenance (see Minnie Bruce Pratt, "Identity: Skin, Blood, Heart"). Williams takes advantage of this by sending George home but he also takes a stand against it by counseling George not to take a job whose implication in violence might have been subtle enough to disavow (as most of us do when we buy goods every day that were made in China).

4. This pun on Kingsley Amis's *Lucky Jim* conjures up a review by Roger Kimball ("Reputations: 'Lucky Jim' at 50," *New York Sun*, April 12, 2004, Arts and Letters, 15), which opens with the following line: "Somewhere obscure and unpleasant—a desolate village in South America, perhaps—there lives the publisher who turned down Kingsley Amis's first novel, 'Lucky Jim,' for 'not having alive or exciting enough characters.'"

5. Williams, "A Critique of Utilitarianism," 117.

6. Williams, "Moral Luck."

7. Honig, "Difference, Dilemmas, and the Politics of Home." Still, it is important to acknowledge that individual integrity in the sense of a principled refusal to compromise one's commitments is, as I demonstrate in chapter 3, a source, often enough, of political integrity. Integrity in government is often shown, as George Kateb reminds me, "when role-imperatives are subordinated to the individual decency of a few."

8. On this see my discussion of Rawls on punishment in *Political Theory and the Displacement of Politics*.

9. *Korematsu v. United States*, 323 U.S. 244, 245 (1944).

10. Clinton Rossiter, *Constitutional Dictatorship*.

11. I discuss this concept in detail in *Political Theory and the Displacement of Politics*, chapter 4, drawing on Derrida's "Deconstruction in America." See also Derrida, "Living On."

12. Emily R. Wilson, *Mocked with Death*.

13. Derrida, "Deconstruction in America," 24–25.

Chapter One

1. He also refers to the paradox of politics as the paradox of sovereignty, the paradox of political founding, and the paradox of politics-sovereignty in *Political Theory and Modernity*, *Identity/Difference*, and *The Ethos of Pluralization*.

2. Connolly, *The Ethos of Pluralization*, 138.

3. Ibid., 137.

4. Rousseau, *On the Social Contract*, bk. I, chap. 7; Johnston, *Encountering Tragedy*, chap. 4.

5. Paulo Virno uses these terms to cast the difference between people and multitude, and calls for renewed attention to the latter, which for him is "a category of political thought which, having been defeated in the theoretical debate of its time, now presents itself again as a most valuable instrument for the analysis of living labor in the post-Ford era" (44).

6. Benhabib, "Deliberative Rationality and Models of Democratic Legitimacy," 28, 29, 30. Benhabib's phrase, "if they were properly enlightened" telegraphs her preference for Kant over Rousseau, for Rousseau's lawgiver does not so much enlighten the people—they seem to have trouble understanding what he is talking about ("the legislator is incapable of using either force or reasoning" [*Social Contract*, bk. II, chap. 7])—as set the agenda and embed the people in material conditions that enable them to coalesce around properly general willing (e.g., he limits the size of the polity, ensuring that all members know each other).

7. Here, as Lefort and others have pointed out, it seems that the "people" try and fail to take the place of the king, in symbolic terms. Under the French monarchy, since the king could do no wrong, injustices were attributed to corrupt advisors or to the queen and her circle. Thus during popular uprising, violations of law were said to be done in the king's name, "*par l'ordre du roi.*" Taylor refers

to the "myth that the good king had been betrayed by his local agents and officers," which, he says, is "age-old." Lefort, *Democracy and Political Theory*, 15,
20; Taylor, *Modern Social Imaginaries*, 127.

8. Rousseau, *Social Contract*, bk. II, chaps. 3 and 6.

9. Ibid., bk. II, chap. 3, cited in Benhabib, "Deliberative Rationality," 28.

10. Benhabib, "Deliberative Rationality," 29.

11. Keenan, *Democracy in Question*; Johnston, *Encountering Tragedy*.

12. Arendt, *The Origins of Totalitarianism*, 106–17.

13. Rousseau, *Social Contract*, bk. II, chap. 6.

14. Honig, *Democracy and the Foreigner*.

15. Habermas, *Between Facts and Norms*, 354–59.

16. Fitzpatrick, *Modernism and the Grounds of Law*, 74.

17. In *Democracy and the Foreigner*, I argue that some of the models of Rousseau's lawgiver were foreign founders so as to mark this lingering foreignness to
a people even of good law. Honig, *Democracy and the Foreigner*, 29–30; cf. Hans
Lindahl, "Sovereignty and Representation in the European Union," 113: "[W]hile
every polity necessarily refers to its origin as 'its own,' the origin remains forever
alien to it."

18. Benhabib, "Deliberative Rationality," 29–30.

19. Honig, *Democracy and the Foreigner*, 21; Keenan, *Democracy in Question*, 17; Fitzpatrick, *Modernism*, 83.

20. *Social Contract*, bk. II, chap. 7.

21. Bennington, *Legislations*, 222.

22. After Mu'awiya's death, his son, Yazid, defeated Ali's younger son Hussein in
battle and then formed the hereditary Ummayad dynasty. But Hussein's son Ali survived to continue that familial line as well. Around these two lines, were formed the
distinct Shia and Sun'ni branches of Islam. Thanks to Noah Whinston on this point.

23. *Social Contract*, bk. II, chap. 7.

24. Bennington, *Legislations*, 222.

25. *Social Contract*, bk. II, chap. 7.

26. In *Democracy and the Foreigner*, I fault Bennington for ignoring the lawgiver's foreignness to focus on other signs of the figure's undecidability (136 n.
27). I also suggest, contra Bennington, durability *can* function as a sign, since the
people are rarely in a pseudocontractual position of deciding in advance on the
authenticity of the lawgiver anyway. They are more likely to be reconsidering
post hoc whether they want to reaffirm their allegiance to the law(giver) by which
they were formed, and in that setting durability can be a consideration. I modify
that criticism here since Bennington's point is that durability is an ambiguous sign
even post hoc since it may bespeak successful force or well-considered founding.
Things are further complicated by what Bennington calls the "temporal après
coup," which means we can change our minds about the quality of a thing based
on how it turns out later. If events unfold in a certain way, it could turn out that
even Moses (a lawgiver idealized by Rousseau) was a charlatan, and there is no
time limit beyond which such a revision in judgment could not, in principle, be
(re)made. I add here a piece of the argument unnoted by Bennington and myself:
Rousseau himself concedes the point. By arguing against those who disagree with

him about the legacy of Moses and Ishmael, he shows he knows that durability, as such, is not a unanimity-producing sign.

I agree with Bennington about the logic of the temporal après coup—of course, in principle, I could turn out to have been wrong all along—but what follows from that? Events could unfold in a way that makes the lawgiver I supported look like a charlatan but (pending a still not known future) I might yet not have been wrong. What could decide that a lawgiver who becomes a charlatan was never a lawgiver in the first place? That a man found to be corrupt was never honest? That a life partner who cheats does not truly love? That a genuinely arrived-at general will was really merely aggregative all along? Bennington does not intend such essentialism (or existentialism), but he risks it. At best, however, his point is that we cannot know for sure whether a lawgiver is real, a friend honest, a partner truly loving, our will general or merely aggregative, and, whatever we think, we can still turn out to have been wrong or change our position on the matter.

27. Benhabib, "Deliberative Rationality." This possibly infinite cycle of leadership and uptake, lawgiver and people/remnant, solicitation and answerability, discernible in Rousseau, is identified in a different context by Franz Rosenzweig. Commenting on the new theology's reinvention of god by man, Rosenzweig references a kabbalist myth: "God speaks: If you do not bear witness to me, then I am not." This statement professes to show the dependence of God on man (as in The New Theology), but, Rosenzweig points out, it is "pronounced precisely as a Word of God." Rosenzweig might have further complicated matters by noting that this pronouncement is itself made by human lips but Rosenzweig is keen to make a different point: Key here is that "God himself, not human presumption makes Himself dependent upon the testimony of man." Rosenzweig opposes this human presumption in order to preserve or acknowledge the alienness of God and the truth of revelation. To that end, he highlights another parable in which it is said God "sells himself" to man. Rosenzweig argues: "[Y]et He who could 'sell' also has a claim to the purchase price" (Rosenzweig, "Atheistic Theology," 23–24; cf. Star of Redemption, 185). This self-limiting divinity who puts himself into the service of man may, as Rosenzweig suggests, be a bad model for theology, insofar as it works against theology's aim of decentering or humbling human aspirations to sovereignty. But it might serve as an excellent model for sovereign power in the political world, which would arguably do very well to enchain itself or see itself as enchained to the population it serves (For such a model and practice of sovereignty, see chapters 3 and 4 below). Or, better, democratic citizens might do well to enchain it, as the theologians criticized by Rosenzweig set out to do to divine sovereign power.

28. Habermas, "Constitutional Democracy," 768.

29. Kramer, The People Themselves.

30. Shklar, "Review of We the People."

31. Jefferson, 216. Jefferson's answer: "The dead? But the dead have no rights."

32. Christodoulidis, "The Aporia of Sovereignty," 126.

33. Schmitt, The Concept of the Political and Political Theology; Mouffe, "Carl Schmitt and the Paradox of Liberal Democracy" and The Democratic Paradox and On the Political.

34. Elster, *Ulysses and the Sirens*; Holmes, *Passions and Constraint*; Ruben-feld, *Freedom and Time*.

35. The phrase "self-consuming artifact" is Fish's. This concern is shared by Hayek who sees constitutions as inoculations against (in Holmes's parsing) "the self-defeating character of constitutionally unlimited democracy." Hayek, *The Constitution of Liberty*, 176–92, cited in Holmes, "Precommitment and the Paradox of Democracy," 196.

36. Arendt, *On Revolution*; Connolly, *The Ethos of Pluralization*; Lefort, *Democracy and Political Theory*; Rancière, *Dis-agreement*; Markell, "The Rule of the People."

37. Nietzsche, *Thus Spoke Zarathustra*, 162.

38. Holmes, *Passions and Constraint*, 135.

39. Holmes, "Precommitment and the Paradox of Democracy" and *Passions and Constraint*.

40. Elster, *Ulysses and the Sirens*; Holmes, "Precommitment and the Paradox of Democracy"; Rubenfeld, *Freedom and Time*; Habermas, "Constitutional Democracy," 774; but see Kramer's *The People Themselves* on the erasure of "popular constitutionalism."

41. Jefferson, 593–98.

42. Paine quoted in Arendt, *On Revolution*, 233.

43. Webster quoted in Rubenfeld, *Freedom*, 18 n.3.

44. Hartley, *The Go-between*.

45. Farrington, "Bengkulu: An Anglo-Chinese Partnership," 111–17; Kennedy, *A History of Malaya*, 68–77. This fact was known to have been elsewhere on Webster's mind.

46. Rubenfeld, *Freedom and Time*.

47. "Constitutional Democracy," 766; 774.

48. *Between Facts and Norms*, 463–90.

49. Ferrara, "On Boats and Principles," 788; Waldron, "Precommitment and Disagreement."

50. Markell, "Making Affect Safe for Democracy?" 45–46; cf. Habermas, *Between Facts and Norms*, 680.

51. Michelman, "Constitutional Authorship"; in Habermas, "Constitutional Democracy," 773.

52. "Constitutional Democracy," 774.

53. Ibid., 772; cf. *Between Facts and Norms*, chap. 9.

54. "Constitutional Democracy," 772.

55. Ibid., 774. Most liberal democratic constitutions do recur to "moral realism"; e.g., the Canadian Constitution Act of 1982 begins: "Whereas Canada is founded upon principles that recognize the supremacy of God and the rule of law ..." and the preamble to the German constitution reads: "Conscious of their responsibility before God and Men, Animated by the resolve to serve world peace as an equal partner in a united Europe, the German people have adopted, by virtue of their constituent power, this Basic Law."

56. "Constitutional Democracy," 774; 776.

57. For a critique of such would-be formalism, see e.g., Butler, *Antigone's Claim*.

58. Habermas, "On the Relation between the Nation, the Rule of Law, and Democracy."

59. "Constitutional Democracy," 768.

60. Ibid.

61. Kant, "Contest of the Faculties," 181; italics original; 182. Lomonaco rightly notes that not everyone in fact joined in the so-called universal sympathy and concludes that universality here functions not as an empirical fact but as the wished-for outcome of an aesthetic judgment, as described in Kant's Third Critique. ("Kant's Unselfish Partisans as Democratic Citizens," 414.) Another (not incompatible) possibility is that Kant is here only committing himself to the view, familiar from his arguments regarding the moral law, that everyone is stirred by it (the moral law, the revolution), even those who do not act on it or give public expression to it. This reading, which does without the 3rd Critique and so may be more amenable to Habermas, might help make sense of Habermas's own empirically false claim in "Constitutional Democracy" that once constitutional "interpretive battles have subsided, all parties recognize that the reforms are achievements" (775), i.e., contrary to my own earlier reply to Habermas, the truth or falsity of this claim of universal recognition is not the point if the claim is not an empirical one. Honig, "Dead Rights, Live Futures," 798.

62. Habermas may misread Kant's essay but he does not misread Kant, whose "persistent championship of the French Revolution even in the face of the Terror, won him the nickname 'the Old Jacobin'" (Korsgaard, "Kant on the Right to Revolution," 300, citing Gooch, *Germany and the French Revolution*, 269). Even so, Kant was wary of enthusiasm, which he cataloged as one of the "Sicknesses of the Head." (Thanks to Peter Fenves on this point.) Habermas shares that wariness, but he sees, according to Jason Frank, the need for something like enthusiasm when he says deliberative democracy may need not just context transcendence but "'another kind of transcendence,'" one that draws (albeit critically) on the "'identity-forming religious traditions.'" Frank, "Besides Our Selves," 390–91, citing Habermas, *Facts and Norms*, 490.

63. "Constitutional Democracy," 768; emphasis original.

64. On this, however, see my "An Agonist's Reply," in which I note how close U.S. patriotism did come to grounding itself in this machine's kiss at founding-era parades that featured printing presses on wheels which printed numerous copies of the Declaration for distribution to the crowds. The machines were the heroes of the spectacle. See Michael Warner, *Letters of the Republic*.

65. "Constitutional Democracy," 774.

66. Reading Habermas's constitutional patriotism, Markell notices a similar problem: "the universal principles toward which constitutional patriotism is supposed to direct our affect are not self-sufficient, but both depend on *and* are threatened by a supplement of particularity that enables them to become objects of passionate identification." Habermas's political practice, however, particularly his invaluable contribution to the German *Historikerstreit* of the 1970s and 1980s, is less susceptible to this critique. In practice, Habermas actually notes the tense relationship between universal and particular rather than "denying or repressing" or (I would say) overriding it. For Markell's Habermas,

If universal normative principles always depend upon supplements of particularity that enable them to become objects of attachment and identification but that are also never quite equivalent to the principles they purport to embody, then constitutional patriotism can best be understood not as a safe reliable identification with some pure set of already available universals, but rather as a political practice of refusing or resisting particular identification—of insisting on and making manifest this failure of equivalence—for the sake of the ongoing, always incomplete, and often unpredictable project of universalization.

(As Markell acknowledges, this way of reading Habermas brings him close to Ernesto Laclau, a thinker with whom we would not normally associate Habermas. Markell, "Making Affect Safe for Democracy?" 40, 59 n. 8.

Habermas's practice in the *Historikerstreit* upholds Markell's important reading, but in that context the particularity we are supposed to resist was a German identity put to pernicious use by Habermas's German nationalist or holocaust revisionist opponents. In the work under examination here, I see Habermas as aware of (but not forthcoming about) a gap between the universal and the particular but since the particular in question is less obviously pernicious (the particulars of American constitutionalism), it is more awkward for Habermas to call for (Markell's notion of) resistance to it. Moreover, I do not see that Habermas would join Laclau to call the gap between particular and universal a *failure* of the universal.

67. Arendt, *On Revolution*; Wolin, *The Presence of the Past*; Kramer, *The People Themselves*. Note, however, that the antifederalists are missing from Arendt's account as well as Habermas's.

68. Holmes, *The Anatomy of Anti-liberalism*.

69. Holmes, *Passions and Constraint*.

70. Kramer, *The People Themselves*.

71. Benhabib sees the challenge to deliberative democratic theory. Building on the tradition we were born into, we encounter "the paradox of bounded communities," in which discourse theory either

cannot articulate *any* justifiable criteria of exclusion, or it simply accepts existing practices of exclusion as *morally neutral* historical contingencies that require no further validation. This would suggest a discourse theory of democracy is itself chimerical insofar as democracy requires a morally justifiable closure that discourse ethics cannot deliver. (Benhabib, *Another Cosmopolitanism*, 18–19)

Benhabib's solution, "democratic iterations," is like Habermas's tapping but she endorses engagements with cultural practices as well as constitutions. Her attention to culture, however, does not seriously alter the deliberative democratic project of universality. On this point, see chapter 5. For a critique of Benhabib's treatment of culture, see Nikolas Kompridis, "The Idea of a New Beginning," and his exchange with Benhabib: Kompridis, "The Unsettled and Unsettling Claims of Culture"; Benhabib, "The 'Claims' of Culture Properly Interpreted."

72. Aristotle, *De Anima*, bk. II, chap. 4, 415b. Roy Sorenson, *A Brief History of the Paradox*, 11; cf. James Lennox, "Are Aristotelian Species Eternal?"

73. The revolutionary spirit "had been formed and nourished throughout the colonial period." After the revolution, "the people remained in undisturbed possession of those institutions which had been the breeding grounds of the revolution"—the townships and town hall meetings, the "original sources of their power and public happiness." Arendt, *On Revolution*, 239.

74. The term, "lucky break" is used by Jonathan Lear in *Happiness, Death, and the Remainder of Life*, and is used to good effect by Eric Santner, in *On the Psychotheology of Everyday Life*, 98–99.

75. Richard Ross, "Communications and Imperial Governance in Colonial British and Spanish America."

76. See, e.g., Arendt, *On Revolution*, 205; Honig, *Political Theory and the Displacement of Politics*, chapter 4.

77. Oakeshott, *On Human Conduct*, 105.

78. Not just deliberativists but also many of their critics perform the same substitution. On Mouffe and the deliberative democrats, see the introduction to my "Between Decision and Deliberation," which this chapter reworks.

79. Cf. Dietz, "Merely Combating the Phrases of This World."

80. Andrew Schaap makes a similar point with regard to another of Mouffe's binaries, her reworked version of Schmitt's friend-enemy distinction, which Schaap argues was implicitly rejected by Arendt in *The Human Condition* on behalf of a more political plurality, which Schaap favors: "[W]hen people are 'only for or against other people,' the world-disclosing potential of action is curtailed; for then 'speech becomes indeed *mere talk*, simply one more means toward the end, whether it serves to deceive the enemy or to dazzle everybody with propaganda; here words reveal nothing.'" Schaap *Political Reconciliation*, citing Arendt, *The Human Condition*, 180.

81. Gould occupies a point on that spectrum when she faults Habermas and his followers for their neglect of "effective decision-making" in favor of "participation as talk or discussion or deliberation." Gould, "Diversity and Democracy," 176.

82. Dietz, "Working in Half-Truth," 158.

83. Also left out are provisions I elsewhere call "aconstitutional constitutional," such as Canada's "notwithstanding clause." Honig, "Dead Rights, Live Futures."

84. The article version of this chapter focused in particular on the debate between deliberation and decision in contemporary democratic theory. See my "Between Decision and Deliberation."

Chapter Two

1. Moses Mendelssohn, *Jerusalem*, 96. See Kant's discussion in "On the Common Saying: 'This May be True in Theory, but It Does Not Apply in Practice,'" 87–88.

2. Kant, "Theory and Practice," 89.

3. Matt Erlin, "Reluctant Modernism," 83.

4. Mendelssohn, *Jerusalem*, 96, quoted in Erlin, "Reluctant Modernism," 83.

5. Kant, "Theory and Practice," 88.

6. Quoted in Alexander Altmann, *Moses Mendelssohn: A Biographical Study*, 540; Mendelssohn, *Gesammelte Schriften*, vol. XIII, 65–66. Translation is from Erlin, "Reluctant Modernism," 87.

7. Erlin, "Reluctant Modernism," 88.

8. Ibid., 84.

9. Although Kant too, of course, had his own run-ins with a supposedly enlightened ruler, after publishing *Religion within the Limits of Reason Alone*.

10. Hensel, *The Mendelssohn Family*.

11. Jean Nordhaus, "The Porcelain Apes of Moses Mendelssohn," 55–56.

12. Kant, "Theory and Practice," 88. Kant's concern about the need to act hopefully is shared by contemporary thinkers such as Jurgen Habermas and Seyla Benhabib. Indeed, in the 1995 volume, *Feminist Contentions*, Benhabib played Kant to Judith Butler's Mendelssohn, castigating Butler for what Benhabib took to be Butler's inability to sustain the grounds of hope among the ruins of her poststructuralism. See esp., on the theme of hope, Benhabib, "Feminism and Postmodernism," 23–25, 30.

13. These questions also frame the perspective from which I assess new institutional developments in the EU and international law in chapter 5.

14. As Slow Food put it in its September 2008 on-line circular, "Slow Food is guided by the belief that pleasure and responsibility are deeply linked." http://www.slowfoodusa.org/index.php/about_us/news_post/slow_food_usa_hires_joshua_viertel_as_president/ (accessed September 17, 2008).

15. Habermas, "Constitutional Democracy," 768, 776, my italics.

16. William Connolly, *The Ethos of Pluralization*, 187.

17. Connolly, *Ethos*, 184 (italics in original).

18. Nietzsche, *Thus Spoke Zarathustra*, 161–62; Arendt, *The Human Condition*, 236–43.

19. On this point Sandel's *Liberalism and the Limits of Justice* is still very useful.

20. On the other hand, his way of thinking about rights and identity is particularly expansive, so the risk is less here than it is with others—liberal and deliberative democratic theorists—who put rights at the center of things.

21. Niklas Luhmann, "Verfassung als evolutionäre Errungenschaft," cited in Emilios Christodoulidis, "The Aporia of Sovereignty," 126, my italics.

22. The mutuality of transformation makes new political coalitions possible, as Connolly points out: "It is often more feasible, say, for gays and straights to enter into alliances ... than it is for heterosexuals and homosexuals to do so. This is because neither constituency, in the first set, is constituted as intrinsically unnatural, abnormal or immoral by the other." Connolly, *The Ethos of Pluralization*, 197.

23. Connolly, *Neuropolitics*, 148

24. Ibid., 161.

25. Connolly, *Pluralism*, 121, italics in original.

26. Giorgio Agamben, *Homo Sacer*, 137, 139.

27. Such lives are also treated as "ungrievable," as Judith Butler points out in *Precarious Life*.

28. The ambiguity may not be deep. Eric Santner brilliantly reads the Schiavo case in a way that shows the commitment of Bush and his supporters not to life per se but to innocent, bare life. See his "Terry Schiavo and the State of Exception."

29. Richard Flathman, *The Practice of Rights*.

30. Agamben, *Homo Sacer*, esp. the last chapter.

31. Cora Diamond, "The Difficulty of Reality and the Difficulty of Philosophy."

32. For Connolly, such work involved practices of agonistic respect, nontheistic reverence for being, and more.

33. Here Wittgenstein anticipates Derrida's critique of Austin, regarding the role of infelicities in speech acts, but Wittgenstein stops short of Derrida's insight regarding the function of those infelicities and their relationship to ordinary language, as I note below.

34. Wittgenstein, *Philosophical Investigations*, nos. 193–94, italics added.

35. Ibid., no. 194.

36. Ibid., no. 195, italics in original.

37. David De Grazia, "Regarding the Last Frontier of Bigotry."

38. There is here in Wittgenstein, as elsewhere, a stubborn empiricism, captured by his repeated admonition to his readers to "Look, don't think!" Nietzsche gives his readers similar instructions. For a discussion of nonlinear time as the product of a hyperempiricism, see M. De Landa, *A Thousand Years of Nonlinear History*.

39. J. L. Austin, *How to Do Things with Words*; Jacques Derrida, "Signature, Event, Context."

40. For more on the political implications of this dimension of Derrida's reading of Austin, see my *Political Theory and the Displacement of Politics*, chapter 4.

41. It may even be causing some of the paradoxes to which it claims to respond, a point I raised in chapter 1 and develop further in chapter 5.

42. Arendt, *The Life of the Mind*, 216–17.

43. I develop in more detail this idea of pleasure as a resource with which to counteract doom in "From Lamentation to Logos: Antigone's Offensive Speech," in *Antigone, Interrupted*.

44. Alice Waters, "Slow Food Nation," *The Nation* (*The Food Issue*), September 11, 2006, http://www.thenation.com/doc/20060911/waters.

45. "Ark products range from the Italian Valchiavenna goat to the American Navajo-Churro sheep, from the last indigenous Irish cattle breed, the Kerry, to a unique variety of Greek fava beans grown only on the island of Santorini. All are endangered products that have real economic viability and commercial potential." Slow Food Foundation for Biodiversity, "Ark of Taste," http://www.fondazione slowfood.it/eng/arca/lista.lasso.

46. Quoted in Alexander Stille, "Slow Food," *The Nation*, August 20, 2001, http://www.thenation.com/doc/20010820/stille.

47. Andrew Finkel, "Food for Thought," *CNN.com*, November 30, 2000, http://archives.cnn.com/2000/WORLD/europe/11/30/time.food/index.html (accessed August 23, 2008).

48. Stille, "Slow Food."

49. See, for example, Mad River Valley Localvore Project, www.vermontlocal
vore.org.

50. See also, below, Carlo Petrini on the good, the clean, and the just. At the
convention of the American Political Science Association in 2006, objections
were raised about the "classist" nature of this movement. Some audience members and the panelists, myself included, responded to these objections by noting
that time was not in such short supply as people think, given the number of hours
spent by most Americans watching television (Jane Bennet), that slow food need
not entail any great expense of time or money (Honig), and that defending the
right of the masses to fast food is itself hugely problematic because of the health
effects of fast food, ranging from heart disease to diabetes (William Connolly).
Just a couple of weeks later, the "Food Issue" of *The Nation* hit the stands on
September 11, 2006, the date itself marking a connection between emergency and
food. Several of its articles, one of which was Waters's, reiterated responses to the
unease expressed by some audience members at the panel.

51. Alice Waters, "Slow Food Nation," italics added; Felicia Mello, "Hard
Labor," *The Nation*, September 11, 2006, http://www.thenation.com/doc/2006
0911/mello.

52. See, for example, Vandana Shiva's discussion of Indian women's noncoop-
eration with the ban in 1998 on mustard oil, one of India's indigenous edible oils,
on grounds of "food safety," which she calls "an excuse," noting that the "re-
strictions on import of soya oil were simultaneously removed. Ten million farmers' livelihoods were threatened." Shiva in Schlosser et al., "One Thing to Do
about Food: A Forum," *The Nation*, September 11, 2006. http://www.thenation.
com/doc/20060911/forum, 4.

53. De Grazia, quoted in Joanne Hari, "'Irresistible Empire': McEurope," *New
York Times*, May 8, 2005, http://www.nytimes.com/2005/05/08/books/review08
HARIL.html?scp=1&sq=hari%20mcEurope&st=cse (accessed August 23, 2008).

54. Petrini in Schlosser et al., "One Thing to Do about Food: A Forum," 5. Cf.
Petrini and Padovani, *Slow Food Revolution*.

55. Again, when this paper was presented publicly, this time at the American
Bar Foundation, it was objected that the Guatemalan coffee growers themselves
drink Nescafe. Their right to taste is not protected, it was said. They cannot af-
ford to drink the high-quality coffee they produce. And there is truth in the claim.
But it seems a weak charge against the Slow Food project that the organization
has succeeded in enabling a community to develop a product whose sale benefits
them more than its consumption would. At bottom, it is true, Slow Food works
with—but also against—the capitalist economy that now dominates our lives.
Were the movement more radically anticapitalist, it would fail or have less salient
effects. Were it less so, it would be less interesting and important. It is also worth
noting that an endorsement of Slow Food is not exclusive. That is, Slow Food
politics is not an entire politics. One can combine this commitment with other
forms of political engagement that are more expressly directed at class issues.
That is, it is not, in my view, a fair criticism of a movement to argue that there are
political problems that it fails to address. No movement could pass the test that
is implied by such a criticism.

56. Arendt, *On Revolution*.

57. Stephen Holmes, "Precommitment and the Paradox of Democracy," 223 n. 89. The distinction between the serious and the nonserious is one to which others have properly drawn critical attention. See for example Jacques Derrida's "Signature, Event Context," 1–23. For further critical response to the call to political theory to focus on the "serious" juridical register, see chapter 5.

58. Holmes, "Precommitment and the Paradox of Democracy," 223.

59. Of those involved in thinking critically about the human-animal divide and its political repercussions, I would name Jane Bennett, Bill Chaloupka, Donna Haraway, Peter Singer, and John Coetzee.

60. For an interesting critique of the quest for the new see Nicholas Kompridis, "The Idea of a New Beginning," 32–59.

Chapter Three

1. Rosenzweig, *The Star of Redemption*, 111, cf. 123.

2. Quoted in Elizabeth Young-Bruel, *Hannah Arendt*, 513 n. 54.

3. Among the most unrelieved in their criticism of Schmitt are William Scheuerman, *Between the Norm and the Exception*, chap. 1, and Stephen Holmes, *The Anatomy of Anti-liberalism*.

4. Analogously, and prior to this struggle between judicial and administrative power, courts themselves were disciplined into the predictable and proceduralized institutions demanded by the rule of law as we have now come to understand it. In the postrevolutionary United States, military courts were used to break the independence and unruliness of jural freedom, an institution that was once, in Akhil Amar's words, a fourth branch of government. See Shannon Stimson's wonderful and now timely *The American Revolution in the Law* and Amar's *Bill of Rights*.

5. Scheuerman would agree with this point, but he would, I think, very much resist its identification with Schmitt, whom Scheuerman sees as totally and unrelievedly decisionistic, by contrast with the history of American liberal democracy. In short, while Scheuerman would agree that the American state has generated many discretionary components of governance that are inadequately accountable to the people over whom they rule, he seems to think it risky indeed to use Schmitt in any way to highlight or identify such dimensions of America's larger politics, insofar as we risk, thereby, taking on board Schmitt's irredeemably fascist conception of law (on Scheuerman's account) and passing on the superior aspiration to weigh in (as Scheuerman does) on the rule of law side, by (for example) calling for the expansion of simple legal language and regularity, e.g. *Between the Norm and the Exception*, 212 and passim.

As William Scheuerman notes in his book, and as William Novak first pointed out to me, the idea that there is a connection between emergency law and administrative law is a point made by Neumann in *Behemoth*. But Neumann's point is a bit different: Neumann criticizes and delegitimates administrative law by noting that its paradigmatic model is the emergency. I am interested in the converse, in thinking about emergency politics in the context of larger and more mundane struggles for state power between advocates of administrative discretion (not necessarily illegitimate, in my view) and proponents of judicial review.

6. Such "settings" include both emergency times and spaces because contra Carl Schmitt and Clinton Rossiter, emergency powers are not just temporal; they may be spatial. Or, better, even when they are temporal, they are also always spatial. For example, in a time of national emergency, we are not all equally subject to emergency rule—some have the wealth or power or profile to opt out of many constraints and remain uncriminalized and even, in some cases, uncriminalizable by new security measures. An example of this is the availability of a pass that for an annual fee allows some air travelers in the United States to be moved more quickly through security.

7. As Lucy Salyer notes: Immigration politics and law are taken to be exceptional in American law, even in American administrative law—a "maverick," she says, citing Peter Schuck, "anomalous," and even an "outlaw" body of law. As Schuck puts it, "probably no other area of American law has been so radically insulated and divergent from those fundamental norms of constitutional right, administrative procedure, and judicial role that animate the rest of our legal system." Indeed, says Schuck, in immigration law, "government authority is at its zenith and individual entitlement is at the nadir." Quoted in Lucy Salyer, *Laws Harsh as Tigers*, xiv. See also David Cole, *Enemy Aliens*, 30 and passim, on the Ashcroft Justice Department's appropriation of immigration law as a tool in detaining people for investigation in the War on Terror.

But Salyer goes on to suggest that the area of immigration law is less an outlaw than Schuck and others assume. Chinese petitioners in the context of the Chinese Exclusion Act were savvy users of law and courts and were surprisingly successful in the federal courts, even when standing before nativist judges, because those judges were bound by institutionalized norms of the court and would not allow even their own nativism to stand in the way of judicial norms of due process. She argues, however, that immigration law, which is still largely administrative, should be further judicialized. That is, Salyer not only studies a time and a place in which the contest between rule of law and administrative governance is visible, or rather is rendered visible by her historical research, she also participates in that scholarly debate while accepting and resecuring its governing terms: the opposition between administrative law or rule of man and the rule of law, judicially enforced.

One merit of Louis Post's case, detailed here, is that it troubles that opposition and highlights the ways in which the rule of law's proceduralism is always dependent to some extent on *some*one's administrative or judicial decision. Mere proceduralism lacks direction and nuance and meaning and offers no guarantees regarding the justice of its outcomes. With this point, we enter into large and ongoing debates in legal theory, which I discuss briefly in the concluding pages of this chapter.

8. In recontextualizing emergency politics in an ongoing institutional setting, I find myself somewhere between Clinton Rossiter and Lucy Salyer: For Rossiter, "crisis government in this country has been a matter of personalities rather than of institutions" (*Constitutional Dictatorship*, 210). For Salyer, administrative discretion has played too large a part in the still exceptional arena of immigration

politics (see n. 7 above), but that discretion has also been mediated in hitherto unappreciated ways by courts and by law in its institutionalized settings. I am looking at emergency politics as a moment in that larger institutional struggle between judicial and administrative power (studied by Salyer in the mostly non-emergency area of immigration politics), while also emphasizing more approvingly than Salyer, I think, the extraprocedural and not always law-governed role played in that struggle by the personalities (Rossiter) and decisions of judges, administrators, elites, legal clients, and all sorts of political actors.

9. See Andrew Arato, "The Bush Tribunals and the Specter of Dictatorship," and Cole, *Enemy Aliens*.

10. See Salyer, *Laws Harsh as Tigers*, and Martin Shapiro, *Who Guards the Guardians?* for the literature on scholarly calls to proceduralize discretionary administrative agency.

11. Alan Dershowitz. *Why Terrorism Works*, chaps. 4 and 5.

12. Bruce Watson, "Crackdown!" 52.

13. Although at the time, of course, it was not so called (the Second Red Scare had not yet occurred). The events were referred to by Post as the "Red" Crusade. The above summary of events draws on William Leuchtenburg, *The Perils of Prosperity 1914–32*.

14. Charles Howard McCormick, "Louis Freeland Post," 731.

15. A vivid sense of the fears surrounding these raids is given by Clancy Sigal, a Hollywood screenwriter whose 2002 op. ed. provides an excellent counter to Leuchtenburg, who downplays popular fears at the time. Says Sigal:

> The anarchist threat was terrifying, just as the terrorist threat is now. Most Americans supported Attorney General Palmer's campaign against the "Reds"— an ill-defined menace that went far beyond the small group of actual anarchists that was blamed for pretty much anything that smacked of social conflict— including at various times, the women's suffrage movement, a Chicago race riot, and a wave of paralyzing industrial strikes.

Sigal's parents were at high risk in such a setting: "foreign-born, Jewish, radical labor organizers, who had actively participated in several turbulent strikes, [they also] had no fixed address and were living in sin. They were arrested, jailed and almost deported during the infamous Palmer Raids of 1920 and 21 [sic]." Later, Sigal learned from his mother that his father had been beaten by federal agents on his way to jail. Both were released later, she after a few days, he after a few weeks, and were not deported, though many of their friends were. "The raids," Sigal continues,

> were a living presence at our house. At a later time, when J. Edgar Hoover's FBI came around to question me during the cold war, my mother politely met them at the door, invited them in for coffee and charmed them out of their intended purpose. But she was pale and terrified when I got home. In an understandable slip of the tongue she said: "The Palmers have been here. What have you done?" (Clancy Sigal, "John Ashcroft's Palmer Raids," *New York Times*, March 13, 2002, Section A, Page 25, Column 1, Editorial Desk).

16. Dominic Candeloro, "Louis Post and the Red Scare of 1920." Caminetti resisted the takeover, of course, but Post replied that "power over deportation

matters had never been given to the bureau [of immigration] and that Caminetti was merely an agent who had been assigned to brief cases for him." As Post later put it in his testimony before the Committee on Rules, "The Commissioner General of Immigration is not the dictator to the Secretary of Labor in warrant cases. It has been assumed by the committee that makes this complaint [the charges made by the Committee on Rules] that he is the dictator in effect, and that the Assistant Secretary [Post himself] was culpable for overruling him." But this assumption was wrong, Post insisted over many hours of testimony, in which he repeatedly characterized the immigration commissioner as a "sheriff" to the Department of Labor and as a mere advisor and, finally and most brutally, as possessed of "no more authority than the private secretary of a Secretary would have." House Committee on Rules, "Investigation of Administration of Louis F. Post," 227, henceforth House Testimony or HT.

17. Dominic Candeloro, "Louis Freeland Post: Carpetbagger, Single-taxer, Progressive," 155–65 inter alia.

18. "The mere innocent member who is guilty of nothing but joining an organization ... I don't think that any man with an *American mind* would wish to have that kind of man deported without showing some evidence that he was culpable." HT, 263.

19. Quoted in Candeloro, "Louis Freeland Post: Carpetbagger," 45, citing Palmer's testimony before the House Committee on Rules. Secretary of Labor Wilson held open hearings on this matter and "stunned Hoover and the Justice Dept." when he ruled "that membership in the Communist Labor party was not a deportable offense because members were not required to know of or subscribe to the Party's goals or tactics as a condition of membership; he flatly rejected Hoover's brief and argument on the subject" Richard Gid Powers, *Secrecy and Power*, 118.

20. "In other words, the principle 'Once a member, always a member,' is not true, in my judgment, in these cases, provided there is a withdrawal from membership in good faith" Post, in HT, 77.

21. Thirty years later, Hannah Arendt articulated one of the insights that motivated Post: That an innocent but stateless person subject to administrative state power could paradoxically improve her position by breaking the law and gaining thereby the scrutiny but also the procedural protections to which those accused of criminal law violations are subject or have a claim. *The Origins of Totalitarianism*, 286–87.

22. Candeloro, "Louis Freeland Post: Carpetbagger," 46.

23. Post said he had Court decisions backing him in this view but none finessed the question (discussed below) of whether it was incumbent on an administrative procedure to hold itself to the more stringent requirements of criminal law. Thus, it is true, as Charles Howard McCormick says, that Post's legal position *anticipated* later court rulings. (McCormick, "Louis Freeland Post"; cf. Candeloro, who says that "Post's dedication to upholding the procedural rights of the defendants anticipated Supreme Court rulings of half a century later." Candeloro, "Louis Freeland Post: Carpetbagger," 46.) I will quarrel with that term— "anticipation"—below. McCormick mentions specifically *Wong Yang Sun v. McGrath* (1950) and *United States v. Brignoni-Ponce* (1975). Post himself invoked

an eighth circuit Court of Appeals case, *Whitfield v. Hanges*, when he said in his testimony, "an alien, once lawfully admitted and resident in this country ... has the same constitutional rights, except as to voting and purely citizenship rights ... that the citizen has," and Post added, this "is good *American* doctrine." HT, 223, emphasis added.

24. Regarding his disregard for statements made by aliens without benefit of counsel, Post said to the House Committee:

> If there is any objection to that stand that I took, the quarrel is with the United States district judge in the West and with the Supreme Court of the United States in its unanimous decision. I based that on the principle of the case of Re Jackson, in the United States District Court for Montana, in which the decision was by Judge Bourquin; and on the case of Silverthorn *v.* The United States, which was an appeal taken to the Supreme Court and decided January 28, 1920. (HT, 78)

Post's ruling on this matter directly reversed an earlier change introduced by Hoover: In response to a pamphlet that advised aliens not to answer questions without benefit of counsel, Hoover amended immigration regulations "to delay the right to a lawyer until the case 'had proceeded sufficiently in the development of the facts to protect the Government's interests.' The amendment took effect on Dec. 31, 1919, one business day before the raids began." Cole, *Enemy Aliens*, 120 and passim.

25. HT, 230. Two other considerations entered into the case for Post, which he mentions at other times at the hearings: Magon had six American-born children dependent upon him and, as a dissident, would very likely have been killed had he been returned to Mexico. Thus, Post said that even had he found Magon deportable, he would have imprisoned him in the United States until such time as he could be assured of the man's safety in Mexico.

26. William Leuchtenburg, *The Perils of Prosperity, 1914–32*, 79; cf. "McCormick, Louis Freeland Post."

27. Leuchtenburg, *The Perils of Prosperity*, 80; cf. Watson, "Crackdown!" Leuchtenburg says that thanks to Post, of the five thousand arrest warrants sworn out in late 1919, "only a few more than 600 aliens were actually deported" (ibid., 81).

28. Salyer (*Laws Harsh as Tigers*, 239), Cole (*Enemy Aliens*, 123), and others suggest Post was impeached or "brought up on impeachment charges," referring to the hearings referred to here. In fact, he was not impeached. An impeachment resolution was introduced "unostentatiously" by Kansas congressman Homer Hoch. But the resolution "did not come formally before the House" and although it should then have gone to a preliminary inquiry by the Committee on the Judiciary, "the Speaker referred it to the Committee on Rules" (whose record is here referred to as House Testimony [HT]). In Post's view, the Speaker took a wise course:

> [T]he Judiciary Committee is a judicial branch of the House. It could not gracefully dispose of such a resolution without reporting its judgment. But the Committee on Rules is a political branch which could, without any breach of judi-

cial deportment, smother the whole proceeding if it discovered that the impetuous Mr. Hoch had gone off on a false scent. Like the nearsighted hunter of the familiar anecdote, the Speaker aimed to hit if the object were a deer, but to miss if it were a calf. (Post, *The Deportations Delirium*, 232–34).

Thanks to Stephen Daniels for pressing me to clarify this point.

29. This, in a nutshell, is the recurring question in the literature regarding administrative power: Lucy Salyer parses it by way of a quotation from attorney Max Kohler, who criticized the Bureau of Immigration's exercises of administrative power under Commissioner Williams (1911): "The discretion wielded by men like Williams to interpret law turned immigration officials from 'law-enforcers' into 'self-constituted lawmaker[s].'" *Laws Harsh as Tigers*, 154.

30. Mr. Johnson, Chair of the House Committee on Rules, in HT, 254.

31. Even such "unfriendly" witnesses as the *Spokesman-Review* (a newspaper so characterized by Post) were entirely persuaded by this clarification. Post, *The Deportations Delirium*. Of course, calling it a "clarification" is itself an ideological move.

32. HT, 80–81, italics added. Note how Post here meets Hoover on his own ground, vying with him for the right to be called the truest American and casting his opponents' violations of proceduralism as un-American. Post found support in this from the rhetoric of District Court Judge George W. Anderson, who reviewed Justice Department activities in hearing *Colyer v. Skeffington*, and said: "Talk about Americanization! What we need is to Americanize people that are carrying out such proceedings as this. We shall forget everything we ever learned about American Constitutional liberty if we are to undertake to justify such a proceeding as this." Quoted in Salyer, *Laws Harsh as Tigers*, 238.

Note too Post's key phrase above: "on an administrative process warrant, a mere police warrant until it gets to the Secretary of Labor." Post signals here his determination to divide the role of accuser from judge in deportation cases. He was very aware that a "police mentality" "develops in institutions such as the Immigration Bureau, in which those who issue the warrants are the very same people as those who ultimately decide the cases (HT, 229 and 239ff.). Unsurprisingly, then, and largely for these structural reasons, the whole spirit of the Bureau, he said, "was the police office spirit of keeping the alien out or putting him out without much regard to facts" (ibid., 229). "Most of the men in this service that I have come into contact with are perfectly honorable and honest men and intend to be good officials" (ibid., 239). And later

> I am not making any imputation against the man: it is human nature—he would naturally feel that it was up to him, if he has asked for a warrant, to see that that warrant was not asked for thoughtlessly, and so as a rule he would be very apt to find that the man whose arrest he had asked for had, upon examination, turned out to be what he had supposed he was in the beginning. Consequently, a police spirit develops naturally.... The effect of that is to turn that inspector into a police investigator. (Ibid., 246)

In short, the problem was structural and so was the solution: separation of investigative and decision powers.

33. Post, *Deportations Delirium*, 254. Notably, with the phrase "strongest reason," Post leaves room for emergency/state of exception considerations.

34. HT, 80–81. That is not the *only* issue, however. Another is the separation of powers. Post's first response to Garrett's first iteration of the question cited above lights on this: "For myself, I do not see how Congress can compel the executive department of the Government to do anything other than execute the law that it passes," HT, 81 (i.e., presumably, Congress cannot compel the executive to implement the law in any *particular* [as Oakeshott might say] *adverbial* fashion).

35. E.g. HT, 68, 230, 248.

36. Wittgenstein, *Philosophical Investigations*, no. 186.

37. HT, 78, 79; emphasis added. Here Post presents himself as bound by law, though in a different sense than I point to in this chapter's last section. Here Post emphasizes his own feeling that he was forced by the law of the land and the responsibilities of his office to do things he thought wrong and unwarranted. By way of protest, Post referred repeatedly to the *usefulness* of the men he was forced to deport. The criterion of usefulness is fully at odds with the more deontic norm of individual liberty to which he also appeals, but it is unsurprising, as a political and historical matter, that Post would appeal to both.

38. Interestingly, Elliot Dorff and Arthur Rosett point out, this requirement of a divided bench "is the exact opposite of the requirement in American law for a unanimous jury" (Dorff and Rosett, *A Living Tree*, 225). I am indebted to Bob Gibb of the University of Toronto for calling this text to my attention.

39. As Dorff and Rosett point out, some of these requirements (I would say all of them) are "extensions of principles that are reasonable in a different form" (ibid, 226). Even basic inference is precluded lest it corrupt the chain of direct sense data evidence. The testimony of witnesses who saw a man with a knife enter a room and then saw him leaving minutes later with the same knife, bloody, in his hands, is insufficient for a capital conviction. Only the most empirically indubitable sense data are acceptable, and the result, of course, is that nothing that meets these evidentiary and procedural standards will ever be found in the empirical world. The Rabbis knowingly defend their amendments (not of the death penalty but of death penalty judgments and the procedures whereby they are reached) as a reasonable requirement given the severity of the punishment in question. but in so doing (for example, when they say the accused must have said, "Even so, I am going to do it"), they call attention to the indefensibility of capital punishment itself, not to any real evidentiary or procedural rigor.

40. See Austin Sarat and Thomas Kearns, "A Journey through Forgetting," 236, 247 and passim, for a useful summary of the debates among Hart, Dworkin, and others on the need of law for interpretation. Note that since it is the generality and breadth of law that stage the scene for the problem/solution of interpretation and technicality, generality and breadth cannot per se, contra William Scheuerman, serve simply as the solutions to the problem of arbitrary administrative power. Scheuerman, "Between Radicalism and Resignation," and *Between the Norm and the Exception*.

41. This is contrary to the example of the Rabbis, which is unusual in this regard: They did broadcast the technicalities in advance. That is because they did

not do case law, per se, they debated matters of interpretation apart from particular cases, using hypotheticals, mostly unlikely and fanciful ones intended precisely to stretch the law and test its capaciousness. These contrived hypotheticals are the very sort that R. M. Hare charges utilitarianism's critics (such as Bernard Williams) with using deliberately and unfairly to discredit that moral and political theory. R. M. Hare, *Moral Thinking*, 19.

42. On the various requirements of the rule of law, see Lon Fuller, *The Morality of Law*, and William Scheuerman's discussion, by way of Locke, in *Between the Norm and the Exception*. For a recent case of the political use of technicality, see "The Way We Live Now," *New York Times Magazine*, Sunday, September 28, 2003, 19: "Librarians Unite: Three Technically Legal Signs for Your Library" (regarding the Patriot Act):—We're sorry! Because of national security concerns, we are unable to tell you if your Internet-surfing habits, passwords, and e-mail are being monitored by federal agents; please act appropriately.—The F.B.I. has not been here. (Watch very closely for the removal of this sign).—Q. How can you tell when the F.B.I. has been in your library? A. You can't. The Patriot Act makes it illegal for us to tell you if our computers are monitored; be aware! From www.librarian.net.

43. Thanks to Laura Beth Nielsen on this point.

44. See John Rawls, "Fair Equality of Opportunity and Pure Procedural Justice," in *A Theory of Justice*, 83–90.

45. The Supreme Court has held that Congress has turned this whole matter over to our administrative department of the Government; that the question of whether an alien shall be allowed to continue to reside in the United States is a question of sovereignty and belongs on the Executive side of the Government and not on the judicial side. Consequently the courts have refused, on writs of habeas corpus, to interfere with the decisions of the administrative side of the Government in these cases unless there is absolute lack of jurisdiction. Where there is no evidence at all to support the case for deportation, the courts will interfere on habeas corpus. But they will not review the merits of the case, because they say, it is a question of sovereignty turned over to the Executive department of the Government and they have no right to cross the line. (Post, Deportations Delirium, 253).

46. Actually, the question *was* posed. Dorff and Rosett cite Makkot 1:10, in which the Rabbis try to change the norms that surround death penalty judgments:

> A court which has put a man to death once in a seven year period is called "a hanging court." Rabbi Elazar ben Azariah says, "Even once in seventy years." Rabbi Tarfon and Rabbi Akiva say, "Were we members of the court, no person would ever be put to death." [Playing Garret to Post's Akiva] Rabban Simeon ben Gamliel retorted: "If so, they would multiply the shedders of blood in Israel" (Dorff and Rosett, *A Living Tree*, 225).

47. HT, 247–48. This response seems to have utterly turned Pou, who then suddenly expressed his admiration for Post—"I want to say, Mr. Secretary, that my feeling is that in what you have done, speaking for myself, I believe you have

followed your sense of duty absolutely"—and ceased his questioning, which, until that point in the proceedings, had been vigorous and aggressive.

48. Candeloro, "Louis Freeland Post: Carpetbagger," 50.

49. Leuchtenburg makes a move in this direction when he says,

> The election of Warren G. Harding, amiable but bumbling Republican presidential candidate in 1920, marked a desire for release from political turmoil and a chance to enjoy the pleasures of peace.... The 1920's, despite their chauvinism and conservatism, were hostile to the spirit of the Red Scare; the decade was one when interest in politics was at its lowest ebb in half a century, and Palmer was defeated less by liberal opponents than by the hedonism of the age. (Leuchtenburg, *The Perils of Prosperity*, 81)

50. A lot rides on how we render these moments in American history.

51. *The Deportations Delirium* is the title of the book Post wrote about his role in the events recounted here.

52. Though it was thought and actually hoped that Hoover, who replaced the corrupt Billy Burns, would, as one reporter put it,

> forget the teachings of Mr. Palmer under the more intelligent leadership of Mr. Stone [who had fought Palmer's crusade and was the new attorney general charged with cleaning up government after the Teapot Dome scandal]. It would be worth a great deal to the American people to be assured that the Department of Justice is what the name signifies and not the Department of Hysteria and Intolerance.

In short, it was hoped, ironically, that Hoover would prove to be more Post than Palmer. This must have irked Hoover, who lost every direct, public battle he had with Post. One of Hoover's responses was to save a nine-stanza poem (excerpted below) about Post in a scrapbook along with a colored-in newspaper photo of Post. Says Powers, "Hoover may have been the artist, he may have been the poet" (Powers, *Secrecy and Power*, 146, 121–22). The poem was titled "The Bully Bolsheviki" and was "Disrespectfully dedicated to 'Comrade' Louie Post." It begins

> In every city and town
> To bring on Revolution
> And the old USA to down.
>   The sixth stanza says:

> And when he's lost his nice fat job
> And is looking around for some work
> They'll ask him to come to Russia
> With the Bolsheviks he'll lurk

The poem instantiates the demonology Rogin studied. Here was Post, a Declaration of Independence radical, tarred as a Bolshevik for standing up for procedural fairness and depicted as Russian for his efforts to limit executive power in a divided government system that is supposed to be committed to such institutional (self-)limitation. I guess Hoover saw the truth of what I am arguing here—

that Post was no mere proceduralist, that he was using proceduralism and technicality as ways to pursue substantive political goals with which Hoover was very much in disagreement.

53. Salyer might see less irony here than I do. She admires Post and his actions, but not so the Progressives'. Of them in the 1900s she says: "Even Progressives who were sympathetic to immigrants' concerns failed to endorse the proceduralist definition of the rule of law, advocating instead better personnel and more elaborate administrative review" (Salyer, *Laws Harsh as Tigers*, xviii). In this as in most other things, Post defies our categories; he was a Progressive, but a qualified one—he championed proceduralism in a way most Progressives did not. On the other hand, Post's proceduralism was, as I remarked above, hardly unqualified. Perhaps then, Salyer's view would be that it is fitting rather than ironic that Post's efforts to proceduralize executive-branch agency were never institutionalized. In the end, Post's innovations were (she might say) too or still dependent upon the good will of a beneficent administrator.

54. David Cole, *Enemy Aliens* and *Justice at War*; David Cole and James X. Dempsey, *Terrorism and the Constitution*; David Cole and Jules Lobel, *Less Safe, Less Free*. Cole has argued numerous civil liberties cases, from the twenty-year legal battle on behalf of the "L.A. eight" to the recent cases of Maher Arar, a victim of "extraordinary rendition," and of prisoners held in Guantanamo Bay. See the Center for Constitutional Rights: http://ccrjustice.org/.

55. This goes some way beyond a position like, for example, Philip Pettit's, in which the liberal rule of law is, as it were, married but not deeply altered by marriage to a republican practice of democratic contestation that is located not in the sphere of law or administration, but rather in civil society, a distant enough place from which law is engaged but also insulated from deep challenges. See Pettit, *Republicanism*, chap. 6: "Republican Forms: Constitutionalism and Democracy."

56. Candeloro, "Louis Freeland Post: Carpetbagger," 46. Cf. ibid., 55: "Post's legal training and human sympathies allowed him to anticipate the judicial trend toward greater attention to the rights of the accused."

57. This picture of law as its own agent, with lawyers and other legal actors just along for its progressive ride, is, as I noted earlier, a key theme in the 2000 film, *Civil Rights and Wrongs: The Fred Korematsu Story*.

58. Candeloro attributes Post's steadfast refusal to be swept up in the anti-red hysteria to his "deep roots in the democratic radicalism of the Declaration of Independence and the Bill of Rights." Candeloro, "Louis Freeland Post: Carpetbagger," 55.

59. Hence the arguments in legal and political theory about how judicial deliberation is more than mere preference-based voting. Similarly, deliberative democrats distinguish aggregative from deliberative democracy: in the former, raw preferences are added up, while in the latter, preferences are transformed and authorized to rule by a legitimating deliberative process. See Iris Young, *Inclusion and Democracy*, on the distinction between aggregative and deliberative democracy, and arguments for the superiority of the latter.

60. Salyer, *Laws Harsh as Tigers*, 85.

61. See Shapiro, *Who Guards the Guardians?*

62. Michael Oakeshott is one of the few theorists of the rule of law who owns the enforcement and policing traits of the rule of law, calling the former "postulates" of the latter in his essay, "The Rule of Law."

63. As I have argued elsewhere, such "taking" is a quintessential democratic practice. See chapters 4 and 5 of *Democracy and the Foreigner*.

64. On the differing and overlapping institutional norms of judges and administrators, see Donald Horowitz, *The Jurocracy*.

65. Michael Rogin, "American Political Demonology." My debt to Michael Rogin's work in this chapter is large. Indeed, I hope this chapter can function as a response to an obituary for Rogin written by Stephen Greenblatt shortly after 9/11. Greenblatt appreciates Rogin's substantial contributions to our thinking about the role of paranoia in American politics, but then adds:

> I want, with an urgency I have never felt before, to phone Mike Rogin. I want to know what he makes of the massive intensification of the national security state. I want to know what happens to his concept of political demonology when there actually are deadly enemies, when they seem genuinely demonic, and when American boundaries have indeed been revealed to be permeable."
> ("In Memory of Michael Rogin," *London Review of Books*, January 3, 2002)

With this, Greenblatt undermines what I take to be Rogin's most important insight: Demonology has little to do with the reality (or not) of one's enemies. Although the term "demonology" seems to suggest that one's enemies are the products of a popular or cultural imagination, the exteriorized reflections of some internal disorder, phantoms cast out and then disavowed, this need not be the case. One's enemies can be real and external and one can still demonize them, or not; one can make one's real enemy stand for a range of things that are opposed to one's idealized self-image, or not. Demonology has to do with how one experiences enmity, how one lives it, how one's politics are branded or warped by it. Demonology involves projecting all that we fear onto another and representing ourselves as pure of any such demonic traits, even as we exhibit behavior startlingly like that of our foe (which we justify by saying we have to counter their subversion using their weapons or lose). In short, just because someone is really out to get you, does not mean you are not paranoid; and just because our enemy is really real does not mean we have not also demonized our foe. Perhaps the best way to answer Greenblatt's question and to gain some perspective on our own particular challenges is to recall the lived reality of earlier enmities that Rogin called demonological or countersubversive not because they were false (they were not) but because of how they were lived. This is one of my aims in writing about Post here.

66. "Nothing is more striking to the European traveler in the U.S. than the absence of what we term Government, or the Administration. Written laws exist in America and one sees that they are daily executed; but although everything is in motion, the hand which gives the impulse to the social machine can nowhere be discovered" (Alexis de Tocqueville, *Democracy in America*, vol. I, p. 70).

[The new science of administration] is not of our making; it is a foreign science, speaking very little of the language of English or American principle. It employs only foreign tongues; it utters none but what are to our minds alien ideas.... If we would employ it, we must Americanize it ... radically, in thought, principle, and aim as well. It must learn our constitutions by heart; must get the bureaucratic fever out of its veins; must inhale much free American air. (Woodrow Wilson, "The Study of Administration," 486)

67. Wilson, "The Study of Administration," 486. Recall that Judge George Anderson's inspiring indictment of the Justice Department also played the foreignness card in this way. See note 32 above.

68. See Sheldon Wolin, *Politics and Vision*, for a democratic perspective on bureaucracy's ills and also for an exploration of a middle way between rule of law versus rule of man, by way of Calvin's ideal magistrate. On the latter point, I am indebted to Eldon Eisenach.

69. The same demonological or purifying logic is discernible in Ronald Dworkin's work as well, in which certain "decisionistic" elements of judicial procedure are excised, undone, or tamed by way of an emphasis on the ineluctable workings of norms in the practice of legal interpretation and, in Dworkin's later work, on the importance of moral rules. (Oakeshott too, his account of law's postulates notwithstanding, gives a purified account of what the rule of law is. Others stress the effects of the norms of the legal profession, or bemoan their ineffectiveness, for the same reasons.) Austin Sarat and Thomas Kearns note this dimension of Dworkin's arguments, rightly capturing the domesticative effect of his interpretative norms. They counter by identifying the law in its entirety with the decisionism that Dworkin seeks to excise by way of interpretative norms. Then, since law is now all decision, they charge that law, as such, is violent ("Journey through Forgetting," 247 and passim). But, oddly, insofar as the intent of Sarat and Kearns is to criticize the rule of law's ideological self-presentation, they repeat the terms of that self-presentation. They repeat the rule of law's prejudice, according to which decision, or the rule of man, is as such violent. They only contest the claim that goes with that, the claim that the rule of law, by contrast, is not.

70. Although of course, regularity and predictability are no less available for capture by diverse parties than is technicality. For example: then Attorney General John Ashcroft's defenders said that it was on behalf of regularity and predictability—uniformity—that he issued in September 2003 a new directive limiting the use of plea bargains in federal prosecutions. The directive required federal prosecutors to charge defendants with "the most serious, readily provable offense" in every case and, with some exceptions, not to engage in plea negotiations thereafter. Reactions to the new directive replay the binaries studied here: According to William W. Mercer, the United States attorney in Montana, fairness is precisely what the directive should achieve. "It's meant to minimize unwarranted sentencing disparities among similarly situated defendants." But one man's fairness is another's efficiency. For Alan Vinegrad, a former United States attorney in Brooklyn, the change represents a philosophical shift from "a focus on justice [to] more of a focus on efficiency." In the space between directive and implementation lies ... discretion: "[I]f history is any guide," the *New York Times* reports, "local prosecutors will retain substantial flexibility but will exercise it quietly and early, before rather than after charges are filed." In other words, every directive, like

every law, has its nuances and technicalities, available for exploitation by law's users (Adam Liptak and Eric Lichtblau, "New Plea Bargain Limits Could Swamp Courts, Experts Say," *New York Times*, September 24, 2003).

Chapter Four

1. The story is told in Carol Greenhouse, *A Moment's Notice*, 19.

2. I find a kindred project in Paulo Virno's *A Grammar of the Multitude*. Against Schmitt's late-in-life concern that "[t]he State as the model of political unity, the state as the holder of the most extraordinary of all monopolies, that is to say, of the monopoly of political decision-making ... is being dethroned" (citing *Concept of the Political*, 10), Virno cautions: "One important addition, however, must be made: this monopoly of decision making can be truly taken away from the State only when it ceases once and for all to be a monopoly, only when the multitude asserts its centrifugal character" (*Grammar*, 44).

3. Quoted in Agamben, *State of Exception*, 72.

4. Ibid.

5. Indeed, Rosenzweig's own treatment of the holiday as combining the extraordinary and the ordinary points precisely in this direction. For his anti-exceptionalist reading of the holiday, see his *On Understanding the Sick and the Healthy*.

6. This possibility informs my reading of Antigone in "Antigone's Laments, Creon's Grief."

7. Carl Schmitt, *Political Theology*, 36.

8. Schmitt (1888–1985) published his early *Political Theology* in 1922, two years after Rosenzweig (1886–1929) published his masterpiece, *The Star of Redemption* (1920). Since Schmitt was two years younger than Rosenzweig, both thinkers were thirty-four years old at the time of these publications.

9. Hilary Putnam, Introduction to *Understanding the Sick and the Healthy*.

10. See his critique of historicist and materialist "atheistic" theology in his early essay, "Atheistic Theology."

11. It is hard not to think of Whitman's "Reconciliation" here: "For my enemy is dead—a man divine as myself is dead."

12. On this point, Simon Critchley is unrelenting (and also more than a little Rosenzweigian). See his *Infinitely Demanding*, 144:

> It sometimes seems to me that the only thing in which many American leftists believe, particularly the Habermasians squirming in their seats since 9/11, is law, particularly international law. International law is a very nice thing, but if it fails to have an anchor in everyday social practices then it leads to a politics of abstraction.

13. Not nonsovereign, but limitedly so, she is careful to say (*The Human Condition*, 245). See also her posthumously published "Introduction into Politics" for a discussion of miracle as that which defies likelihood, an example of which is, on her account, the birth of life from inanimate matter ("Introduction," 111). As this treatment of miracle shows, for Arendt the rupture of new beginning is

immanent rather than (as in Schmitt) transcendent. Strikingly, Habermas enters the debate about theology and (non-)causality too, identifying a difference within the concept of creation that sets in motion both material causal chain and the creativity of free moral agents.

> Because he is both in one, God the Creator and God the Redeemer, this creator does not need, in his actions, to abide by the laws of nature like a technician.... From the very beginning, the voice of God calling into life communicates within a morally sensitive universe.... Now, one need not believe in theological premises in order to understand what follows from this, namely, that an entirely different kind of dependence, perceived as a causal one, becomes involved if the difference assumed as inherent in the concept of creation were to disappear. (Habermas, "Faith and Knowledge," 115)

14. For more on this point, see my *Political Theory and the Displacement of Politics*, chapter 4.

15. Arendt, *The Human Condition*, 180, italics added. Arendt's rebuttal of Schmitt begins, however, in her dissertation on Augustine, as John Wolfe Ackerman points out, when she juxtaposes to Schmitt's political theology of decision her own alternative political theological focus on the "encounter" (John Wolfe Ackerman, "The Memory of a Common World: Hannah Arendt, Carl Schmitt and Politics After Totalitarianism," (citing Arendt: Der Liebesbegriff bei Augustin, pp. 52–53) given at the conference, "Concentrationary Memories: The Politics of Representation 1945–1985," University of Leeds, UK, 23–25 March 2009, paper on file with author.

16. Arendt mentions Schmitt explicitly in three footnotes in *Origins*: 251 n. 76, 266 n. 110, 339 n. 65.

17. Historically, it is entirely possible the Schmitt knew of Rosenzweig's work, since he was in contact with two others who did: Walter Benjamin and the theologian, Karl Barth. Rosenzweig is footnoted and referenced by Benjamin in his *Trauerspiel*, so Schmitt and Arendt would have known of him.

18. Schmitt, *Political Theology*, 36–37, italics added.

19. This suggests, perhaps, that secular theorists who prize willfulness, such as Nietzsche or Richard Flathman, may owe an uncomfortable debt to a certain (post)theological tradition.

20. As, indeed, Eric Santner points out when he says that Rosenzweig's concept of miracle suspends the torsion of norm-exception in which Schmitt's miracle is mired. On the sense of stuckness, see Santner, "The Neighbor," 103 and passim. See also chapter 3 in this book, on Louis Post, and my response to David Cole regarding the rights-exception circle, "A Legacy of Xenophobia."

21. Rosenzweig, "Prayer for Sacrifices," 352.

22. On the holiday, see "Convalescence" in *On Understanding the Sick and Healthy*, 95–99.

23. As Else-Rahel Freund notes, *The Star of Redemption* begins with the words "From death" (mere life) and concludes with the words "into life" (more life). Freund quoted in Zachary Braiterman, "'Into Life?' Franz Rosenzweig and the Figure of Death."

24. Nahum Glatzer, Introduction to *Franz Rosenzweig: His Life and Thought*.

25. Rosenzweig, *Star*, 284. Thanks to Leora Batnitzky for reminding me of this passage and its relevance here.

26. *Star*, 103.

27. This is Santner's parsing, "Miracles Happen," 79. See Rosenzweig, "Atheistic Theology."

28. In short, for Rosenzweig, the hostility of atheistic theology to miracle both, as it were, canceled and preserved the miracle. For him, exception and law, miracle and lawfulness are co-constitutive and, to really fulfill the Enlightenment Project (of rationality, progress, etc.), miracle would have to be rethought, not rejected. A different miracle or exception needs to be thought—this is the challenge of what he calls the new thinking—rather than a championing of the old miracle or decision against the law that seeks to replace it or render it moot. See Santner, "Miracles Happen," 102–3 on the need to suspend the state of exception itself to get out of the "Gordian knot" of law-exception or, as I call it, the rights exception circle. On Rosenzweig's effort to move beyond the limits of Cohen's neo-Kantianism, see Paul Mendes-Flohr, "Rosenzweig's Concept of Miracle"; Leora Batnitzky, *Idolatry and Representation*.

29. *Star*, 104.

30. On the miracle as portent, see Mendes-Flohr, "Rosenzweig's Concept," 55; on the event as portent, see Kant on the French Revolution, "The Contest of the Faculties," 181–82.

31. Quoted in Mendes-Flohr, "Rosenzweig's Concept," 55.

32. Thus far, this is the view taken as well by mid-twentieth-century scientist Immanuel Velikovsky, who sought to show that biblical miracles did not contravene but rather occurred in accordance with laws of nature. Velikovsky, *Worlds in Collision*.

33. Mendes-Flohr, "Rosenzweig's Concept," 66; 63.

34. Rosenzweig, "On Miracles," 290.

35. Arendt, *The Human Condition*, 43, 322. We may recall here Arendt's similar concern, specifically about the hegemonic character of behavioral explanation but also (and here she converges a bit with Rosenzweig) about historicism, which in its folding of action into narrative time and its explanation of events in terms of causes or precedents tended to embed action into the stream of time and deprive events of their inaugural and interruptive, indeed, for her—their miraculous—quality. Rosenzweig's response to the problem is to concede that yes the miracle occurs on that time continuum but not only there: Plural time marks the miracle. Arendt similarly argues that action opens up a new linear time sequence. It leaves the timeline on which it occurred and partitions a new time. Arendt also echoes Rosenzweig when she emphasizes the importance of judgment in prizing and preserving the exceptionality of action; he emphasizes orientation, receptivity, all elements of judgment, as Arendt scholars (e.g., Disch, Bickford) have pointed out.

36. Kant, *Religion within the Boundaries of Mere Reason*.

37. *Star*, 104.

38. Ibid., 105. A similar binary structure is at work in Rosenzweig's discussion of miracle's dependence upon true prayer:

The sole precondition for [a miracle's] coming to pass is that one seeks it in prayer. But with true prayer, and that means prayer apart from will, not with willed prayer, which is the magic practiced by the medicine man. But when true prayer is possible, then the most impossible becomes possible, and if true prayer is impossible then the most possible becomes impossible. Thus it may be possible that the dead awaken and impossible that the sick be healed. (Rosenzweig, "Jehuda Halevi," 83, cited in Mendes-Flohr, "Rosenzweig's Concept," 64.)

39. Mendes-Flohr, "Rosenzweig's Concept," 53.

40. See chapter 1.

41. Santner, "Miracles Happen," 84.

42. American Jewish World Service. Weekly Torah Commentary, Parshat Chukat Balak, 5766, July 8, 2006, http://ajws.org/viewer.html#http://www.ajws.org/ what_we_do/education/resources/dvar_tzedek/sfarim-books-5766.pdf. Of course, Aaron is similarly deprived, but that provokes little commentary.

43. Santner, "Miracles Happen," 84–85, citing Robert Paul, *Moses and Civilization*, 106.

44. Abravenel to Bamidbar, 20:12.

45. Impatience? Why ? Didn't it "work" the first time? *Why* didn't it "work" the first time? Because the first time was already a violation of the order.

46. Rashi says he struck the rock instead of speaking to it; that's all; Rashi to Bamidbar, 20:12.

47. On crises of investiture see Santner, *My Own Private Germany* and *On the Psychotheology of Everyday Life*. On the rule of the talents, see *Psychotheology*.

48. The slippage of Moses from prophet to sorcerer may be in a sense enabled by the absence of sorcerers with whom to contrast him. Moses's credentials as a leader were established in Egypt *by contrast* with the Egyptian magicians who could do what he could, almost. Typical is the episode of the rod and the snake. Moses says his rod will turn into a snake; it does; and then the court magicians perform the same trick with many rods and many snakes seeking to show they can outdo him. But then Moses's snake eats theirs, and thus we see who is the true prophet and who are the mere magicians. This example is rehearsed by Rosenzweig who sees in it confirmation of his distinction between true miracle and mere magic. In Meribah, however, it is just Moses and the Israelites, and the question of whose prophecy is true is, as we shall see, up for grabs.

49. The idea that the people need or ought to be pandered to is also resisted by Rosenzweig, who criticizes Maimonides for his claim that the institution of sacrifice was "a mere pedagogical concession on the part of Moses" (anticipating Kant's identical objection to miracles and ritual, as such). Instead, Rosenzweig argues, ritual in general and sacrifice in particular make manifest "the relationship between the natural necessity of taking food on the one hand and Him who gives food on the other." Here mere life opens the way to more life. Ritual makes the metaphorical concrete. Immediately thereafter, however Rosenzweig concedes the pedagogic function, but it is not "mere." It addresses—and this is his continuing counter to Maimonides—not a lack in the Jewish people, but rather a facet of the human condition as such: Some prayers or rituals respond to human need

(spontaneous prayer). Others, however, exist to create a felt need in humans who might not otherwise experience it (liturgical cycle). An example of the latter is the prayer for the coming of the Messiah—"Man is sufficiently rooted in all life, even the most difficult, so that, although he may have good reason to long for a partial change, he fears a radical one.... yet he must learn to pray for this radical change [the messianic age] even though that prayer may be difficult for him until the change actually occurs" ("Prayer for Sacrifices," 352–53). This necessarily am- bivalent relation to the messianic is thematized many times by Derrida and ap- plies as well to his messianic figure, democracy-to-come. In Rosenzweig, in par- ticular, though, we get the connection (rather than the more usual opposition) between the rootedness in and of mere life and the promise of more, in this case messianic, life.

50. Mendelssohn to BaMidbar 20:6, 12. See *Biur*.

51. Cf. Ibn Ezra to Bamidbar 20:6.

52. Spinoza, *Theological-Political Treatise*, 214; Hardt and Negri, *Empire*, 65; thanks to Julie Cooper on this point.

53. Rashi sees the connection, but not the implications of it. He literalizes, claiming that as long as Miriam was alive, a portable well followed the people in the desert, as reward for her virtue. When she died, the well disappeared, and so the Israelites—whose merits are always in question and do not deserve the well on their own merits—cried for water (but, the implication is, *not* for Miriam).

54. On the politics of lamentation in fifty-century Athens, see my "Antigone's Laments, Creon's Grief."

55. That Moses may have been himself vulnerable, because grieving the loss of Miriam, is a point called to my attention by Hannah Ferenc.

56. So may Rosenzweig know this, and perhaps better than Rousseau. This awareness may underlie Rosenzweig's own attenuation, elsewhere, of the distinc- tion between false and true prophecy or messiah. That attenuation occurs in a note to a poem by Judah ha-Levi, called "The True and the False Messiah." In that note, Rosenzweig argues that

> the false Messiah is as old as the hope for the true Messiah. He is the changing form of this changeless hope. He separates every Jewish generation into those whose faith is strong enough to give themselves up to an illusion, and those whose hope is so strong that they do not allow themselves to be deluded. The former are the better, the latter the stronger. (Rosenzweig, "The True and the False Messiah," 350)

Rousseau takes a dimmer view of the former, calling them "blind factionalists" as we saw in chapter 2.

57. Martin Buber, *Prophetic Faith*, 2–3:

> [T]he connection of the nabi with the future is not that of one who predicts. To be a nabi means to set the audience, to whom the words are addressed, before the choice and decision, directly or indirectly. The future is not something al- ready fixed in this present hour, it is dependent upon the real decision, that is to say the decision in which man takes part in this hour.

And *Prophetic Faith*, 103:

[T]he Israelite prophet utters his words, directing them into an actual and defi-
nite situation. Hardly ever does he foretell a plainly certain future. YHVH does
not deliver into his hand a completed book of fate with all future events written
in it, calling on him to open it in the presence of his hearers. It was something
of this kind the "false prophets" pretended.... Their main "falsity" lay not in
the fact that they prophesy salvation, but that what they prophesy is not dependent on question and alternative. The attitude is closer to the divination of the
heathen than to true Israelite prophecy. The true prophet does not announce an
immutable decree. He speaks into the power of decision lying in the moment,
and in such a way that his message of disaster just touches this power.

I owe this reference to George Shulman, by whose *American Prophecy* I was
well instructed.

58. It also directs our attention to a curious thing about the performative of
prophecy: When this sort of speech act is felicitously received (when it has its
desired effect, which is to induce repentance or rapprochement), the speech act
appears to fail; it fails as prediction. It is rendered constatively false (the predicted
punishment does not come to pass) to the extent that it is performatively effective
(the addressees repent, and so the predicted punishment does not come). Is it the
case, then, that the arc of fulfillment that Rosenzweig saw as central to true
prophecy is undesired by prophecy, which when most effective is least fulfilled?
This certainly seems to be the case if we privilege the perspective of predictive
prophecy. But prophecy may also be remonstrative or hortatory. The two are intertwined but may be analytically distinguished: Predictive prophecy makes providence manifest (behold!), while remonstrating prophecy calls the people to repent lest they be punished for their sins (or else!). The first seems to be the model
that Rosenzweig assumed, the second that presupposed by Buber. The problem
noted here (in which performative success renders prophecy constatively false)
applies more to Buber's sense of remonstrative/decision-oriented prophecy than
to Rosenzweig's predictive/orientation-oriented prophecy. In a way, Rosenzweig
is repeating a version of Spinoza's distinction between prophecy and philosophy
(as Julie Cooper casts it in "Freedom of Speech and Philosophical Citizenship in
Spinoza's Theologico-Political Treatise"). What Spinoza calls prophecy, in which
the people remain dependent upon a leader, is what Rosenzweig brands sorcery
or magic. And what Spinoza calls philosophy is what Rosenzweig calls prophecy,
philosophically understood. A marriage of theology and philosophy was the aim
of Rosenzweig's project. The two kinds of prophecy are connected, however, or
mutually contaminative, for the first kind of prophecy, prediction, often serves
also as a kind of exhortation (second kind of prophecy). Most important, it is a
kind of interpellation: The speech act puts the witness in something like the situation of miracle, and solicits his/her attention and assent.

59. Batnitzky emphasizes the miracle's character as an eventful encounter between human and divine. In this sense, miracle here is the opposite of what she
calls idolatry. It is revelation, or even, if she is correct, representation. Below, I
will ask how *this* definition of miracle would change Schmitt's view of sover-

eignty. That is, how would our view of not just divinity but also sovereignty change if we emphasized encounter rather than command, and (as we shall see Rosenzweig does) orientation *rather than* obedience?

60. Moreover, Bilaam himself poses for readers the question of true versus false prophecy: Rabbi Brant Rosen reads the episode as comic: Bilaam

> is toyed with by God at every turn. Bilaam, the great seer cannot even see what his own ass (pardon the expression) sees.... When Bilaam finally arrives at the Israelite camp, his humiliation deepens: try as he might to curse the Israelites, God makes sure that he can only bless them. Ironically, his blessings over Israel are among the most powerful Biblical poems of praise (including the famous verses *"Mah tovu ohalecha ya'akov"*—"How beautiful are your tents, O Jacob!" which have since become a permanent part of the Jewish morning liturgy). Though some commentators view Bilaam in positive terms, the conventional understanding of this story is as a monotheistic polemic against pseudo-prophets. Indeed, although Bilaam blesses Israel in the end, his blessings are the product of divine manipulation, not authentic piety. It is difficult to read this story and not, on some level, view Bilaam as something of a fraud.

I would add that if the ass can see god's angel and Bilaam cannot, that may be because the ass has experienced subjection (having one master, it may be more alert than a would-be sovereign subject like Bilaam to divinity, a different master), whereas Bilaam who thinks he is a prophet, is not similarly habituated. He is used to self-mastery and so misses the solicitation to mindfulness. Brant Rosen, comment on "Bilaam's Folly and the Evangelical Right," Shalom Rav Blog, posted June 29, 2007, http://rabbibrant.com/2007/06/29/bilaams-folly-and-the-evangelical-right (accessed August 20, 2008).

61. Rosenzweig. *On Jewish Learning*, 22–23. Note, the miracle speaks out of the open Torah but, like the proverbial tree that falls in the woods with no one there to hear it, that is not sufficient. Someone must be listening—in fulfillment of the commandment to do so, we must open our ear.... But, if we can hear what speaks to us, it is because we have put ourselves into a context that opens our ears. In Rosenzweig's case here, he is in synagogue, among others, participating in the Sabbath liturgy, etc., i.e., he has put himself into a material context that opens his ears to hear (notwithstanding his more voluntaristic language).

62. Rosenzweig here and throughout emphasizes the importance of hearing not sight, the word not the gesture, language not spectacle. The eyes, one infers, may be fooled by sleights of hand, as Rousseau knew. True, the witness says "I saw it with my own eyes" but the sense data of vision are surely remote in an episteme governed by an invisible god. The ears are better entrusted with the task of opening us up to the other, and the otherness, of miracle or its possibility. A world in which it is possible to experience miracle is one in which the human is not (self-)sovereign. In the event of encounter between human and divine, the human gives up the will to mastery, and one way to symbolize this is to privilege not sight but hearing. (Batnitzky emphasizes a different aspect of Rosenzweig, arguing persuasively that he took very seriously the powers of sight and visual representation, arguing for their permissibility and power even in the context of

Judaism's ban on idolatry, a ban he took to signal not a prohibition against images but rather a prohibition against mis-taking such images for the divine. As Batnitzky puts it, the problem was not *what* we worship [the object] but rather *how* we worship [the practice].)

63. Jason Frank. *Constituent Moments*.

64. "Taking Exception to the Exception." Conference: Cornell University, September 2006.

65. William Connolly, *Pluralism*, 140.

66. Ibid., 142.

67. Ibid.

68. This possibility extends in a new direction my earlier argument that Moses is a foreign founder. See my *Democracy and the Foreigner*, chapter 2.

69. Michael Walzer, *Exodus and Revolution*, 110.

70. *Star*, 284. In this respect, Louis Post, the subject of chapter 3, whose exploits I admire, and himself a member of the executive branch, was a radical exception.

71. Walzer, *Exodus*, 59–61, 66. I owe this insight to Andre Munro.

72. Talmud, Bava Metzia 59b.

73. Beyond, that is, its function as a tale of procedural autonomy, which is how it is usually treated today. See for example Noam Zohar, "Midrash: Amendment through the Molding of Meaning."

74. Talmud, Bava Metzia 59b.

75. On the role of fables in attenuating the paradox of politics (which I there cast as a paradox of founding), see my article, "Declarations of Independence." On stories and the importance of their beginnings and endings as a resource in attenuating that same paradox, see chapter 1. On the insufficiency of Arendt's fable of founding to secure her politics, see James Martel, *Subverting the Leviathan*, chapter 5.

Chapter Five

1. "1988 Presidential Debates," *CNN.com*, http://www.cnn.com/ELECTION/2000/debates/history.story/1988.html (accessed August 25, 2008).

2. Arendt did, Benhabib acknowledges, write in the Postscript to *Eichmann in Jerusalem* that it "is inconceivable ... that [an international] court would be a criminal tribunal which pronounces on the guilt or innocence of individuals" (*Eichmann in Jerusalem*, 298, quoted in *Another Cosmopolitanism*, 15), but Benhabib pronounces this statement "baffling" and explains that it is symptomatic of Arendt's "civic republican vision of political determination" (*Another Cosmopolitanism*, 15), a vision in need of mediation or overcoming. Benhabib's lectures, positioned as they are, as an effort to mediate between cosmopolitan norms and republican self-determination in part by way of practices of democratic iteration, might well be seen as Benhabib's own iterative effort to offer Arendt the middle way she did not see or might have refused. (But which is it?).

3. For an insightful account of Arendt's *Eichmann in Jerusalem* as a critical engagement with rather than an endorsement of neutral legal proceduralism, see

Lida Maxwell, "From Procedural to Legal Justice: A Reading of Arendt's *Eichmann in Jerusalem*" (paper presented at the annual meeting of the Association for the Study of Law, Culture and the Humanities, Berkeley, CA, March 28–29, 2008).

4. I have in mind here Kant's famous discussion of the absolutism of the prohibition against lying, even to save the life of someone who has sought sanctuary with you, a topic attended to in some detail by Derrida, who casts it as a violation of hospitality.

Cosmopolitics is the term under which Pheng Cheah and Bruce Robbins gather a collection of essays exploring themes of hospitality, transnational debt, and international engagement (*Cosmopolitics: Thinking and Feeling Beyond the Nation*). Derrida identifies Kant with a mere "cosmopolitics" and notes that Levinas never used that term, nor the more usual "cosmopolitanism," preferring instead: "universalism." Derrida suggests that Levinas abjured the term "cosmopolitanism" or "cosmopolitics" (Derrida does not here distinguish the two) for two reasons:

first, because this sort of political thought refers [to] pure hospitality and this peace to an indefinite progress [which also always "retains the trace of a natural hostility," which is its point of departure in Kant]; second, because of the well-known ideological connotations with which modern anti-Semitism saddled the great tradition of a cosmopolitanism passed down from Stoicism or Pauline Christianity to the Enlightenment and to Kant. (Derrida, *Adieu—to Emmanuel Levinas*, 88)

5. Derrida, *Rogues*, 145; 173 n. 12, citing *Of Hospitality, On Cosmopolitanism and Forgiveness*, and *Adieu*.

6. Derrida, *Adieu*, 47; *Of Hospitality*, 25–27.

7. Derrida, *Rogues*, 173 n. 12.

8. See Derrida, "Hostipitality."

9. This is reminiscent of Rogers Smith's effort to identify ascriptive moments in United States history not with the liberal tradition but with alternative ascriptive rivals to that tradition (Rogers M. Smith, "Beyond Tocqueville, Myrdal, and Hartz"). On Smith, see Jacqueline Stevens, "Beyond Tocqueville, Please!" and my *Democracy and the Foreigner*, chaps. 1 and 5.

10. As Derrida puts the point in the "Force of Law": "The undecidable remains caught, lodged, as a ghost at least, but an essential ghost, in every decision, in every event of decision. Its ghostliness deconstructs from within all assurance of presence, all certainty or all alleged criteriology assuring us of the justice of a decision" (Derrida, "Force of Law," 253).

11. Derrida, *Rogues*, 172 n. 12.

12. Arendt, *The Origins of Totalitarianism*, 296.

13. Arendt, *On Revolution*, 82–87.

14. A similar point is made by Etienne Balibar, who says that Arendt's

"right to have rights" does not feature a *minimal* remainder of the political, made of juridical and moral claims to be protected by a constitution; it is much more the idea of a *maximum*. Or, better said, it refers to the continuous process in which a minimal recognition of the belonging of human beings to the "common" sphere of existence (and therefore also work, culture, public and private speech) *already* involves—and makes possible—a totality of rights. I call this the "insurrectional" element of democracy, which plays a determinant role in every constitution of a democratic or republican state. (*We, the People of Europe?* 120).

(Note that democracy, quite properly, is not here cast as insurrectional, but as having an "insurrectional element.")

15. For another take on the paradox of rights, to which I refer elsewhere in this book, see Wendy Brown, "Suffering the Paradoxes of Rights."

16. Indeed, Benhabib herself confesses in the final version of the lectures that she may have been, with regard to the French headscarf case, overly optimistic, given events in the subsequent year (*Another Cosmopolitanism*, 75 n. 8.). Etienne Balibar, by contrast, is not less optimistic. He is cutting: The Maastricht definition of European citizenship that awards EU citizenship to nationals of any constituent national state, he says, "immediately transforms a project of inclusion into a program of exclusion," given the size of the resident alien population in Europe at the time and given the dependence of Europe on that population's labor. *We, the People of Europe?* 122.

17. Balibar, *We, the People of Europe?* 122, 162 and passim. For example, "European citizenship, within the limits of the currently existing union, is not conceived of as a recognition of the rights and contributions of *all* the communities present upon European soil, but as a postcolonial isolation of 'native' and 'nonnative' populations" (ibid., 170).

18. I am thinking here of Arendt's discussion of the Dreyfus case as well as of her argument that police powers developed to deal with the stateless after World War II would, if left unchecked, soon be used against the general population. Arendt, *Origins of Totalitarianism*, pt. I, chap. 4; pt. II, chap. 9.

19. In her discussion of the French Marianne (*Another Cosmopolitanism*, 59–61), Benhabib leaves the terrain of law altogether to mark out the importance of cultural politics, with which I agree. In only one instance does Benhabib leave the terrain staked out by the binary of formal law versus democratic contestation to acknowledge the abundant powers of administrative discretion, and the example she mentions is a positive one of discretionary power used to the good: "Although officially the wearing of the 'turban' (a form of headscarf worn by observant Muslim women) is banned [in Turkey], many faculty members as well as administrators tolerate it when they can" (ibid., 79). On discretion and the rule of law, see chapter 3 above.

20. *Another Cosmopolitanism*, 60.

21. Ibid.

22. Ibid., 61. Here she seems almost to echo Julia Kristeva, whose (more) French universalism I criticized in detail in *Democracy and the Foreigner*, chapter 3.

23. Derrida, *Of Hospitality*, 15.

24. This claim is one I defend at length vis–à–vis Rawls and Sandel in *Political Theory and the Displacement of Politics*, chapter 5.

25. *Another Cosmopolitanism*, 17. Compare with her earlier casting of the paradox:

Rousseau's distinction between the "will of all" and "the general will," between what specific individuals under concrete circumstances believe to be in their best interest and what they would believe to be in their collective interest if they were properly enlightened, expresses the paradox of democratic legitimacy. Democratic rule, which views the will of the people as sovereign, is based upon the regulative fiction that the exercise of such sovereignty is legitimate, i.e., can be normatively justified, only insofar as such exercise of power also expresses a "general will," that is, a collective good that is said to be equally in the interests of all. (Benhabib, "Deliberative Rationality and Models of Democratic Legitimacy," 28–29)

26. *Another Cosmopolitanism*, 35; 18.

27. Ibid, 19.

28. That is to say, democratic iterations will converge with cosmopolitan norms and the international and national law that give expression to them.

29. *Another Cosmopolitanism*, 34.

30. Ibid., 67. Benhabib finds it likely that the experience of standing up to the state will provide the girls with the resources to "engage and contest the very meaning of the Islamic traditions that they are now fighting to uphold."

31. In Canada, alien suffrage was ended at the same time as some women (military wives) were first given the vote (1917–18). Until then, coresidents were assumed to share a fate, a shared future, if not a past. This is different from the German court's invocation of "fate" in its decision on alien suffrage, in which, it seems, the fact that people moved once (in a cross-border migration; presumably other residents had moved too but not across national borders) was taken as license to script those people as always about to leave. (This, it seems to me is the real offense, insofar as it bespeaks the unimaginability of real immigration. They may have come here but they are never really here because, having come from elsewhere, they will certainly leave; they will be called home? Or expelled, deported?) In other words, the fact of proximity, so important in this chapter, is radically undone by a symbolic politics that scripts the immigrant not as one who is here but rather as one who is always on his way out (evidence for which, as it were, is that he came here in the first place).

32. At the lectures Benhabib responded, as Habermas also has to objections like this one, by acknowledging the fact of the regress, saying OK, "one step forward two steps back." This response is different from the double gesture called for here insofar as it rescues progress from any evidence against it, and preserves the linearity of its timeline: Progress and regress are two sides of the same coin and regress is here suffered due to the promise of progress. Thus, the alternative to progressive time is not regress but rather plural temporalities, an idea developed by William Connolly (along with some useful thoughts on cosmopolitanism) in his recent work, *Pluralism*, and commented upon by me in chapter 2, above.

33. *Another Cosmopolitanism*, 46.

34. Derrida, *The Other Heading*, 48.

35. I take Wendy Brown to have something like this approach in mind when she talks about "suffering the paradoxes of rights," in *Left Legalism, Left Critique*.

36. *Another Cosmopolitanism*, 47.

37. The same might be said as well for the new human rights regime itself, which as Derrida points out, is a new site of sovereignty and counters sovereignty with sovereignty, not with nonsovereignty.

38. Nevzat Soguk, *States and Strangers*. On the camps, see Etienne Balibar, "Europe as Borderland."

39. Giorgio Agamben, *Homo Sacer*.

40. Here Benhabib provides a minor amendment to Habermas, who treats constitutionalism as if it were merely the rule of law. He does not attend to constitutions as expressions of particularity. (I, myself, criticize him on this point, as does Alessandro Ferrara. See our replies to Habermas: Honig, "Dead Rights, Live Futures"; Ferrara, "On Boats and Principles.") Benhabib, by contrast, does emphasize the character of the act of political self-legislation as an act of self-constitution in which the "we" defines itself as a "we" in relation to a territorialized setting.

41. *Another Cosmopolitanism*, 67, 53.

42. Aldon Morris, *The Origins of the Civil Rights Movement*.

43. Derrida, *Of Hospitality*, 65.

44. Ibid., 57.

45. *Another Cosmopolitanism*, 57.

46. See my *Democracy and the Foreigner*, chapter 3, for a detailed discussion of this issue.

47. Most of the arguments relevant here are well summarized by Anand Bertrand Commissiong in the review of David Held, *Global Covenant: The Social Democratic Alternative to the Washington Consensus*, published in *Logos*, May 2005.

> The challenges the authority and execution of international legal regimes face in controlling these [i.e., antimodern] forces [both of Bush's messianism and of Islamic extremists] illustrate further the complexities of the stalemate. As Tocqueville noted, courts in a democracy represent an undemocratic strain essential to the system's proper functioning. The relation between natural law and democratic will, a key component of modernity, was accomplished over several hundred years partly through the compromise of political negotiation in successful national formation processes in Europe and North America. But this process in many cases also violently ruled out effectively dissolutionary elements that sought to establish smaller, autonomous units (Tilly). Even in some Western countries these forces were not entirely pacified and still simmer.... [Held's] vision can only be realized if some sense of world-wide solidarity, or covenant if you will, develops to take shared control of these networks.

48. Michael Rogin, *Ronald Reagan, the Movie*; Derrida. *On Cosmopolitanism and Forgiveness*.

49. Santner, *Creaturely Life*, 207, original emphasis.

50. *Star*, 252; see also Santner, *Creaturely Life*, 207.

51. Alex Kotlowitz, "The Politics of Ibrahim Parlak: How did a political refugee who became a popular café owner in a small Michigan town suddenly become a terrorist in the eyes of the government? A post 9/11 story," *New York Times Magazine*, March 20, 2005, 46.

52. U.S. District Judge Avern Cohn set bail at $50,000 for Parlak on May 21, 2005, deciding that he should be free while he appeals his deportation. As the *Chicago Sun-Times* reported, Judge Cohn reasoned that otherwise Parlak "was likely to be held for an unreasonable time period, given the complexity of his deportation case." Released on bond on June 3, Parlak is back in Harbert, Michigan, for the time being while his lawyers prepare his appeal. *Ibrahim Parlak v. Robin Baker* (Detroit Field Office Director, US Immigration and Customs), U.S. District Court for the Eastern District of Michigan Case No. 05-70826. See also Monifa Thomas, "Jailed Immigrant to Get Out on Bond," *Chicago Sun-Times*, May 21, 2005, 6; Jeff Romig, "Family, Friends Embrace Parlak," *South Bend Tribune*, June 4, 2005, A1, and http://www.harborcountry-news.com/articles/2006/03/23/news/story2.txt.

53. http://www.freeibrahim.com.

54. On sister cities, see chapter 3, *Democracy and the Foreigner*, and the several sources cited therein. Derrida also looks to cities as a source of promise for a new cosmopolitanism: See *On Cosmopolitanism and Forgiveness*.

55. Entry into citizenship and entry into marriage, at least normalized, permitted marriage, are two of those moments (paradoxically permanent moments) at which the state's role as authorizer empowers it over those who seek its recognition and rewards. States, the United States in particular, insist that we treat both institutions romantically, not instrumentally. Both are contracts that we must enter into with the least contractual motives, out of a noninstrumental desire to belong, or to share, or to contribute but never out of a desire to profit in any way from the relationship. This indeed is the quandary faced by those who seek refuge in states like France and the United States. Neediness marks the would-be immigrant as an undesirable. But, as Etienne Balibar points out in *We, the People of Europe?*, who but the needy would come? I discuss the connections between marriage and citizenship in "Foreign Brides, Family Ties, and New World Masculinity," in chapter 4 of *Democracy and the Foreigner*.

56. Balibar calls also for works of citizenship addressed to economic power, or that put religious knowledge in comparative perspective in "Difficult Europe," in *We, the People of Europe?* 173 and passim.

57. Robert M. Cover, "The Supreme Court, 1982 Term, Foreword: Nomos and Narrative."

58. Benhabib, *Another Cosmopolitanism*, 15; 190.

59. For an analysis of Arendt's critique of moralized politics and of the Kantian injunction that politics should bend its knee to morality, see my *Political Theory and the Displacement of Politics*, chapter 4.

60. But Arendt's legalism is different from Benhabib's. On this, see Lida Maxwell, "From Procedural to Legal Justice."

61. *Eichmann in Jerusalem*, 223–24. For an alternative, more empathic and insightful treatment of the K-Zetnik episode, see Shoshana Felman, *The Juridical Unconscious*.

62. Benhabib, *Another Cosmopolitanism*, 60–61.

63. Ibid., 161; 163.

64. On the politics of (non)seriousness see chapters 1 and 2, with regard to Holmes and Slow Food. See also Simon Critchley, who knows that "comical

tactics can hide a serious political intent" (though, I would add, sometimes the tactic *is* the intent). Critchley, *Infinitely Demanding*, 124.

65. Benhabib, *Another Cosmopolitanism*, 164.

66. For a brief in favor of irrelevance see my "Against Relevance."

67. Here are some quotations from my original reply that evidence a more nuanced position ("Another Cosmopolitanism," 102–27):

> Arendt's unconditional right to have rights is as good a motto as any for that project, as long as we understand rights to imply a world-building that is not incompatible with the project of building juridical institutions and safeguards, but also reaches beyond that project because it is wary of the sedimentations of power and discretion that accrete in such institutional contexts.

> [W]e can enact *droits de cité*—by taking people in, harboring them, offering them shelter, finding sympathetic agents of discretionary power who are willing to look the other way—while also risking the re-authorization of law's authoritative institutions by working through them to win papers or amnesty for those who are here.

> Meanwhile a group called Free Ibrahim has formed. Their slogan is "Ibrahim for Citizen" and they have succeeded in getting Senator Carl Levin and two representatives to introduce two bills in the House and Senate to make Parlak a permanent resident should he fail to prevail in the courts.

> We should "approve of movements like Free Ibrahim, and of those that demand alien suffrage for co-residents—'because they are here.' But advocates of an agonistic cosmopolitics would work at the same time to prevent the energies of those movements from being lost once their state-centered and state-affirming goals are won."

> Were all this to happen and to be visible to us (for it does happen, but it is often not visible) through lenses that do not *privilege* (although they do take note of and seek to engage, improve, and democratize) formal legal, state, state-like, and interstate institutions, then we might see more worldliness, in Hannah Arendt's sense of care for the world.

68. Benhabib, *Another Cosmopolitanism*, 164.

69. Ibid., 163.

70. Ibid., 164.

71. On one impact of those phantasms, see Penelope Deutscher's contrast of Derrida and Blackstone on the decision: Derrida, she says,

> emphasizes ... the importance of recognizing the incalculability and "undecidability" of law. Compare with Blackstone, for example, whose aim is to make the law as calculable and predictable as possible. Though this is what we most often expect from the law, Derrida nonetheless emphasizes the simultaneous importance of the undecidable factor in legal decision-making. (Deutscher, *How to Read Derrida*, 97)

72. *Another Cosmopolitanism*, 162; 159.

73. *All Too Human*, §466, and *The Gay Science* §108.

74. For an account of Rosenzweig and Derrida on the generative possibilities of repetition, see Zachary Braiterman, "Cyclical Motions and the Force of Repetition in the Thought of Franz Rosenzweig." See also Arendt: "Experiences and even the stories which grow out of what men do and endure, of happenings and events, sink back into the futility inherent in the living word and the living deed unless they are talked about over and over again" (OR, 222). On the need to inhabit and not just argue for a position, I recur to the passage from Rosenzweig with which this volume's Introduction began:

> Everyone should philosophize at some time in his life, and look around from his own vantage point. But such a survey is not an end in itself. The book is no goal, even a provisional one. Rather than sustaining itself, or being sustained by others of its kind, it must itself be "verified." This verification takes place in the course of everyday life.

Aftermath

1. This is Jonathan Lear's project for a postnarrative psychoanalysis as well, in *Happiness, Death, and the Remainder of Life.*

Bibliography

Ackerman, John Wolfe. "The Memory of a Common World: Hannah Arendt, Carl Schmitt and Politics After Totalitarianism" given at the conference, "Concentrationary Memories: The Politics of Representation 1945-1985," University of Leeds, UK, 23-25 March 2009, paper on file with author.

Agamben, Giorgio. *Homo Sacer: Sovereign Power and Bare Life.* Translated by Daniel Heller-Roazen. Stanford, CA: Stanford University Press, 1998.

———. *State of Exception,* translated by Kevin Attell. Chicago: University of Chicago Press, 2005.

Altmann, Alexander. *Moses Mendelssohn: A Biographical Study.* Tuscaloosa: University of Alabama Press, 1973.

Amar, Akhil. *Bill of Rights.* New Haven: Yale University Press, 1998.

American Jewish World Service. Weekly Torah Commentary, Parshat Chukat Balak, 5766 (8 July 2006). http://ajws.org/viewer.html#http://www.ajws.org/what_we_do/education/resources/dvar_tzedek/sfarim-books-5766.pdf.

Arato, Andrew. "The Bush Tribunals and the Specter of Dictatorship." *Constellations* 9, no. 4 (Winter 2002): 457–76.

Arendt, Hannah. *On Revolution.* New York: Penguin Books, 1963.

———. *The Life of the Mind.* New York: Harcourt, 1981.

———. *The Origins of Totalitarianism.* New York: Harcourt, 1985.

———. *Eichmann in Jerusalem: A Report on the Banality of Evil.* New York: Penguin Books, 1994.

———. *The Human Condition,* 2nd Edition. Chicago: University of Chicago Press, 1998.

———. "Introduction into Politics." In *The Promise of Politics.* Edited by Jerome Kohn. New York: Schocken, 2005.

Aristotle. *De Anima.* Translated by Hugh Lawson-Tancred. New York: Penguin Books, 1986.

Austin, J. L. *How to Do Things with Words.* Edited by J. O. Urmson and Marina Sbisà. Cambridge, MA: Harvard University Press, 1975.

Badiou, Alain. *Saint Paul: The Foundation of Universalism.* Translated by Roy Brassier. Stanford: Stanford University Press, 2003.

Balakrishnan, Gopal. *The Enemy: An Intellectual Portrait of Carl Schmitt.* London: Verso, 2000.

Balibar, Etienne. *We, the People of Europe?* Translated by James Swenson. Princeton: Princeton University Press, 2003.

———. "Europe as Borderland." Paper presented as the Alexander von Humboldt Lecture in Human Geography, University of Nijmegen, November 10, 2004. http://www.ru.nl/socgeo/n/colloquium/Europe%20as%20Borderlandpdf.

Batnitzky, Leora. *Idolatry and Representation: The Philosophy of Franz Rosenzweig Reconsidered.* Princeton: Princeton University Press, 2000.

Benhabib, Seyla. "Democracy and Difference: Reflections on the Metapolitics of Lyotard and Derrida" *Journal of Political Philosophy* 2, no. 1 (March 1994): 1–23.

———. "Deliberative Rationality and Models of Democratic Legitimacy" *Constellations* 1, no. 1 (December 1994): 26–52.

———. "Feminism and Postmoderism." In *Feminist Contentions: A Philosophical Exchange*. Edited by Seyla Benhabib, Judith Butler, and Drucilla Cornell. New York: Routledge, 1995.

———. *The Claims of Culture: Equality and Diversity in the Global Era*. Princeton: Princeton University Press, 2002.

———. "The 'Claims' of Culture Properly Interpreted: Response to Nikolas Kompridis." *Political Theory* 34, no. 3 (June 2006): 383–88.

———. *Another Cosmopolitanism. The Tanner Lectures*. Edited by Robert Post. New York: Oxford University Press, 2008.

Bennington, Geoffrey. *Legislations*. New York: Verso, 1994.

Bickford, Susan. "In the Presence of Others: Arendt and Anzaldúa on the Paradox of Public Appearance." In *Feminist Interpretations of Hannah Arendt*. Edited by Bonnie Honig. University Park: Penn State Press, 1995.

Braiterman, Zachary. "'Into Life?' Franz Rosenzweig and the Figure of Death." *AJS Review* 23, no. 2 (1998): 203–21.

———. "Cyclical Motions and the Force of Repetition in the Thought of Franz Rosenzweig." In *Beginning/Again*. Edited by Aryeh Cohen and Shaul Magid. New York: Seven Bridges Press, 2005.

Brown, Wendy. "Suffering the Paradoxes of Rights." In *Left Legalism/Left Critique*. Edited by Wendy Brown and Janet Halley. Durham: Duke University Press, 2002.

Buber, Martin. *Prophetic Faith*. New York: Harper and Row, 1960.

Butler, Judith. *Antigone's Claim: Kinship Between Life and Death*. New York: Columbia University Press, 2000.

———. *Precarious Life: The Powers of Mourning and Violence*. London: Verso, 2006.

Candeloro, Dominic. "Louis Post and the Red Scare of 1920." *Prologue: The Journal of the National Archives* 2, no. 1 (Spring 1979).

———. "Louis Freeland Post: Carpetbagger, Single-taxer, Progressive." Ph.D. diss., University of Illinois at Urbana-Champaigne, 1970.

Center for Constitutional Rights. http://ccrjustice.org/.

Cheah, Pheng, and Bruce Robbins, editors. *Cosmopolitics: Thinking and Feeling Beyond the Nation*. Minneapolis: University of Minnesota Press, 1998.

Christodoulidis, Emilios A. "The Aporia of Sovereignty: On the Representation of the People in Constitutional Discourse." *The King's College Law Journal* 12, no. 1 (2001): 111–33.

Cole, David. "Their Liberties, Our Security." *Boston Review*. December 2002/January 2003, http://bostonreview.net/BR27.6/cole.html (accessed August 29, 2008).

———. *Enemy Aliens: Double Standards and Constitutional Freedoms in the War on Terrorism*. New York: New Press, 2003.

———. *Justice at War: The Men and Ideas That Shaped America's War on Terror*. New York: New York Review Books, 2008.

Cole, David, and James X. Dempsey. *Terrorism and the Constitution: Sacrificing Civil Liberties for National Security*. New York: New Press, 2006.

Cole, David, and Jules Lobel. *Less Safe, Less Free: Why America Is Losing the War on Terror*. New York: New Press, 2007.

Commissiong, Anand Bertrand. "Review of David Held, *Global Covenant: The Social Democratic Alternative to the Washington Consensus*." *Logos* 4, no. 2 (Spring 2005), http://www.logosjournal.com/issue_4.2/commissiong.htm (accessed August 29, 2008).

Connolly, William E. *Political Theory and Modernity*. Ithaca: Cornell University Press, 1993.

———. *The Ethos of Pluralization*. Minneapolis: University of Minnesota Press, 1995.

———. *Why I Am Not a Secularist*. Minneapolis: University of Minnesota Press, 1999.

———. *Identity/Difference: Democratic Negotiations of Political Paradox*. Expanded Edition. Minneapolis: University of Minnesota Press, 2002.

———. *Neuropolitics: Thinking, Culture, Speed*. Minneapolis: University of Minnesota Press, 2002.

———. *Pluralism*. Durham: Duke University Press, 2005.

Cooper, Julie E. "Freedom of Speech and Philosophical Citizenship in Spinoza's Theologico-Political Treatise." *Law, Culture and the Humanities* 2, no. 1 (2006): 91–114.

Cover, Robert M. "The Supreme Court, 1982 Term, Foreword: Nomos and Narrative." *Harvard Law Review* 97, no. 4 (1983): 4–69.

Critchley, Simon. *Infinitely Demanding: Ethics of Commitment, Politics of Resistance*. London: Verso, 2007.

De Grazia, David. "Regarding the Last Frontier of Bigotry." *Logos* 4, no. 2 (Spring 2005), http://www.logosjournal.com/issue_4.2/degrazia.htm (accessed August 29, 2008).

De Landa, Manuel. *A Thousand Years of Nonlinear History*. New York: Zone, 1997.

Derrida, Jacques. 1985. "Deconstruction in America: An Interview with Jacques Derrida." Edited by James Creech, Peggy Kamuf, and Jane Todd. *Critical Exchange* 17 (Winter 1985): 1–32.

———. "Signature, Event, Context." In *Limited Inc*. Edited by Gerald Graff. Translated by Jeffrey Mehlman and Samuel Weber. Evanston: Northwestern University Press, 1988.

———. *The Other Heading: Reflections on Today's Europe*. Translated by Pascale-Anne Brault and Michael B. Naas. Bloomington: Indiana University Press, 1992.

———. *Adieu to Emmanuel Levinas*. Translated by Pascale-Anne Brault and Michael B. Naas. Stanford: Stanford University Press, 1999.

———. *Of Hospitality*. Translated by Rachel Bowlby. Stanford: Stanford University Press, 2000.

———. "Force of Law: The 'Mystical Foundation of Authorty.'" In *Acts of Religion*. Edited by Gil Anidjar. New York: Routledge, 2001.

———. "Hostipitality." In *Acts of Religion*. Edited by Gil Anidjar. New York: Routledge, 2001.

———. *On Cosmopolitanism and Forgiveness*. Translated by Mark Dooley and Michael Hughes. New York: Routledge, 2001.

———. "Living On." Translated by James Hulbert. In *Deconstruction and Criticism*. By Harold Bloom et al. New York: Continuum, 2004.

———. *Rogues: Two Essays on Reason*. Translated by Pascale-Anne Brault and Michael B. Naas. Stanford: Stanford University Press, 2005.

Dershowitz, Alan. *Why Terrorism Works*. New Haven: Yale University Press, 2002.

Deutscher, Penelope. *How to Read Derrida*. New York: W. W. Norton, 2006.

Diamond, Cora. "The Difficulty of Reality and the Difficulty of Philosophy." In *Reading Cavell*. Edited by Alice Crary and Sanford Shieh. London: Routledge, 2006.

Dietz, Mary G. "Merely Combating the Phrases of This World: Recent Democratic Theory." *Political Theory* 26 (February 1998): 112–39.

———. "Working in Half-Truth." In *Turning Operations*. New York: Routledge, 2002.

Disch, Lisa. "On Friendship in 'Dark Times.'" *Feminist Interpretations of Hannah Arendt*. Edited by Bonnie Honig. University Park: Penn State Press, 1995.

Dorff, Elliot, and Arthur Rosett. *A Living Tree: The Roots and Growth of Jewish Law*. Albany: State University of New York Press, 1988.

Elster, Jon. *Ulysses and the Sirens: Studies in Rationality and Irrationality*. Cambridge, UK: Cambridge University Press, 1984.

Erlin, Matt. "Reluctant Modernism: Moses Mendelssohn's Philosophy of History." *Journal of the History of Ideas* 63, no. 1 (January 2002): 83–104.

Farrington, Anthony. "Bengkulu: An Anglo-Chinese Partnership." In *The Worlds of the East India Company*. Edited by H. V. Bowen et al. Woodbridge: Boydell Press, 2002.

Felman, Shoshana. *The Juridical Unconscious: Trials and Traumas of the Twentieth Century*. Cambridge, MA: Harvard University Press, 2002.

Ferrara, Alessandro. "On Boats and Principles: Reflections on Habermas's 'Constitutional Democracy,'" *Political Theory* 29, no. 6 (December 2001): 782–91.

Fish, Stanley. *Self-Consuming Artifacts: The Experience of Seventeenth-Century Literature*. Berkeley: University of California Press, 1972.

Fitzpatrick, Peter. *Modernism and the Grounds of Law*. New York: Cambridge University Press, 2001.

Flathman, Richard. *The Practice of Rights*. New York: Cambridge University Press, 1976.

———. *Willful Liberalism: Voluntarism and Individuality in Political Theory and Practice*. Ithaca: Cornell University Press, 1992.

Frank, Jason. "'Besides Our Selves': An Essay on Enthusiastic Politics and Civil Subjectivity." *Public Culture* 17 (Fall 2005): 371–92.

———. *Constituent Moments: Enacting the People in Postrevolutionary America*. Durham: Duke University Press, forthcoming.

Fuller, Lon. *The Morality of Law*. New Haven: Yale University Press, 1969.

Glatzer, Nahum N. Introduction to *Franz Rosenzweig: His Life and Thought*. Edited by Nahum N. Glatzer. Indianapolis: Hackett, 1998.

Goldman, Emma. *Living My Life*. New York: Dover, 1970.

Gooch, G. P. *Germany and the French Revolution*. New York: Russell and Russell, 1966.

Gould, Carol. "Diversity and Democracy: Representing Differences." In *Democracy and Difference: Contesting the Boundaries of the Political*. Edited by Seyla Benhabib. Princeton: Princeton University Press, 1996.

Greenhouse, Carol J. *A Moment's Notice: Time Politics across Cultures*. Ithaca: Cornell University Press, 1996.

Habermas, Jürgen. *Between Facts and Norms: Contributions to a Discourse Theory of Law and Democracy*. Translated by William Rehg. Cambridge, MA: MIT Press, 1996.

———. "On the Relation between the Nation, the Rule of Law, and Democracy." In *Inclusion of the Other*. Cambridge, MA: MIT Press, 1998.

———. "Constitutional Democracy: A Paradoxical Union of Contradictory Principles?" Translated by William Rehg. *Political Theory* 29, no. 6 (December 2001): 766–81.

———. "Faith and Knowledge." In *The Future of Human Nature*. Malden: Polity Press, 2003.

Halevi, Jehuda. "Jehuda Halevi: Fünfundneunzig Hymnen und Gedichte deutsch und hebräisch." Translated by Franz Rosenzweig. In *Franz Rosenzweig, Der Mensch und sein Werk. Gesammelte Schriften IV.1*. Den Haag: M. Nijhoff, 1983.

Hardt, Michael, and Antonio Negri. *Empire*. Cambridge, MA: Harvard University Press, 2000.

Hare, R. M. *Moral Thinking: Its Levels, Methods and Point*. New York: Oxford University Press, 1982.

Hartley, L. P. *The Go-between*. London: H. Hamilton, 1953.

Hayek, Friedrich. *The Constitution of Liberty*. Chicago: University of Chicago Press, 1960.

Hegel, G.W.F. *Philosophy of Right*. Translated by T. M. Knox. New York: Oxford University Press, 1967.

Hensel, Sebastian. *The Mendelssohn Family 1729–1847, from Letters and Journals*, 2nd Edition. Translated by by Carl Klingemann. New York: Harper and Brothers, 1882.

Holmes, Stephen. "Precommitment and the Paradox of Democracy." In *Constitutionalism and Democracy*. Edited by Jon Elster and Rune Slagstad. Cambridge, UK: Cambridge University Press, 1988.

———. *The Anatomy of Anti-liberalism*. Cambridge: Harvard University Press, 1993.

———. *Passions and Constraint: On the Theory of Liberal Democracy*. Chicago: University of Chicago Press, 1995.

Honig, Bonnie. "Declarations of Independence: Arendt and Derrida on the Problem of Founding a Republic." *The American Political Science Review* 85, no. 1 (1991): 97–113.

———. *Political Theory and the Displacement of Politics*. Ithaca: Cornell University Press, 1993.

———. "Difference, Dilemmas and the Politics of Home." In *Democracy and Difference*. Edited by Seyla Benhabib. Princeton: Princeton University Press, 1996.

———. "Dead Rights, Live Futures: A Reply to Habermas's 'Constitutional Democracy.'" *Political Theory* 29, no. 6 (December 2001): 792–805.

———. *Democracy and the Foreigner*. Princeton: Princeton University Press, 2001.

———. "Against Relevance." Paper presented at the Perestroika Reception during the annual meeting of the American Political Science Association, Boston, MA, September 2002.

———. "A Legacy of Xenophobia: A Response to David Cole's 'Their Liberties, Our Security.'" *Boston Review: A Political and Literary Forum* (December 2002/January 2003), http://bostonreview.net/BR27.6/honig.html (accessed August 29, 2008).

———. "An Agonist's Reply." *Rechtsfilosofie en Rechtstheorie* 2 (2008).

———. "Antigone's Laments, Creon's Grief: Mourning, Membership and the Politics of Exception." *Political Theory* (February 2009).

———. "From Lamentation to Logos: Antigone's Offensive Speech." *Antigone, Interrupted*. Book manuscript on file with the author.

Horowitz, Donald. *The Jurocracy: Government Lawyers, Agency Programs and Judicial Decisions*. Lexington: Lexington Books, 1977.

House Committee on Rules. "Investigation of Administration of Louis F. Post, Assistant Secretary of Labor, in the Matter of Deportation of Aliens." CIS-NO: H247-4. April 27, 30, and May 7, 8, 1920. Cited as HT in notes.

Jefferson, Thomas. *Political Writings*. Edited by Joyce Appleby and Terrance Ball. New York: Cambridge University Press, 1999.

Johnston, Steven. *Encountering Tragedy: Rousseau and the Project of Democratic Order*. Ithaca: Cornell University Press, 1999.

Kant, Immanuel. "Contest of the Faculties." Translated by H. B. Nisbet. In *Kant: Political Writings*. Edited by Hans Reiss. New York: Cambridge University Press, 1991.

———. "On the Common Saying: 'This May Be True in Theory, but It Does Not Apply in Practice.'" Translated by H. B. Nisbet. In *Kant: Political Writings*. Edited by Hans Reiss. New York: Cambridge University Press, 1991.

———. *Groundwork of the Metaphysics of Morals*. Edited by Mary Gregor. New York: Cambridge University Press, 1998.

———. *Religion within the Boundaries of Mere Reason and Other Writings*. Translated by Allen W. Wood and George Di Giovanni. New York: Cambridge University Press, 1998.

———. *Critique of the Power of Judgment*. Translated by Paul Guyer and Eric Matthews. New York: Cambridge University Press, 2001.

Kapuściński, Ryszard. *Shah of Shahs*. New York: Vintage International, 1992.

Kateb, George. *The Inner Ocean: Individualism and Democratic Culture*. Ithaca: Cornell University Press, 1992.

———. *Patriotism and Other Mistakes*. New Haven: Yale University Press, 2006.

Keenan, Alan. *Democracy in Question: Democratic Openness in a Time of Political Closure*. Stanford: Stanford University Press, 2003.

Kennedy, J. *A History of Malaya*. 2nd Edition. London: Macmillan, 1970.

Kompridis, Nikolas. "The Idea of a New Beginning: A Romantic Source of Normativity and Freedom." In *Philosophical Romanticism*. Edited by Nikolas Kompridis. New York: Routledge, 2006.

————. "The Unsettled and Unsettling Claims of Culture: A Reply to Seyla Benhabib." *Political Theory* 34, no. 3 (June 2006): 389–96.

Korsgaard, Christine M. "Kant on the Right to Revolution." In *Reclaiming the History of Ethics: Essays for John Rawls*. Edited by A. Reath, B. Herman, and C. M. Korsgaard. Cambridge: Cambridge University Press, 1997.

Kramer, Larry. *The People Themselves: Popular Constitutionalism and Judicial Review*. New York: Oxford University Press, 2004.

Lear, Jonathan. *Happiness, Death, and the Remainder of Life*. Cambridge: Harvard University Press, 2002.

Lefort, Claude. *Democracy and Political Theory*. Translated by David Macey. Minneapolis: University of Minnesota Press, 1988.

Lennox, James. "Are Aristotelian Species Eternal?" In *Aristotle on Nature and Living Things*. Edited by Allan Gotthelf. Pittsburgh: Mathesis Publications, 1985.

Lessing, Gotthold Ephraim. *The Education of the Human Race*. In *Philosophical and Theological Writings*. Translated and edited by H. B. Nisbet. New York: Cambridge University Press, 2005.

————. *Nathan the Wise*. Translated by Edward Kemp. London: Nick Hern, 2003.

Leuchtenburg, William. *The Perils of Prosperity, 1914–32*. Chicago: University of Chicago Press, 1958.

Lever, Annabel. "The Politics of Paradox: A Response to Wendy Brown." *Constellations* 7, no. 2 (June 2000): 242–54.

Lévinas, Emmanuel. "Cities of Refuge." In *Beyond the Verse: Talmudic Readings and Lectures*. Translated by Gary D. Mole. London: Athlone Press, 1994.

————. "Les villes-refuges." In *L'Au-delà du verset: Lectures et discours talmudique*. Paris: Editions de Minuit, 1982.

Lindahl, Hans. "Sovereignty and Representation in the European Union." In *Sovereignty in Transition*. Edited by Neil Walker. Oxford: Hart Publishing, 2003.

Lomonaco, Jeffrey. "Kant's Unselfish Partisans as Democratic Citizens." *Public Culture* 17 (Fall 2005): 393–416.

Luhmann, Niklas. "Verfassung als evolutionäre Errungenschaft." *Rechtshistorisches Journal* 9 (1990).

Mad River Valley Localvore Project. www.vermontlocalvore.org.

Markell, Patchen. "Contesting Consensus: Rereading Habermas on the Public Sphere." *Constellations* 3 (January 1997): 337–400.

————. "Making Affect Safe for Democracy? On 'Constitutional Patriotism.'" *Political Theory* 28, no. 1 (February 2000): 38–63.

————. "The Rule of the People: Arendt, Archê, and Democracy." *American Political Science Review* 100, no. 1 (February 2006): 1–14.

Martel, James. *Subverting the Leviathan: Reading Thomas Hobbes as a Radical Democrat*. New York: Columbia University Press, 2007.

Maxwell, Lida. "Between Law and Lawlessness: Democratizing Law in Montesquieu, Burke, and Arendt." Ph.D. diss., Northwestern University, December 2006.

————. "From Procedural to Legal Justice: A Reading of Arendt's *Eichmann in Jerusalem*." Paper presented at the annual meeting of the Association for the

Study of Law, Culture and the Humanities, Berkeley, CA, March 28–29, 2008.

McCormick, Charles H. Entry: "Louis Freeland Post." *American National Biography*. Vol. 17. Edited by John Garraty and Mark C. Carnes. New York: Oxford University Press, 1999.

Mello, Felicia. "Hard Labor." *The Nation*, September 11, 2006. http://www.the nation.com/doc/20060911/mello (accessed August 23, 2008).

Mendelssohn, Moses. *Gesammelte Schriften. Jubliäumsausgabe*. Edited by Alexander Altmann et al. Stuttgart: F. Frommann, 1971.

———. *Jerusalem*. Translated by Allan Arkush. Hanover: University Press of New England, 1983.

Mendes-Flohr, Paul. "Rosenzweig's Concept of Miracle." In *Jüdisches Denken in einer Welt ohne Gott. Festschrift for Stephane Moses*. Edited by Jens Mattern, Gabriel Motzkin, and Shimon Sandbank. Berlin: Verlag Vorwerk 8, 2001.

Michelman, Frank I. "Constitutional Authorship." In *Constitutionalism: Philosophical Foundations*. Edited by Larry Alexander. Cambridge, UK: Cambridge University Press, 1998.

Morris, Aldon. *The Origins of the Civil Rights Movement*. New York: Free Press, 1984.

Mouffe, Chantal. "Carl Schmitt and the Paradox of Liberal Democracy." In *The Challenge of Carl Schmitt*. Edited by Chantal Mouffe. New York: Verso, 1999.

———. *The Democratic Paradox*. New York: Verso, 2000.

———. *On the Political*. New York: Routledge, 2005.

Neumann, Franz. *Behemoth*. London: V. Gollancz Ltd., 1943.

Nietzsche, Friedrich. *Thus Spoke Zarathustra*. Translated by R. J. Hollingdale. New York: Penguin Books, 1969.

———. *The Gay Science*. Translated by Walter Kaufmann. New York: Vintage, 1974.

———. *Human, All Too Human: A Book for Free Spirits*. Translated by R. J. Hollingdale. New York: Cambridge University Press, 1966.

Nordhaus, Jean. "The Porcelain Apes of Moses Mendelssohn." In *The Porcelain Apes of Moses Mendelssohn*. Minneapolis: Milkweed Editions, 2002.

Oakeshott, Michael. *On Human Conduct*. Oxford: Oxford University Press, 1975.

———. "The Rule of Law." In *On History and Other Essays*. Totowa: Barnes and Noble, 1983.

Paul, Robert A. *Moses and Civilization: The Meaning behind Freud's Myth*. New Haven: Yale University Press, 1996.

Petrini, Carlo, and Gigi Padovani. *Slow Food Revolution: A New Culture for Eating and Living*. Translated by Francesca Santovetti. New York: Rizzoli, 2006.

Pettit, Philip. *Republicanism: A Theory of Freedom and Government*. New York: Oxford University Press, 1997.

Pocock, J. G. A. *Politics, Language and Time: Essays on Political Thought and History*. London: Methuen, 1972.

Post, Louis. *The Deportations Delirium*. Chicago: C. H. Kerr, 1923.

Powers, Richard G. *Secrecy and Power: The Life of J. Edgar Hoover*. New York: Free Press, 1987.

Pratt, Minnie Bruce. "Identity: Skin, Blood, Heart." In *Yours in Struggle: Three Feminist Perspectives on Anti-Semitism and Racism*. By Elly Bulkin, Minnie Bruce Pratt, and Barbara Smith. Ithaca: Firebrand Books, 1984.

Putnam, Hilary. Introduction to *Understanding the Sick and the Healthy: A View of World, Man, and God*. By Franz Rosenzweig. Cambridge, MA: Harvard University Press, 1999.

Ranciere, Jacques. *Dis-agreement: Politics and Philosophy*. Translated by Julie Rose. Minneapolis: University of Minnesota Press, 1999.

Rawls, John. *A Theory of Justice*. Cambridge, MA: Belknap Press, 1999.

Rogin, Michael. "American Political Demonology: A Retrospective." In *Ronald Reagan, the Movie*. Berkeley: University of California Press, 1987.

Rosen, Brant. Shalom Rav Blog. http://rabbibrant.com/.

Rosenzweig, Franz. "On Miracles." In *Franz Rosenzweig: His Life and Thought*. Edited by Nahum N. Glatzer. Indianapolis: Hackett, 1998.

———. "Prayer for Sacrifices." In *Franz Rosenzweig: His Life and Thought*. Edited by Nahum N. Glatzer. Indianapolis: Hackett, 1998.

———. "The True and the False Messiah." In *Franz Rosenzweig: His Life and Thought*. Edited by Nahum N. Glatzer. Indianapolis: Hackett, 1998.

———. *Understanding the Sick and the Healthy: A View of World, Man, and God*. Translated by Nahum N. Glatzer. Cambridge, MA: Harvard University Press, 1999.

———. "Atheistic Theology." In *Philosophical and Theological Writings*. Translated and edited by Paul W. Franks and Michael L. Morgan. Indianapolis: Hackett, 2000.

———. *On Jewish Learning*. Edited by Nahum N. Glatzer. Madison: University of Wisconsin Press, 2002.

———. *The Star of Redemption*, Translated by Barbara E. Galli. Madison: University of Wisconsin Press, 2005.

Ross, Richard J. "Communications and Imperial Governance in Colonial British and Spanish America." In *Cambridge History of Law in America*. Edited by Christopher L. Tomlins and Michael Grossberg. Cambridge, UK: Cambridge University Press, 2006.

Rossiter, Clinton. *Constitutional Dictatorship: Crisis Government in the Modern Democracies*. New York: Harcourt, Brace, and World, 1963.

Rousseau, Jean-Jacques. *On the Social Contract*. Translated by Maurice Cranston. New York: Penguin Books, 1968.

Rubenfeld, Jed. *Freedom and Time: A Theory of Constitutional Self-Government*. New Haven: Yale University Press, 2001.

Salyer, Lucy. *Laws Harsh as Tigers*. Chapel Hill: University of North California Press, 1995.

Sandel, Michael. *Liberalism and the Limits of Justice*. New York: Cambridge University Press, 1998.

Santner, Eric. *My Own Private Germany: Daniel Paul Schreber's Secret History of Modernity*. Princeton: Princeton University Press, 1996.

———. *On the Psychotheology of Everyday Life: Reflections on Freud and Rosenzweig*. Chicago: University of Chicago Press, 2001.

————. "Miracles Happen: Benjamin, Rosenzweig, Freud, and the Matter of the Neighbor." In *The Neighbor: Three Inquiries in Political Theology*. By Slavoj Zizek, Eric Santner, and Kenneth Reinhard. Chicago: University of Chicago Press, 2005.

————. "Terry Schiavo and the State of Exception." University of Chicago Press, posted March 29, 2005, http://www.press.uchicago.edu/Misc/Chicago/05april_santner.html (accessed August 29, 2008).

————. *On Creaturely Life: Rilke, Benjamin, Sebald*. Chicago: University of Chicago Press, 2006.

Sarat, Austin, and Thomas R. Kearns. "A Journey through Forgetting: Toward a Jurisprudence of Violence." In *The Fate of Law*. Edited by Austin Sarat and Thomas R. Kearns. Ann Arbor: University of Michigan Press, 1991.

Schaap, Andrew. *Political Reconciliation*. London: Routledge, 2005.

Scheuerman, William E. *Between the Norm and the Exception: The Frankfurt School and the Rule of Law*. Cambridge, MA: MIT Press, 1994.

————. "Between Radicalism and Resignation: Democratic Theory in Habermas' *Between Facts and Norms*." In *Habermas: A Critical Companion*, edited by Peter Dews. Oxford: Blackwell, 1999.

————. *Liberal Democracy and the Social Acceleration of Time*. Baltimore: Johns Hopkins University Press, 2004.

Schlosser, Eric, et al. "One Thing to Do about Food: A Forum." *The Nation*, September 11, 2006. http://www.thenation.com/doc/20060911/forum (accessed August 23, 2008).

Schmitt, Carl. *Political Theology: Four Chapters on the Concept of Sovereignty*. Translated by George Schwab, foreword by Tracy B. Strong. Chicago: University of Chicago Press, 2005.

Shapiro, Martin M. *Who Guards the Guardians? Judicial Control of Administration*. Athens: University of Georgia Press, 1988.

Shklar, Judith. "Review of *We the People: Foundations*, by Bruce Ackerman." *American Political Science Review* 86 (September 1992): 775–76.

Shulman, George. *American Prophecy: Race and Redemption in American Political Culture*. Minneapolis: University of Minnesota Press, 2008.

Slow Food Foundation for Biodiversity. "Ark of Taste." http://www.fondazione slowfood.it/eng/arca/lista.lasso (accessed August 23, 2008).

Smith, Rogers M. "Beyond Tocqueville, Myrdal, and Hartz: The Multiple Traditions in America," *American Political Science Review* 87, No. 3 (Sep., 1993): pp. 549–66.

Soguk, Nevzat. *States and Strangers: Refugees and Displacements of Statecraft*. Minneapolis: University of Minnesota Press, 1990.

Sorenson, Roy. *A Brief History of the Paradox: Philosophy and the Labyrinths of the Mind*. Oxford: Oxford University Press, 2003.

Spinoza, Benedict de. *Theological-Political Treatise*. Translated by Michael Silverthorne and Jonathan Israel. New York: Cambridge University Press, 2007.

Stevens, Jacqueline. "Beyond Tocqueville, Please!" *American Political Science Review* 89, no. 4 (December 1995): 987–95.

Stille, Alexander. "Slow Food." *The Nation*, August 20, 2001. http://www.the Vnation.com/doc/20010820/stille (accessed August 23, 2008).

Stimson, Shannon. *The American Revolution in the Law*. London: Macmillan, 1990.

"Taking Exception to the Exception." Conference: Cornell University, September 2006.

Talmud, *The Steinsaltz Edition: Tractate Bava Metzia*. New York: Random House, 1990.

Taylor, Charles. *Modern Social Imaginaries*. Durham: Duke University Press, 2004.

Tocqueville, Alexis de. *Democracy in America*. Edited by Phillip Bradley. New York: Alfred A. Knopf, 1966.

Velikovsky, Immanuel. *Worlds in Collision*. Garden City: Doubleday Books, 1950.

Virno, Paulo. *A Grammar of the Multitude*. Cambridge, MA: Semiotext(e), 2003.

Waldron, Jeremy. "Precommitment and Disagreement." In *Constitutionalism: Philosophical Foundations*. Edited by Larry Alexander. Cambridge, UK: Cambridge University Press, 1998.

Walzer, Michael. *Exodus and Revolution*. New York: Basic Books, 1986.

Warner, Michael. *The Letters of the Republic: Publication and the Public Sphere in Eighteenth-Century America*. Cambridge, MA: Harvard University Press, 2006.

Waters, Alice. "Slow Food Nation." *The Nation*, September 11, 2006. http:/www.thenation.com/doc/20060911/waters (accessed August 23, 2008).

Watson, Bruce. "Crackdown!" *Smithsonian* 32, no. 11. February 2002. http://www.smithsonianmag.com/people-places/redsquare.html (accessed August 23, 2008).

Whitman, Walt. "Reconciliation." In *Walt Whitman: The Complete Poems*. Edited by Francis Murphy. New York: Penguin Books, 1996.

Williams, Bernard. "A critique of utilitarianism." In *Utilitarianism: For and Against*. By J. J. C. Smart and Bernard Williams. New York: Cambridge University Press, 1973.

———. "Moral Luck." In *Moral Luck: Philosophical Papers, 1973–1980*. New York: Cambridge University Press, 1981.

Wilson, Emily R. *Mocked with Death: Tragic Overliving from Sophocles to Milton*. Baltimore: Johns Hopkins University Press, 2004.

Wilson, Woodrow. "The Study of Administration." *Political Science Quarterly* 56, no. 4 (December 1941): 481–506.

Wittgenstein, Ludwig. *Philosophical Investigations*, 3rd Edition. Translated by G. E. M. Anscombe. Oxford: Blackwell, 2001.

Wolin, Sheldon. *Politics and Vision*. Boston: Little Brown, 1960.

———. *The Presence of the Past: Essays on the State and the Constitution*. Baltimore: Johns Hopkins University Press, 1990.

Young, Iris. *Intersecting Voices*. Princeton: Princeton University Press, 1997.

———. *Inclusion and Democracy*. Oxford: Oxford University Press, 2000.

Young-Bruehl, Elizabeth. *Hannah Arendt: For Love of the World*. New Haven: Yale University Press, 2004.

Zohar, Noam J. "Midrash: Amendment through the Molding of Meaning." In *Responding to Imperfection: The Theory and Practice of Constitutional Amendment*. Edited by Sanford Levinson. Princeton: Princeton University Press, 1995.

Index